Double Deception

Double Deception

Ford D. Barrett

Copyright © 2011 by Ford D. Barrett.

Library of Congress Control Number: 2011909487
ISBN: Hardcover   978-1-4628-8551-0
                 Softcover   978-1-4628-8550-3
                 Ebook   978-1-4628-8552-7

All rights reserved. No part of this book may be reproduced or transmitted in any form or by any means, electronic or mechanical, including photocopying, recording, or by any information storage and retrieval system, without permission in writing from the copyright owner.

This book was printed in the United States of America.

To order additional copies of this book, contact:
Xlibris Corporation
1-888-795-4274
www.Xlibris.com
Orders@Xlibris.com
99954

ACKNOWLEDGEMENTS

Thank you to my family and friends for the support.
A special thanks to Carla, Tifffany, James, Ngozi,
Vanessa, Jo-Ann and Anna for the extra ideas
and boosting up my creativity and confidence.
There are a lot of other people that I can thank
but I am only limited to so much space!! (LOL)

CHAPTER ONE

Antonio stood in front of the blank canvas that rested on the easel. He had a lot on his mind tonight, but crawling into bed to sleep seemed the only thing he could think of to do. Antonio worked for a well-known established art gallery in the fashion district of downtown Kingsway named Mahogany, which over the past decade generated lots of revenue, media attention and a great reputation. For the last four years, Mahogany was listed as one of the top ten successful and biggest earning companies, pulling almost close to a $100 million dollars annually, unheard of from an art gallery. At twenty-eight years old, Antonio had accomplished a lot. He had graduated from Oxbridge University downtown with honors in Art and Philosophy, his work has been featured in a number of magazines and museums, and, last year, one of his paintings had sold for almost $100,000. His success had allowed him to move out from his parents' home in the suburbs, and he now lived in a two-level studio apartment in the heart of the city. Antonio had no social life and the word "dating" sounded foreign to him. Before his success, Antonio had an active social life was constantly going on dates. Today, Antonio found himself, tired, overworked and alone in his apartment. Raindrops fell, smacked, and bounced off the window, and Antonio felt more depressed.

He dropped his paint palate and brushes on the table and walked over to sit on his leather sofa. As he sunk down, he felt for the remote control buried between the seats and turned on the television.

Flipping through the channels, the phone rang.

Antonio rolled his eyes. "God, who is it now?"

Antonio began to reach for the phone, but stopped midway and sunk back in the couch, muttering, "Let the machine take care of it."

The answering machine beeped. "Yo Tony! Tony! Pick up the phone! I know you're there, Tony. Pick up the phone!" repeated the voice over the machine.

Antonio sighed as he reached for the phone and picked it up. "What do you want, Greg?"

Greg was always hyperactive, always calling Tony for the latest updates that occurred in the gallery. "Tony, you know that last painting you did with the silhouette of the woman?"

Antonio scratched his head. "Yeah, why?"

"There's a client who wants to buy your painting for $6,000! Yo, isn't that great?"

Antonio yawned. "Wow, that's great."

"What do you mean *wow that's great?*" Greg had quickly sensed Antonio's mood. "What's your problem?"

"Listen I'm not in the mood right now, OK? I'll talk to you tomorrow."

"What do you mean you're not in the mood?"

"Listen Greg, I am not in the mood for talking. Comprendeh?"

Greg sighed. "OK. Fine then. I'll talk to you tomorrow, but you don't sound so good."

"I'm just exhausted."

"OK then, later." Greg hung up.

"Yeah, later," Antonio said as he hung up. Antonio shook his head, rubbing his palms on his temples. He turned off the T.V., stretched, yawned and walked towards the window. Raindrops hit the parked cars on the street below like pebbles. The moon emerged from behind dark clouds, illuminating the streets below with a yellow haze.

Antonio turned away from the window and walked upstairs towards his bedroom. He stood in front his dresser mirror and told himself, "Antonio, I think, it is time for you to find a woman. Don't know when, who, where, or how, but you need someone." His expression unchanged, Antonio yawned, changed and went to bed.

CHAPTER TWO

Greg grunted as he lifted his dumbells. Without looking at Antonio, he said, "You know, you've been acting really weird lately."

Antonio got up from doing a pushup. "Greg, I'm just tired. You know, there's so much work to be done and all."

Greg raised his eyebrow. "Yeah right."

"What do you mean *yeah right*?"

"Tony, please. Work's not the problem—it's something else."

Greg leaned in. "Dated any girls lately?"

Antonio retreated. "Why do you want to know?"

"I was just asking one simple question."

Antonio eyes shifted across the room to an attractive young woman using the Stairmaster. He couldn't help but notice the way her fluorescent blue spandex and black midriff shirt hugged her curves.

Greg noticed the free show and leaned in. "She looks nice, eh?"

Antonio dabbed his forehead with his towel. "Yeah, she's alright."

"Go over and talk to her."

"I can't."

"Why?"

"Because I can't."

"What the hell's wrong with you? Look at her!"

"Greg this is a gym, not some nightclub."

Greg screwed his face. "Whatever man, you are such a wuss."

Antonio glared at Greg. "Fine." He threw his towel at Greg and marched over towards the woman. She noticed Antonio and smiled.

Antonio approached the woman. He coughed and mumbled "Hi."

The woman smiled. "Hi."

Antonio's hands shook. "Um, have I seen you before?"

She shook her head. "Um, no I don't think so."

"Oh . . . um . . . OK, I thought I had seen you before maybe downtown or something." Antonio hated himself for using such a lame pick up line.

She smiled. "Is that the line you always use when you want to talk to a woman?"

Antonio felt beads of sweat dripping down his forehead. "Oh, um, no."

"You could have fooled me."

Antonio smirked. "OK fine, you got me."

She smiled again. "You work out here often?"

"Oh . . . yeah. A couple times a week."

"I can tell," the woman said as she considered Antonio's arms.

Antonio laughed.

Greg stood across the gym floor observing Antonio and smiled. "Atta boy Tony. There you go." Greg and Antonio had known each other since highschool and remained friends ever since. Though best friends Antonio and Greg had polar differences. Antonio was tall, had a lean athletic build, dark complexion and quiet. Greg was shorter and a bit stocker lighter complexion and loud. Though ladies often considered Antonio the better of the two, Greg was still considered attractive by ladies and often charmed them with his sense of humour. Something that Antonio felt he lacked dearly.

"Sorry, I didn't' catch your name," Antonio remembered.

"Natasha. And yours?"

"Antonio."

Natasha stretched out her hand. "Nice to meet you, Antonio."

Antonio shook her hand. "Likewise."

Natasha stepped down from her exercise machine and wiped her forehead. "Well, I should be heading out of here. My girlfriend is waiting for me outside."

"Oh, not a problem. I don't want to keep your friend up."

Natasha bit her lip and smirked. "Yeah, well I better get going."

Antonio cleared this throat. "OK . . . yeah I guess I'll see you sometime."
Natasha nodded.

Antonio watched Natasha walk towards the changing room. At the door stood a slender, dark-skinned woman with cropped hair wearing a grey Nike T-shirt and red shorts. Natasha spoke to her and both looked in Antonio's direction.

They women smiled momentarily, giggling as they walked into the changing room.

Greg approached Antonio. "So?"

"So what?"

"So what happened?"

"Nothing."

"What do you mean *nothing*?"

"Nothing?"

"Well did you get her number?"

"No."

"Why didn't you?"

"Because I didn't. Man, Greg, would you get off my damn case?"

Greg shook his head. "Tony I really need to teach you some lessons on how to get a woman."

Antonio pretended to ignore him.

Greg said goodbye and hung up.

Antonio grabbed his car keys from his pocket. "What does Lisa want?"

Greg slid his cell phone into his pocket. "Oh, some client coming in wanting us to show them stuff and blah blah b." Greg froze. "Um . . . Tony?"

"What?"

Greg pointed out across the street. "Isn't that the girl you were talking to across in the parking lot?"

Antonio looked across the street to see Natasha and the older woman from the gym chatting. He smiled. "Yeah it . . ." he began, but he couldn't finish his sentence. He watched in awe as Natasha leaned in towards the other woman and gave her a passionate kiss.

Greg dropped his briefcase. "Daaaamn!"

Antonio's heart sank.

"Yo, Tony are you seeing this? That girl is into chicks! Fuckin' wild, man!"

Antonio looked up into the clear sky. "Dear God, why me? I give up."

Greg chuckled. "Hey man, at least lesbians find you attractive."

* * *

Antonio and Greg entered the lobby of the art gallery museum.

Antonio approached Lisa who sat reading a novel behind her desk. "Any messages for me?"

"Just Larry asking you when would you will be able to complete the next painting," Lisa answered, absently handing Antonio a sticky note while still reading.

Antonio nodded and headed towards the elevator doors, but Greg intercepted him before he reached them. "Tony, I totally forgot. We have another client that will be coming here for one of your paintings."

Antonio sighed and closed his eyes. "Great. Who? How much for? And what time?"

"This client is a woman who'll be here at one o'clock. I'm not quite sure how much she wanted to buy your painting, but I heard she's quite wealthy," Greg said.

Antonio rolled his eyes.

"What's wrong with you? You're so goddamn depressing it's making me sick! It's that lesbian, isn't it?"

The elevator doors opened. "No, it's not the lesbian. I just need a vacation."

Greg did not believe him. "Yeah, right. In any case, don't forget the appointment."

Antonio had reached the elevator. "Yeah, I'll remember."

One o'clock arrived. Antonio had missed lunch and was trying to accomplish a number of assignments and appointments with potential clients.

He glanced at his watch. "Shit, the appointment!" Quickly gathering some files and papers, he fled out his office and took the elevator down towards the gallery. The beige painted art gallery was filled with paintings and sculptures. Spotlights hung over each exhibit, illuminating every crevice, paint stroke, and colour of each canvas. Antonio hurried into the front entrance and glanced at his watch that read 1:09 p.m. He adjusted his tie and fixed his jacket in front of a mirror wall beside the elevator.

The elevator bell rang and the elevator doors opened. Inside, a woman accompanied by two large men dressed in long leather jackets and sunglasses stood scanning the gallery. The woman exited the elevator, and the two men followed.

She approached Antonio. "Hello, my name is Simone Jackson, I'm here for an Anthony . . . or Antonio Madison."

Antonio nodded. "Yes, I am Antonio. Nice to meet you." He shook her hand.

Simone took off her sunglasses. "I'm awful sorry that I am late. I had some other stuff to take care of, and I lost track of time, and . . ."

Antonio laughed. "Don't apologize, it's OK." Simone's shoulder-length black hair reached midway down her back, and her brown fur coat lay heavy on her toned, slim body. Her honey-hazel eyes contrasted with her smooth, dark skin, and her glistening, thick lips were painted a fire-engine red. Her diamond earrings shimmered, almost blinding Antonio.

Simone smiled.

"This way, please." Antonio gestured, walking ahead.

Again Simone smiled.

Antonio would treat Simone like any other client. He would start off with some conversation to make sure they all felt relaxed. While conversing he would show them his work as well as the work of others and give his client some insight and information about the artwork. However, Simone didn't act like any other client. Every time Antonio would make a comment she'd just smile and nod. Antonio hated this kind of response—smiling this much was a sign of boredom. Antonio hated this part of his job. He felt like a yellow-plaid-jacket-wearing, greasy, sex-deprived, used car salesman trying to sell anything to make his commission so he can blow it all at the strip joint. The two bodyguards who stood at the entrance of the gallery like massive twin towers did not make the situation any better. Every time

Antonio glanced over to them, they glared at him through their shades. Antonio felt as if, any minute, the Hells Angels were going to raid the gallery and kill him.

Wiping the sweat off his brow, Antonio approached his final painting of a nude man and woman lying down, their arms and bodies intertwined on a white carpet. Dashes of red, pink, and white scattered the background and birds encircled the two figures.

Simone's eyes widened. "Oh my God! That's so beautiful! It has so much *zeal*. I've got to have it."

Antonio felt himself relax as his smile grew wider.

Simone turned to Antonio. "How much?"

"I'm selling that picture for about $500."

"No," Simone said firmly. "I'm not buying this picture for $500."

Antonio hated bargainers, especially the cheap kind. He adjusted his tie. "Ok, so how much were you thinking of?"

Simone paused. "How about I give you $2,000 for it?"

Antonio stopped adjusting his tie. "Sorry, you wanna run that by me one more time?"

Simone leaned in. "$2,000."

Antonio's hands twitched. "Uh, Mrs. Jackson, that's a very generous offer, but I don't think . . ."

"What about $3,000?"

Antonio froze. "Mrs. Jackson, please. You don't have to . . ."

"$4,000?"

Antonio felt paralyzed.

Simone grabbed her purse. "You know, how about I raise it to $5,000? That'll make you happy, wouldn't it?"

Antonio wiped his forehead, shook his head and coughed. *$5,000? She wants to buy my painting for $5,000?!* Antonio's lip twitched. Adjusting his collar, he swallowed. "Um . . . OK, yes, sold."

Simone smiled, Antonio nodded, and the twin towers glared down at Antonio.

Antonio leaned in. "Mrs. Jackson, you don't have to do this."

"Please. I like you, and your paintings are absolutely stunning. By the way, don't call me Mrs. Jackson. Call me Simone, alright?"

Antonio half smiled nodded. *I like you? Call me Simone?*

Simone grabbed her cheque book and wrote the amount. She paused, gazed up at Antonio, smiled, and continued writing. She ripped out the cheque and handed it to Antonio. "Nice doing business with you."

Antonio gazed at the cheque. "You too, Mrs. Jackson . . . . uh . . . I mean Simone. "

One again Antonio glanced at the twin towers. "Um, how are the arrangements going to me made for you to pick up the painting?"

"Do you do deliveries?" She said.

"Yes we do, I can arrange a courier to . . ."

Simone put on her sunglasses. "Can *you* deliver it?"

Antonio lowered his eyebrow. "Well, I don't think I can . . ."

"Oh please, why waste your time with a courier. I *want you* to deliver it to my house."

Antonio suddenly knew where this was going. "Mrs. Jackson, in all honestly, I don't think that—"

Simone grabbed a business card from her pocket. "Here. That's my address. Deliver the painting to my house next Friday. My phone number is on that card. If you have any problems, call me."

"Mrs. Jackson, I really don't think it would be feasible for me to deliver . . ."

"Antonio, I am sure your boss will be extra nice to you when he hears that you sold a painting for $5,000."

Antonio could not deny that. Mr. Huntingwood would buy drinks for everyone in the office when he heard about this. Antonio nodded unconsciously.

"Great." Simone said. She spun around and snapped her fingers. The twin towers followed her to the elevator.

Antonio followed Simone like as if he had lost his own will. "It was great doing business with you Simone." He reached for his business card from his pocket. "I should have given you my number."

Simone turned around, took off her sunglasses and smiled. "Don't worry. I have your number."

Antonio stopped. "Oh you do?"

"Yes I do." The elevators doors opened. The twin towers and Simone entered, and Simone smiled at Antonio before the doors closed.

Antonio looked down at the cheque and shook his head. "Wow."

* * *

Antonio arrived home late from the art gallery. He threw his jacket on the floor and approached the answering machine. Unloosening his tie, he pressed "play."

The first was from Greg. "Antonio, We're having an auction Saturday night at the gallery at 8 o'clock. I would have told you earlier on, but those lesbian seems to be bothering you."

Antonio glared at the answering machine. "Stupid jackass," he cursed.

"Dress code of course is in strict effect. Remember, that's this Saturday. So if you have any dates, which I doubt you do, cancel them. I'll see you there. Later."

"The next time I see Greg I am gonna punch his face in." Antonio muttered as he walked into the kitchen to grab a glass of water.

Beep. "Hi, Antonio, it's your mother. Don't forget to come over and help me and your father paint the guest room on Sunday. Remember to buy some paint brushes. Love you. See you on Sunday."

Beep. Antonio listened, but this one was nothing but dead air.

"Why do people do that? Antonio wondered. Just as he was about to erase the message, a voice came on.

"Mmmmmm, so sexy." Then click.

Antonio choked on his drink. "What the fuck?"

He replayed the message: "Mmmmmm, so sexy."

Antonio could not make out the voice or where the person was calling from. He didn't allow his imagination to roam and figured it must be some childish prank, probably from Greg.

CHAPTER THREE

"What are you talking about?" Greg said as he munched on his Big Mac.

Antonio sipped his Coke. "The message, with some girl saying 'sexy'. Nice try, idiot."

Greg stopped chewing and said, "Buddy, what the hell are you talking about?"

"The message that you left last night.

"What? About Saturday?"

"No, the other one."

"What other one?"

"The one with some girl saying *sexy*."

"I never left you any message like that."

"Oh, give me a break Greg. I know it was you. You always harass me when it comes to dating because I am not Mr. Ladies Man like you."

Greg resumed his eating. "OK, Tony. First of all, the only message I left on your machine was regarding Saturday. And second of all, why would I leave a message like that?"

Antonio did not want to bother getting into an argument with Greg. Their arguments often resembled those of a married couple, who you would see arguing in a store and many people thought they were lovers. Greg laughed at the idea, but Antonio hated it.

Antonio slammed his drink back down on the counter. "Anyhow, forget about it. What I wanted to tell you is about that appointment I had yesterday."

"Yeah, how did it go?"

"Really well. She purchased one of my paintings."

"Right on, how much?"

Antonio smirked. "Man, you are not going to believe it."

Greg shrugged his shoulders. "I dunno, $400? $500?"

"She wrote me cheque for my painting," Antonio said as he leaned in, " . . . for $5,000."

Greg dropped his Big Mac in his tray and yelled. "$5,000?!"

Everyone around them fell silent.

"Shhhhh! Keep it down, man!"

Greg leaned in. "$5,000?"

Antonio nodded.

Greg rubbed his eyes. "Let me get this straight. This woman, a supposed 'client' comes into the art gallery . . ."

Antonio nodded.

"And then you and her do business, and you show some of your paintings, correct?"

Again Antonio nodded.

"She then stumbles upon that painting you did and buys it for $5,000?"

Once more Antonio nodded.

Greg shook his head. "Bullshit," he said definitively.

"You don't believe me?"

"Yeah I believe you. I also believe that men have PMS and can have babies."

"Fine, you don't believe me? I'll prove it to you." Antonio dug into his wallet and pulled out the cheque and handed it to Greg. "Here."

Greg's eyes widened. "Holy shit! This woman was serious."

"Believe me now?"

Greg sat up. "I have two questions," Greg said. "Why, and how?"

Antonio shrugged his shoulders. "I don't know, maybe it's my natural good looks."

"Yeah, which has done nothing for you but attract lesbians."

"Greg, seriously, fuck off with that."

"Chill, man, I was just playing with you. You've really changed. You're so serious all of a sudden. You need to lighten up."

Antonio ignored Greg and stared at his cheque. He too wondered why and how.

"Any calls for me, Lisa?" Antonio said approaching her desk.

"No, except for one." Lisa said. "Some woman was asking for you, so I just transferred her to your voicemail."

Greg stood beside Antonio and patted his shoulder. "Ahh . . . a girl. Who could that be?"

"Knock it off, Greg."

Lisa leaned towards Greg. "Is he still bent off about that lesbian at the gym?"

Antonio turned toward them. "What?"

Greg's eyes darted away. "Nothing."

"Greg, exactly how many people did you tell about what happened yesterday morning?"

Lisa rubbed Antonio's hand. "It's OK Antonio, the last guy I had a crush on turned out to be gay. No biggy."

Antonio jerked his hand away and gave them both the evil eye. "I'll be in my office."

"Gee, someone didn't have their Frosted Flakes in the morning." Lisa sneered.

Antonio pressed play on his answering machine.

Beep: "Mmmmmm . . . so sexy," purred the voice. Then there was a click.

"Seriously, again?" Antonio said. "Who the hell is doing this?" Antonio immediately called Lisa.

Lisa yawned when she picked up. "Yeah, Antonio?"

"Lisa, question: that woman you transferred me to, did she leave a name or anything?"

"Nope. She just asked for you and that was it."

"Thanks, Lisa."

"No problem. Listen Antonio, I'm really sorry if I offended you."

Antonio sheepishly accepted her apology and hung up. He stood up and looked down through his window at the busy streets below. "Who the heck is leaving these messages?"

* * *

Antonio looked at his watch. "Is it seven already?" he wondered. Antonio was scrambling to get his stuff together when he heard a knock at the door.

"It's open." Antonio yelled from his chair.

The door flung open and Greg stood with some files in his hands.

Antonio smirked. "Oh, it's you."

"Yes, it's me," Greg mimicked. "What are you smirking at?"

"Listen Greg, I know I've been cranky for a while and I apologize, but really man, you don't have to get one of your friends to leave messages at work to boost my ego."

Greg raised his eyebrow. "Huh?"

"The message on my machine."

"Tony, I told you, I had nothing to with that."

"Even the one that was left this afternoon here?"

"Huh?"

Antonio rubbed his chin. "You really don't know what I am talking about, do you?"

Greg shook his head. "Guy, you keep talking about these messages. Honestly, I don't know what you are talking about."

Antonio sat in his chair. "Then who the hell is doing it?"

"What does it say on this message?" Greg said.

"Well, there is a brief pause and this girl then comes on saying 'sexy.'"

Greg laughed. "Sexy? Oh give me a break."

"Yo, I am serious. Listen for yourself." Antonio played the message.

Greg listened and then began to laugh. "So, which psycho girl do you have stalking your black ass?"

"This is stupid!" Antonio said. "Some woman is leaving these messages and it's annoying."

"Who?"

"That's just it! I don't know," Antonio replied. Antonio instantly thought of Simone Jackson. Her smiles from that day at the art gallery were obviously flirtatious. Her insistence on the idea that he "personally" deliver his artwork to her house was certainly questionable—also the fact that she already had his phone number. Where did she get that from? Antonio had handed his business cards to people, but they only had his cell phone number on them. Everything about the encounter seemed more than coincidental, but it was still not enough to draw too many conclusions.

"Maybe it's that client woman that you dealt with," Greg said.

"You obviously read my mind."

"Tony, women are capable of doing all kinds of weird stuff."

Antonio scratched his head. "Yeah but I really don't think it's her."

"Then who could it be?"

Antonio weakly shrugged his shoulders. "I guess I'll never know."

* * *

Antonio threw his jacket on the floor and rushed towards the answering machine. Ever since the messages had started, he'd felt like an obsessive neurotic eagerly waiting to listen to his messages. Antonio had dated his fair shares of psychos and idiots and was hoping this wasn't one of his ex-girlfriends. Deep down, though, he was hoping it was Simone.

Beep: "Tony, it's your mom again. Remember I told you pick up some paint brushes? I also forgot to ask you to pick up four rolling pans. Home Hardware has them on sale for $9.99 each. They limit you to two, but do what I told you do before. Buy the two, drop them off in your car, and go back and buy another two and go to a different cashier. OK, Tony? Remember! See you Sunday. Oh, your father says, hi. Anyways see you Sunday."

Antonio laughed at the message. Even though he was fewer than two years from being thirty, his mother still treated him like he was ten. It was a great feeling to know that he had a mother that cares for him so much, but it was also annoying. She seemed to forget that he was old enough to vote, drink, and, well, do whatever else he wanted.

Beep: "Yo Tony, it's Larry. I'm calling from Central Square about Saturday. I forgot to tell you that another one of your paintings is going to be auctioned. Uh, the one with the two people on the beach. Or was it a forest? Well you know which one I'm talking about. Anyway, gotta go, I see a cop about to put a parking ticket on my car. Later."

Antonio slapped his hand on his forehead. "Shit! I totally forgot about Saturday night." He was in the kitchen by the time the third message came on.

Beep: "Sexy . . . . . . mmmmm, so sexy."

Antonio spun around and hurried to the answering machine. There was another brief pause and then a click. Antonio checked the phone display to see who would it was. It was listed "Private."

Antonio continued to stare at his answering machine. Whoever this was, she didn't seem like she was going to stop. Antonio shook his head but Simone's image remained imprinted in his mind.

CHAPTER FOUR

Saturday night arrived so fast that Antonio did not even have time to enjoy the day. He had so many errands to run that leaving his place to go to an auction was the last thing he wanted to do.

Antonio stood in front of the mirror adjusting his tie when there was a knock on the door.

"Who is it?" Antonio shouted.

"It's me," Greg shouted from behind the door.

"The door's open."

Greg skanked into the apartment with a cane, black blazer, navy pants, and white shoes.

Antonio screwed up his face. "Hey, the audition for Ronald McDonald is down the street."

"Oh shut up," Greg said. "Don't I look fly?"

Antonio laughed. "You need to fly away from here and put on something decent."

Greg shot a look at Antonio. "Whatever man. You ready?"

"Greg are you seriously going to the function looking like that?"

"Antonio, this is an art gala for crying out loud. We are dealing with artists, not executives."

Antonio rolled his eyes. "Whatever man, you can't be in an art gallery with white shoes and a cane. You look like a rejected pimp."

Greg ignored Antonio's comment. "Are you ready?"

"Yeah I'm ready."

Greg spun his cane around with one hand. "There are women at that gallery that are going to be looking good." Greg turned around in a circle and paused in front of Antonio. "Now tell me Tony, do I, or do I not look like Mr. America?"

"Well it looks like Mr. America forgot something." Antonio said

"What?"

Antonio pointed at Greg's zipper. "Mr. America forgot to zip his all-American fly."

Embarrassed, Greg zipped up his fly and then posed. "Now how do I look?"

Antonio sat down and pulled on his shoes. "Greg, I am going to remind you one more time. We are going to an art gallery, not a club."

"You're so naïve, Antonio," Greg said. "Our paintings are starting at $500. Rich women will be there."

Antonio got up. "Speaking about women, I got that stupid message again?"

"Again?"

"Yep."

"OK Tony, what immature chick do you know who is doing this?"

"Guy, I don't know, but it's getting kind of annoying."

"Yeah tell me about it. You think it's Simone, don't you?"

Antonio did not reply.

"You do, don't you?"

"Kind of."

"Why?"

"Well, that afternoon when she came to the gallery she was all flirty with me."

Greg rubbed his chin. "Well whoever this chick is, she really wants you."

Antonio laughed. "Yeah, she wants me so bad she can't even tell me who she is or what her number is."

Greg nodded. He then tapped Antonio's shoulder. "Hey, you mentioned Simone right?"

"Yeah, why?"

"She might be there tonight."

"And what does that have to with anything?" Antonio said, grabbing his jacket.

"You can ask her if she was leaving those messages."

"Greg I can't do that."

"Why not?"

"Because I can't just go up to her and be like 'um excuse but are you leaving steamy messages on my answering machine?' Please!"

Greg opened the door. "Hey, it was just a suggestion."

It was a suggestion, and Antonio was now considering it as they walked out the door.

* * *

Sade's "Your Love is King" was playing as Antonio and Greg entered the building. Strangers moved about with wine glasses and in their hands. Antonio and Greg both grabbed glasses of red wine from a table when a voice spoke out from the front of the room.

"Excuse me, everybody, may I have your attention. The auctioning of the paintings is going to begin in ten minutes. We'd ask everyone to have a seat. Thank you."

Antonio's stomach turned. He turned to Greg. "Greg, I am nervous. I hope my paintings sell well."

"Why are you worrying?" Greg reassured him. "Your paintings will do great."

Everyone was now finding their seats, and Greg and Antonio snuck up at the front where they found two vacant seats beside each other.

A short, middle-aged man with grey hair and thick-rimmed glasses stepped up behind the podium. "Good evening everybody, and thank you for attending our auction this evening."

Greg tapped Antonio's shoulder. "Check out the girl with the long black hair."

Antonio leaned in. "Who?"

"Her." Greg answered, gesturing behind them.

"Greg, not now. Quiet."

The auctioneer continued. "We will now start our auctioning with a wonderful painting by Antonio Madison from Mahogany." The audience clapped as the red velvet curtains opened. Antonio's painting sat on a gold-trimmed easel. The lights illuminated every single stroke his brush had made on the canvas. Two naked bodies lay in a green forest, their chocolate-skinned bodies intertwining. Antonio's recent paintings had all been naked couples in the act of lovemaking— something that he was quite aware of. He told everyone that he enjoyed capturing the art of two people sharing an intimate moment together, which was a bold-faced lie. In reality, his recent paintings sought to capture what Antonio was lacking in his life: a relationship.

"We will begin the bidding at $200," The MC began.

One person in the audience raised her hand.

"I see $200," the MC continued. "Do I see $250?"

Another hand from the audience shot up.

"I see $250, do I see $300?"

Another hand sprung up from the audience. Each bid the MC offered, a hand raised from the audience. Antonio gleamed as the bid reached $800.

The bidder continued. "Do I see $850?"

A voice suddenly sounded from the back of the room. "I bid $2,000!"

All heads in the room turned around to see who had spoken.

Antonio whispered to Greg, "Holy shit! $2,000? Fuck, who is so desperate for my work?"

Greg shrugged his shoulders. "I don't know, but shut up and be happy."

The MC's eyes widened as he adjusted his tie, coughed, and rubbed his brow. "Uh . . . OK . . . uh, I've got . . . well . . . $2,000. Going once, going twice . . ."

Everyone fell silent.

"Sold to the woman in the back," the MC said, clapping. Everyone clapped while muttering to their neighbors. Antonio tried to get a good view of the woman.

"Damn, who was that woman who bought your painting?" Greg said.

"I don't know but I am sure—" Antonio's heart stopped. He gaped at the woman walking up to the podium.

"Tony, what's wrong?" Greg said.

The woman spotted Antonio, stopped, and smiled. Then, she then continued on her way.

Greg nudged Antonio. "That was the girl I was pointing at."

Antonio did not reply.

"She must be rich," Greg said. "She looks fit too."

Antonio turned to Greg. "Dude, that is the woman who bought my painting the other day for $5,000."

Greg and Antonio both leaned back, stunned.

* * *

Antonio felt uncomfortable the entire evening. Simone had bid on almost all of his work. Usually Antonio would be high as a kite, but not tonight. This woman was making Antonio uncomfortable in ways that he couldn't put his finger on. When the auctioning was over, Antonio quickly darted into the lobby to avoid the strangers at the auction. He grabbed a glass of red wine from the table and gulped it down. A sea of people were gathering around Simone Jackson as she exited the auctioning room. Everyone started asking her questions as if she were the latest Hollywood celebrity.

"How do you know Antonio Madison? Do you know him personally?" asked one searching patron.

"No I don't," she answered. "But we have met before and he is a very talented artist." Her twin towers stood at either side of her, making sure no one got too close to her. Antonio watched from the table and wanted to throw up. This all seemed so bizarre and somehow pathetic that he was hoping that his alarm clock would buzz any minute now and he would wake up.

"So you are gonna talk to her?" Greg said from behind.

Antonio jumped. "Shit man, you startled me. Greg, if I approached her, God knows what I would say."

"Tony, she likes your paintings and she obviously likes you too."

"This is too weird for me," Antonio said, gazing at Simone from across the room. Simone turned to look at him and their eyes locked. Simone smiled, but Antonio grimaced inwardly. Simone whispered something to one of her bodyguards and squeezed her way through the crowds towards Antonio.

Antonio choked. "Dear God, she's coming this way."

"Oh, shut up and take it like a man."

"Greg, the woman has bought almost all my paintings— some of which are probably garbage. And I have this strong feeling that she's been leaving me those so-called 'secret messages' on my machine. God knows how she got my number and . . ."

"Well save your complaining for Jerry Springer, 'cause here she comes," Greg warned him.

Simone approached the two. "Well good evening, gentlemen," she said looking at each man individually. "Enjoying the evening?"

"Yes." Greg piped up.

Simone stretched out her hand. "Hi, my name is Simone Jackson. And you are?"

Antonio remembered his manners. "Oh, this is Gregory Brownstone."

"Hi, Mrs. Jackson." Greg said. "You can just call me Greg." He quickly glanced at Antonio. "Ask her how she is doing tonight, dummy," Greg muttered between his teeth.

Antonio coughed. "So, how are you this evening?"

Simone beamed. "Great."

Antonio stared at the floor. "Uh, the paintings—you really shouldn't have. I'm not that great."

"Are you kidding me?" Simone said. "Your paintings are terrific."

Greg stepped in. "Yeah, he paints damn good."

Antonio glared at Greg.

"Antonio, can you meet me outside in fifteen minutes? I want to speak to you." Simone said.

Antonio's hands shook, his lips twitched, and his face felt hot. "Of course. Sure."

"That's great." she said. She turned to Greg. "Nice meeting you, Gregory," she said, disappearing into the anonymous crowd.

Greg turned to Antonio. "Well, you heard her. *She wants to talk to you alone.*"

Antonio sighed. "Yeah, I wonder what for?"

Antonio downed his fourth glass of wine while he paced outside the gallery. Nervousness and anxiety raveled his body. Part of him felt excited and exuberated that Simone had purchased his paintings at such a high price, but mostly, he felt uncomfortable because she hardly knew him or his artwork and had been willing to drop thousands of dollars on work he'd believed was worthless. A pair of heels clicked against the concrete, echoing closer and closer before stopping behind him. He turned around to face Simone.

Antonio smiled. "Hey."

She smiled back at him. "Antonio, would you like to sit over by that bench where it's more quiet?"

"Sure."

They both walked over by the entrance of the building. Antonio stopped. His conscience bothered him. He deeply wanted to know why Simone was leaving those messages on his machine. What was so attractive about Antonio that Simone couldn't resist? Did she even leave those messages?

Antonio adjusted his tie. "Simone, I want to ask you something."

"Yes?" Simone said.

"I hope you don't mind my asking . . . and if you find this rude, I apologize because this has been on my mind for days. You said you have my phone number?"

"Yes, but I don't understand why would that be rude."

Antonio sighed. "Well, lately I've been getting messages from some anonymous woman."

Simone raised her eyebrow. "Really?"

"Yeah, and I just wanted to know . . . have you attempted to call me?"

"No. Why?"

Antonio forced a laugh. "OK this is really embarrassing to say this but this woman keeps calling my place and all she says on the message is "sexy."

Simone laughed. "You're kidding me, right?"

"No . . . as embarrassing and stupid as it sounds."

"You think it's me who is leaving those messages?"

"Well I didn't say that."

"Well good. I would never do such a thing. If I want something, I ask for it up front."

Antonio darted his eyes away in embarrassment.

Simone continued. "Which is why I wanted to see you."

"Uh, what did you want see me for?"

"Well, I know you are dropping off that painting at my house next Friday, but I was wondering if we could schedule a business lunch or dinner."

Antonio did not know how to respond to her request. He went with his gut feeling. "Sure."

Simone moistened her lips. "I am so intrigued by your paintings, and I would like to talk some business with you."

"Well thank you. Business? What kind of business?"

"We will talk about that over lunch."

Antonio nodded. "OK, what time were you thinking?"

"Is Wednesday at 1pm fine with you?"

"That should be fine, but I might have to double-check my schedule just to make sure if . . ."

Simone reached out for Antonio's cold, clammy hands. "I'm sure you can accommodate me, Antonio."

Antonio grinned. "Well considering you bought almost all my work tonight, of course."

Simone laughed.

"So it's next Friday that I'm delivering your picture and this Wednesday I am having lunch with you. What about the paintings you bought tonight? Who is gonna deliver those to you?"

"Oh, I'll get Juan and Zeus to take care of them."

"Oh. OK," Antonio said. He did not bother asking who Juan and Zeus were but assumed they were the twin towers.

CHAPTER FIVE

Antonio awoke to his phone's insistent ringing. Yawning loudly, he reached to answer the phone. "Hello?"

"You're not up yet?" Greg asked.

Antonio gazed at his alarm clock. "Greg, it's only nine in the morning on a fuckin' Sunday. Why are you calling me so early?"

"Larry's treating us to lunch." Greg announced proudly.

Antonio rubbed his eyes, yawned again, and groaned. "Let me guess. He and Sabrina broke up?"

Greg deepened his voice as if they were on a game show. "Yes, Antonio Madison, you are correct."

"This is ridiculous. Why is it that every time Larry breaks up with his girlfriend, he has to celebrate being single again? What an idiot!"

"That's Larry for you." Greg said. "One minute he's engaged. The next minute he's single."

"So where's he treating us, and what time?"

"Mama Fautino's, at twelve."

"Well I can't stay out too late. I have to go to my folks' house to help them paint. Is he picking us up?"

"Yes, as always."

"Fine I'll see you later then."

"Yeah, later buddy. Wait a minute, what happened between you and Simone last night? When you arrived back at the art gallery, you didn't say anything about her."

"I'll tell you at lunch."

31

* * *

Greg dropped his fork. "In your bed?"

Larry stared at his plate of lasagna and sighed. "Yep."

Antonio shook his head. "I don't believe that slut! The woman sleeps with *two* men *at the same time* in *your bed*? What the fuck?!"

"I know, Tony, I was shocked as hell." Larry said.

Greg took a sip of his wine. "I am sorry, but if that was my woman, and I saw her in my bed with two guys, the only tears you would see in my eyes would be when the judge gave me life imprisonment for first degree murder. For real!"

Antonio and Larry laughed.

Greg continued. "But hold on one second. I'm sorry. Call me a little bit old-fashioned and not liberated, but the thought of banging a girl with another guy in bed just doesn't sit well with me. Personally, I'm not feeling that."

"Threesomes don't always have to be a guy and two girls. Greg." Larry said. "Shit, you would know—you have a ridiculous porno collection."

"Yeah, but those dudes get paid for that shit. I am talking about reality here. Tony, would you have sex with a girl with some guy in the room, at the same time, all three of you naked together? Would you feel comfortable with that?"

"Personally, no. I wouldn't do it."

"Greg, what difference does it make?" Larry said. "You are both fucking her. It's not like you are all of a sudden gonna accidentally mistake her pussy for his ass and go 'oh sorry, wrong hole.'"

Antonio and Greg both looked around to see if anyone could hear them.

Larry persisted. "What? You know I'm right." Larry worked at Mahogany and like Greg was involved with accounts and sales for the gallery. Larry was your typical bachelor who dated many women and often bragged about his sexual adventures to Antonio and Greg. Larry came from a mixed family background where his mother was Irish and his father was

Jamaican so women often complimented about his bright blue eyes though he appeared more black.

Antonio cleared his throat. "Yeah, so anyhow, what did you do after?"

"Well, after beating the crap out one of the guys because the other one took off—and oh by the way, one of them was Mark."

Antonio and Greg's mouths gaped open. "MARK?"

"Yep, Mark." Larry nodded.

"I don't believe this. Malibu surfer-boy Mark? In bed with your girlfriend plus some other guy. You know I knew that guy was an undercover freak," Greg said.

Antonio had been enjoying his wine, but now he needed to get things straight. He set down his glass. "Wait a minute. Mark? That explains why he had a black eye Wednesday morning. So Larry, you beat up Mark?"

Greg interjected. "Yeah, I remember that too. Tony, remember you asked him what happened to his eye, and he said some bullshit about hammering and somehow hitting his eye?"

Larry laughed. "Yeah, I hammered him good though."

Greg leaned in. " So Tony, you wanna tell Larry who *you* hammered last night?"

"Greg, shut up. I didn't hammer anyone." Antonio said, focusing again on his wine.

"You hammered someone? Who?" Larry asked.

"I didn't hammer anyone, you idiots." Antonio said.

"Remember that women who bought all of Antonio's paintings at the gala Friday night?" Greg asked.

Larry turned to Antonio. "Her? You're banging her?"

Antonio's nostrils flared. "I'm not banging her or even dating her!"

Larry started on his lasagna. "I heard people talking about her last night. That woman is loaded. I wanted to go see who she was but I was busy with other stuff."

Antonio jabbed his fork into his spaghetti. "Yeah, tell me about it."

Larry leaned in. "So, you asked for her digits?"

Greg stopped him. "Didn't have to. You already have them, don't you, Tony?"

"Greg, you're acting like I told you this already. I didn't tell you anything about what happened last night."

"Last night? So something did happen last night." Greg said.

Antonio dropped his fork. "Alright fine, I'll tell you what happened last night, you desperate fuck."

Larry and Greg leaned in.

"Well it all started on Thursday afternoon when I had a meeting at one o'clock with this woman. About five minutes after I get down to the gallery, she enters. She wears this long fur coat and she has these two bodyguards at each side of her who look like WWF wrestlers. Well anyway, we begin talking business and she sees one of my paintings. You know that painting I did with the two naked people?"

Larry rolled his eyes. "Well it is kind of hard, Tony, because most of your paintings are of naked couples."

Antonio ignored him. "Well, when she saw that painting, she claimed that she had to have it. Then she offered me $5,000 for the painting."

Larry paused. "Hold on, she bought another one of your paintings? And for $5,000?"

"But, wait. There's more." Greg happily interrupted.

Antonio took a sip from his wine. "Well, after accepting her offer and blah, blah, blah, that night, I check my voice mail and there's this one mysterious message—this woman on my machine saying 'sexy.'"

Larry screwed up his face. "Did she leave you that message?"

Antonio shrugged his shoulders. "I dunno, man. I asked her myself when we talked last night outside the gallery and she said no."

Greg wiped his mouth with a napkin. "So what did you guys talk about?"

"She wants to have lunch with me so we can discuss some business."

"Business? What kind of business?" Greg said.

"Beats me." Antonio said.

What's her name again?" Larry asked.

"Simone Jackson." Antonio answered.

Larry scratched his temple. "Simone Jackson? Wait, I know that woman. I've seen her name some place, but I can't remember where. What does she do?"

"I don't know." Antonio said. "I'll find out on the lunch date."

Larry continued scratching his temple. "Where have I seen her name before?"

CHAPTER SIX

Antonio's parents were civilized yet boisterous individuals. Antonio's mom was especially outspoken. If she saw something that didn't look right, she just had to comment, regardless of the situation. At times, it got her into arguments with others, but she didn't seem to care. Antonio's father was similarly outspoken, but he was more controlled about his arguments. Except of course if the subject was football.

Antonio's mother stood on the front porch with her arms folded. Her soft grey hair rested on her shoulders. A stained but brightly-flowered apron covered her black slacks. The wrinkles around her eyes and mouth grew pronounced as she smiled, welcoming him. She rolled her eyes. "Well, you're a bit late."

Antonio kissed her on her cheek. "Sorry mom. I had lunch with the guys this afternoon and . . ."

"Let me guess. Larry's girl cheated on him and he's celebrating?"

Antonio grinned sheepishly.

"Oh for heaven's sake, what is wrong that boy? He needs to go on Oprah and get himself a girl."

"Mom, what is Oprah gonna do for him?"

"Knock some common sense in his damn head, that's what," Antonio's mom said, wiping her hands on her apron.

Antonio walked inside, dropped his coat and bag, and stood at the edge of the stairway. "Dad, what's up?"

"I'm upstairs," Antonio's father shouted.

Antonio proceeded upstairs to the guest room, which was the first room at the top of the stairs. His dad was in the room laying down plastic over all of the carpet. Sprinkles of blue and black painted dotted his white overalls. A hole peeped from the side of his worn, brown Giants T-shirt.

"I see we are making progress." Antonio said.

"You mean, I'm making progress," his father laughed. He got up and gave Antonio a hug. "So what's up with you?"

"Nothing, nothing at all." Antonio said, turning his Nike baseball cap backwards. "So how are you and mom?"

"The same," Antonio's father said. "You know how your mother and I are. We're still the only ones on the block saying whatever is on our minds. Tony, you would never believe this."

"What?"

"Remember the Johnstons who lived a couple of houses down from us?"

"Yeah, what?"

"Well, rumor has it that their son—the one they've been bragging about claiming that he was going to be better than everybody else—well, the bastard's bankrupt."

"Really?"

"It's true. I heard that bastard got himself bankrupt because some woman scandalized him."

Antonio grabbed a paintbrush from the pail. "What woman?"

"I don't know. Apparently this woman had the hots for Johnston's son but only used him for his assets," Antonio's father said.

Antonio's mom walked in. "Clarence, you're telling Tony about Matthew?"

"Yes, sugar."

"Tony, I hope that teaches you a lesson."

Antonio chuckled. "What? Not to go bankrupt?"

"No, that you need to be tough enough to deal with us women. We women are strong and can manipulate any man we want."

"That has got to be the silliest thing I ever heard." Antonio's father said.

"Do *you* have anything so wise to say, Clarence?" Antonio's mother retorted.

"Marla, a woman is a woman," Antonio's father began. He turned to Antonio. "Take this from a male perspective. Tony, a woman will always be a woman, and women will do everything to get what they want. You need to recognize these signals. She could be rich, pretty, or even ugly. Don't let her make you into her puppet, because she controls the strings."

Antonio looked over to his mother. She had her hands on her hips. "See Tony, this is what I have to put up with every night when I go to bed. Your father telling me he knows best."

Antonio's father got up and gave Antonio's mother a kiss. "That's why we've been married for almost forty years."

Antonio laughed. That settled it. They all began painting the guest room. After four hours of painting, all three stood in the middle of the newly-painted room and looked around at their hard work.

"Finished at last." replied Antonio's mother.

Antonio's father let out a satisfied sigh, and Antonio followed suit.

Antonio turned his mother. "Well, I'm tired. I'd better get going."

"Better get going?" Antonio's mom echoed. "Relax yourself. You've just painted this whole room and you already want to leave?"

"Sorry Mom, but I have some stuff to take a look at when I get back." The only thing Antonio wanted to do when he got home was to see if another message had been left on his machine.

"But I made dinner for you . . ." Antonio's mother began.

Antonio felt guilty. "OK, fine. I'll stay for food but I do have to leave after."

Antonio stayed longer than he'd expected. His father turned on the TV, and he and his father settled on a Western. Antonio's father was fascinated by Westerns. His favorite was *Butch Cassidy and the Sundance Kid*. Antonio remembered his father playing that movie over and over again to the point where Antonio knew every single line in the movie. This evening, though, they were watching one he didn't know entitled *Desert Guns* about two families caught in crossfire between rivalry country police and native Indians. Though the movie seemed interesting, he couldn't get into it. His thoughts kept drifting back to Simone. Simone. Simone was such a *woman*—so inviting yet mysterious. She was obviously wealthy, but what she did or exactly who she was remained a mystery to Antonio.

When Antonio got home, he did his usual routine, He flung his jacket on the floor and approached the answering machine. There was a message.

"I bet myself $10 I am gonna hear that stupid message again," Antonio said as he pressed play.

Beep: "Yeah, Tony, it's Greg, I can't find that file on the account with the Crocker company. I think I left it on your desk on Friday. Tomorrow first thing, can you please check if it's still there? Thanks, buddy."

Beep: "Yes, it your mom. Just checking to see if you got home in one piece. You're probably laying on the couch watching TV while you listen to this. Talk to you later, son."

Beep: There was dead air. Antonio seemed skeptical this time, but then he heard it.

"Mmmmmm sexy . . . sexy . . . sexy. Oh, so sexy." Then click.

Antonio made a fist. "Who the fuck is doing this?"

And then the phone rang.

Antonio looked at his watch. He didn't like receiving calls after 11pm and found it quite odd that someone would call him this late.

Without looking at the call display, he picked up the phone. "Greg I got your message, so you don't have to call me again to remind me."

"Hi . . . Antonio?" said the voice.

Antonio froze. "Simone?"

CHAPTER SEVEN

"Hi, Antonio." Simone said brightly. Her voice sounded as fresh as if she'd just awoken from a massage. "Sorry for calling you so late."

"No, that's OK. I just got in." Antonio said.

Simone fell silent.

"Why, is there is something wrong?" Antonio said.

Again, Simone did not reply.

"Simone . . . . uh . . . you OK?"

Simone sniffled. "Oh, I am fine. It's just . . . oh, never mind."

"No, no . . . Is there is something wrong with the paintings? Did you want to consider the payment of . . ."

"No, no," Simone said. "It's not that. Actually, I really shouldn't be calling you. I'm sorry to call you this late."

"Hey, it's fine. No, really, it is. What's wrong?"

Simone sighed. "Well, it's kind of personal. I've been just going through some stuff and I guess I just need someone to vent to."

Antonio was surprised by her comment. Why would she call him to vent her problems? Where were her friends? But Antonio didn't give these questions a second thought. He cleared his throat. "What's wrong?"

And then, suddenly, Simone began to pour out her problems to Antonio. She was a widow and still felt depressed from her late husband's death. He had died in a car accident over a year ago when the brakes gave out on his car. She now had taken over his share of some computer software company. The business was so successful internationally that her company had been featured on the front page of the *Financial Star*; however, the pressure and stress of running the company had worn her out. Simone and her husband had once had hopes of having children, but she'd had two miscarriages, and now there'd be no children.

Wishing to turn the conversation away from her, she began, "Both your parents—they still live together and are married?"

"Yeah, for about forty years." Antonio said.

Simone gasped on the other end. "Really? That's really good. My father unfortunately passed away when I was twelve, and my mother passed away when I was twenty-one."

"Sorry to hear that."

"But from their passing I've been able to develop into a strong, independent woman."

"I can tell."

Simone cleared her throat. "So Antonio, where did you learn to draw like that?"

Antonio laughed. "I don't know, it's really just a kind of talent."

"Is that the only talent you have?"

Antonio sensed their conversation turning direction. "What do you mean?"

"Well, aren't there any other things that you can do with your hands?"

Antonio always thought these sexual innuendo games were a waste of time and—they were immature, he told himself. But tonight he felt different. "Um, let me see . . . I can write, and I can cook."

"Is that it?" Simone teased.

"Uh . . . I can pick up the TV remote, too."

Simone laughed.

"Simone, can I ask you a question?"

"Sure, what is it?"

"Who told you about my work? And how did you get my number?"

"I heard about you through an acquaintance who said your work was superb."

"Who's that?"

"I believe her name was Jennifer Henry."

Antonio did not recognize the name at all. "Doesn't ring a bell."

"Well, anyway, she loved your work and recommended that I go visit you."

Antonio nodded. "Cool. But I don't remember giving her my home phone number."

"Well it's written on the back of your business card." Simone said.

Antonio still couldn't remember who Jennifer Henry was or why he would have written his home number on the card, but he decided not to dwell on it any further. They continued talking. Simone found herself very comfortable talking with Antonio. His smooth, soothing, and deep voice made her feel relaxed, calm and warm. The conversation seemed endless; she, on her king-sized bed caressing her pillow, and he, on his leather sofa staring up at the ceiling as they ranged effortlessly among topics—from art, to politics, to relationships.

Antonio looked at the clock. "Shit, its 2:30am."

Simone gasped. "Oh my God, really?"

"Yeah it is. I have to be up early in the morning."

"Yes, so do I!"

"Yeah, you should. I mean you have a lot of work ahead and . . ."

Simone cut him off. "Antonio, let me tell you something. I'm might be forty-two years old, and I might have some problems. But I am independent and control my situations. And so . . ."

This time Antonio cut her off. "Wait a minute! How old did you say you were again?"

"Forty-two years old," Simone said. She then giggled. "And damn proud of it, too. Is there a problem?"

"In the last three hours, you never mentioned your age."

"You didn't ask me."

"Was I supposed to?"

"Antonio, come on. I don't go around telling everybody my age."

"I thought you were proud of your age."

"Being proud of something is one thing. Going on around and bill-boarding yourself is another."

"Do you know how old I am?"

"Judging from our talk, you are probably thirty-five."

"I'm twenty-eight."

Simone perked up "Oh?"

Antonio smiled. "Does it make you feel weird that you are talking to someone fourteen years younger than you?" Antonio said.

"Do you find it weird to talking to a woman who's fourteen years older than you?"

"No, but . . ."

"Case closed."

Antonio laughed. "Yeah, you are domineering. So you don't feel uncomfortable?"

"Why should I? Dating younger men is a big turn-on for me."

"So indirectly what you are saying is that I turn you on."

"Nice try, Antonio."

"So you have gone out with younger guys like myself?"

"Yes, but not so young. The youngest guy I talked to was thirty-three. He was such a sweetheart." Simone paused.

"What's wrong?"

"Oh, nothing. I'm fine. I was just daydreaming—or I guess I should say 'night dreaming.' Anyhow, enough about me and my depressing sob story."

"No problems." Antonio yawned. "OK, it's getting really late. I should head off here."

"Yeah me too."

They both said good night to each other and hung up. Antonio stretched his arms, yawned loudly, gazed up at the ceiling, and, for the first time in a while, smiled because he was content.

Simone lay on her luxurious bed staring at Antonio's painting that had been hung up on a wall facing her. She stared at the naked couple. Her eyes felt heavy as she yawned, and she curled up with her pink satin pillow as she sunk deep into slumber. Moments later, she felt warmth against her eyelids. As she opened them, bright light stung her eyes. She squinted as she got up. Surrounding her were dense maple, oak, and evergreen trees. The warm air, clear sky, and large lake in front of her made Simone feel relaxed. She gazed up, placed her hands on her naked chest and gasped. She then smiled, licked her lips, and beckoned for the towering figure standing in front of her to approach her. Kneeling down in front of her was a young naked man whose face was obscured by the blinding light. She pulled him close as he opened his lips. Their tongues swirled against one another. The young man caressed her shoulders before proceeding down her neck. Simone shivered and let out a sigh. The young man continued covering her neck with kisses. Simone felt her naked body weaken. Her senses were overloaded by the intimacy. The young man's hands trailed towards her stiff breasts, and Simone let out a moan. His tongue darted along the valley between her breasts. Simone wanted to explode, and he wouldn't stop. Her legs quivered as the man flung her thighs over his shoulders. He gazed into Simone's face before proceeding further between her legs. Simone squinted trying to see who this lover was. It was a mystery: she didn't know where she was, and she didn't know who this man was, either. The young man stopped, gazed at Simone and forcefully grabbed Simone's legs and propped them on his muscular shoulders. Simone gasped in anticipation as the young man's hand trailed down between her moist, hungry thighs. Closing her eyes, Simone groaned loudly as her legs quivered.

"And that was Marvin Gaye, with his classic song, "Let's Get It On," a voice interrupted.

Simone froze. She quickly opened her eyes. The sun beamed into her bedroom, the birds chirped, and her clock radio blared.

She yawned and looked at the time, which blinked 7:30am.

Simone gazed up at the painting and smiled.

"Good morning, Antonio." she said to herself.

CHAPTER EIGHT

Mondays were so predictable: congestion on the roads, long lines at the coffee shop and the unshakeable lack of energy that everyone feels when going to work. Everyone except Antonio. For the first time in weeks, Antonio felt revived, refreshed, and content.

Lisa looked up from her computer screen and screwed up her face as Antonio walked pass by her desk. His happy mood intrigued her.

"Good morning, Lisa," Antonio said, waving as he passed.

"Good morning. Gee, did someone get lucky last night?" Lisa snorted.

"Don't be ridiculous. I just feel good, that's all." Antonio said.

"You? Feel good on a Monday?" Lisa teased.

Antonio walked over to Lisa. "Do I really look that happy?"

"Uh, yeah. You're really happy. It's almost making me sick. Let me guess, the lesbian finally took you back?"

Antonio laughed. "No, my little uneducated one."

Lisa screwed up her face even more. "My little uneducated one? God, you *are* too happy, and I think I am going to puke."

"Don't be silly, Lisa."

Lisa rolled her eyes. "Yes, you are."

"Whatever Lisa. I just feel refreshed this morning—that's it." Antonio headed toward the elevator. "See you later."

Lisa ignored Antonio and shook her head. In the meantime, Greg had entered the office and waved to Lisa. Lisa got up from her desk and beckoned him over.

"What's up?" Greg said.

"OK, who did Antonio sleep with last night?"

Greg leaned back. "Come again?"

"Tony slept with someone last night, didn't he?" Lisa said.

"No. Well I don't think so. Why? Does he have that extra spring in his step?"

"Yes, he does," Lisa said. He came in the office and he looked so energetic."

Greg rubbed his chin. "Wow. And today's Monday."

"Precisely my point." Lisa said.

Greg knocked on Antonio's door.

"Come in." Antonio yelled.

Greg opened the door. Antonio sat at his desk working on some files. He looked up at Greg. "What's up?"

"Nothing," Greg replied, "What's up with you?"

"Nothing much." Antonio replied.

Greg stared at him. "Yeah, right."

"What do you mean *yeah right*?"

Tony, I've known you since we were twelve. Something happened last night. What did you do last night?"

"Greg, first of all we only knew each other since we were fifteen, not twelve."

Greg rolled his eyes. "Whatever, same thing."

Antonio got up from his desk and headed towards the door, He closed the door and turned around. "She called me."

"Simone?"

"Yep, she called me."

"What time?"

"Before midnight sometime."

"She called you before midnight? That sounds professional."

"Greg, shut up."

"Well, what happened?"

"We just talked, basically . . . for three hours."

"Three hours?"

"Yep."

"What did you'll talk about?"

"Pretty much everything."

Greg settled himself into the chair in front of Antonio's desk. "Ok man, don't be stingy. Let's hear it." Greg said.

Antonio took a deep breath. "Greg, how old am I?"

"Twenty-eight, why?"

"How old do you think Simone is?"

"I don't know, thirty? Thirty-one? Thirty-two?"

"Try forty-two."

Greg eyes widened. "Forty what?"

"I'm not joking."

"Simone Jackson is forty-two years old?"

"Yep."

"Whoa, cradle robber."

"I know."

"And you're cool with this?"

"Cool? Well, it's not like we're dating."

Greg shook his head. "Holy shit! I don't believe this! Forty-two years old!"

Antonio walked towards his desk. "Greg, I swear to God, don't tell anybody, not even Larry."

"Tony, I don't know what to say. You're the man!"

Antonio stopped. "Huh?"

"Come on Tony, how many guys your age go out with older rich women?"

"Greg, stop your bullshit."

"Tony, I am serious. You are rocking the boat with an older lady."

"Greg, you're not helping me out here."

"Why the hell do I need to help you out? You are now living out the ultimate fantasy that every young guy out there wants to live. You're 'in conversation' with an older woman."

"And why is that such an ultimate fantasy?"

"Don't you watch the Discovery Channel or TLC? Women reach their *prime* in their forties. Their sex drives are just as high as horny teenage boys. You're twenty-eight years old, and she's forty-two. That's basically two trains running into each other."

Antonio shook his head. "Oh brother."

"Tony, if you have sex with this woman, you'll have the most wild time of your life. She'll ride you out! God, why couldn't this be me?"

"OK, let's get something straight here. First of all, I am not having sex or planning to have sex with Simone. Second of all, she is my client. I do not mix business with pleasure."

"Whatever man. So what else did you guys talk about?"

"Just stuff."

"Do you like her?"

Antonio didn't reply.

Greg got up from his seat. "See? That says it all, my friend."

"I didn't even say anything."

"Yeah, but it's written all over your face."

Again, Antonio fell silent.

* * *

Antonio left the office early. He had a painting in mind that he had left untouched for weeks, and he wanted to complete it. Antonio avoided the answering machine when he arrived home. There were messages he ought to hear, but he wanted to avoid that annoying "sexy" message. He wouldn't let the messages get to him tonight. He went upstairs, changed, and got ready to paint. A boost of energy made him ready to face the unfinished canvas that sat on his easel. He picked up his paint brush and started painting. Voices of people on the sidewalks below reached him through the open window. The sun was going down, but its warmth remained, and a light breeze caressed his neck as he continued working. Hours passed, and Antonio never once left his canvas. It was transforming, populated by vibrant, colourful, vivid images. Shades of navy blue filled the top half of the canvas, while accents of red, brown and yellow filled the middle.

Antonio yawned and glanced at the clock that read 12:01am. He stared at his new painting that now told a story. The sun had set and the sky was dark. In the background was an empty playground. A young boy sat in the sand with his hand outstretched, offering a rose to an older girl. She was leaning in to give him a kiss on the cheek. The young boy's yellow shirt and blue shorts were dusted with sand, and his black shoes were unlaced. The girl wore navy overalls, a black T-shirt, and white shoes.

Antonio mused at his painting and then turned to the answering machine. The blinking light was nagging at him, and he knew he wouldn't sleep until he had listened to the messages.

Beep: A man's voice was first. "Hello? Mr. Antonio Madison? Hello, my name is Maxwell Teak, and I'm interested in some of your paintings. My phone number is 342-9863. Please call me back. Thank you."

Antonio went into the kitchen to grab himself a drink.

Beep: "Yeah, it's Greg. Mr. Hill wants to know when you'll have the next painting completed. I know, I know, he's an asshole. But the man wants to know. Ring me later. Later."

Beep: There she was, even more insistent and deliberate: "Mmmmm . . . sexy . . . sexy . . ." Her soft panting voice pured like warm kitten but oozed a sense of raw sexuality.

Fourth Call: Mmmmmm . . . sexy . . . sexy . . . you are one sexy *motherfucker*, Antonio."

Antonio froze. She had gone too far, and every nerve in his body was tense with frustration.

The phone rang. Antonio grabbed the phone. "Who is this?"

"Antonio?" Simone said innocently.

Antonio changed his tone. "Oh hi, Simone, sorry."

"Um, did I call you at a bad time?"

Antonio sighed. "No but I'm just kind of losing it right now."

"You sound pissed. What's the matter?"

"I got another of those stupid messages."

"Again?"

"Yes."

Simone paused. "Why don't you tell the police if it bothers you?"

"Nah, it's not worth it. The only thing I could possibly do would be to change my home number."

"Well I hope it ends soon," Simone said.

Antonio had relaxed considerably hearing Simone's voice. "Yeah, me too."

"So how was your day?" Simone asked.

"Not bad at all. Got a lot of accomplished. Just finished another painting."

"Really?"

"Yeah."

"What is it?"

"Well, that is for you to find out."

Simone giggled. "Come on, Antonio, you aren't going to tell me?"

"Nope."

"Fine, be that way."

Antonio laughed. "You are something, you know that?"

Simone didn't reply.

"Anyhow, I should be getting to bed soon."

"Don't forget about Wednesday for lunch." Simone said.

"I won't. Good night."

"Good night," Simone said, hanging up. She laid on her bed, her black negligee hugging her hips and bosom. She held her cell phone to her chest, closed her face, and sighed.

Just then her phone rang.

Simone answered it. "Hello?"

"Where the hell have you been? I've been trying to contact you," scolded a deep male voice.

Simone sat up. "Ronnie, what do you want?"

"I want to know when we're gonna execute this plan of yours," Ronnie said.

Simone sighed. "Ronnie not now, it's too early in the plan for this."

"Listen, I don't have time for this. You gotta let me know when this is all gonna happen. I can't keep postponing my boys, you know. They have other *missions* to complete."

Again Simone sighed. "Ronnie, I told you. I will let you know when things are moving ahead, and then I will give you the signal."

Ronnie paused. "So have you started to talking to this painter yet?"

"Yeah," Simone said. "He's a real sweetheart."

"Listen, remember. You do not have time fall in love with that boy."

Simone didn't reply.

"Listen to me. We have a mission to complete and you need to follow the plan by plan, step by step. Bossman is gonna get real pissed if he hears that you are fucking the—"

"Ronnie, shut up! Just leave me alone. Anyhow listen, I told you I have a lunch appointment with him on Wednesday. Just do what I told you to do beforehand, OK?"

"Yeah. Fine," Ronnie said. He hung up.

Simone laid on the bed staring at Antonio's painting. She sighed, pulled up the covers, turned off the bedside lamp and went to bed.

CHAPTER NINE

Antonio chuckled. "You've got to be kidding me. He really said that?"

Simone sipped her red wine. "Yes he did, and I told him to get lost or else I would make him regret what he said."

It was Wednesday afternoon and Simone and Antonio were having their lunch meeting on the patio of Vito's Steak and Pasta Grillhouse on Broadway. The afternoon sun beamed on the patio, and people milled about on the streets next to them.

Antonio shook his head. "Simone, you are a brave woman."

Simone smiled as she twirled her fork in her pasta. She gazed into Antonio's eyes. Her lip twitched.

"You know, I am sure you have a lot of ladies who are after you," Simone said.

Antonio set down his fork, looked up at Simone, and laughed. "Me? Yeah right! I can't even get a woman to give me change for the phone, much less her number."

Simone laughed. "You are such a joker."

"I am serious! I've been really bad at getting ladies lately and I don't know what it is."

Simone gazed into Antonio's eyes and smiled. "It's because you are too cute."

"Cute?" Antonio said. "No, babies are cute. I am not cute."

Simone leaned in. "OK fine. You are sexy."

Antonio swallowed hard. "Um, thanks, but . . ."

Simone continued. "Antonio, please. You are an attractive man who has it going on. I mean, I am having lunch with you right now, right?"

Antonio nodded. "Yeah, but that doesn't mean anything."

"Antonio, I am going to have to teach you some things."

Antonio leaned in. "Simone, don't worry I've been schooling myself. I'm a graduate."

Simone's eyes widened. "Oh did we graduate with honors?"

"Triple A+"

Simone suddenly stopped flirting, arrested by the sight of a blue van with tinted windows that had parked at the corner of Broadway and 10th.

Antonio noticed her reaction. "I'm sorry, did I say something I shouldn't have?"

"Oh, no, nothing," Simone said distractedly. "I just feel dizzy, that's all."

The afternoon progressed as Simone and Antonio sat across from one another, engaged and sharing stories and new, private jokes. It was after 3pm when Antonio decided he had to head back to the office.

"Well, I had a wonderful time this afternoon." Antonio said.

Simone stared at her black shoes, pressed her lips to her napkin, smiled, and then looked up. "So did I."

Antonio smiled and scratched his chin. He suddenly didn't know what to do with his hands.

Simone grabbed his hand from across the table. "Antonio, tell me this. Do you find me attractive?"

Antonio stared at their entwined hands. "Um, well why do you ask?"

"Sorry, I just feel so insecure at times after everything that has happened to me."

Antonio grabbed her hand. "I know. As I said, you are a brave, strong woman."

Simone smiled sadly. "Thank you Antonio."

She had noticed that the blue dark van was still parked at the corner of the street.

Now her hands trembled. "Listen, I should let you go now, it's getting late."

"Yeah it is. I really should head back to the office."

"Well, thank you. We should do this again."

Antonio scratched his temple. "I was thinking. Maybe I could take you out for dinner some time."

Simone shimmered. "Really? Well I appreciate that. I will take that into consideration."

* * *

Antonio arrived home late that evening. When he opened the door he approached his answering machine. There were no messages.

"That's a first," Antonio thought to himself.

He went to the fridge to grab a beer when his phone rang.

He picked it up. "Yeah Greg, what's up?"

"Dude, I need a favor from you." Greg said.

"Greg I told you. You put on the deodorant *before* you put on your clothes."

"Whatever man, I need to ask you a favor."

"Shoot."

"Do you have Larry's cell number?"

"I think so, why?"

"Because Larry wanted me to call him so I can hook him up with a lawyer."

"A lawyer? For what?"

"Turns out that mail boy who had a fling with his ex is now suing him."

"Suing him? For what?"

"For 'bodily harm.'"

Antonio laughed. "What the hell? He slept with the dude's girlfriend, for fuck's sake! What kind of harm is that?"

"Tony, I don't know. The whole thing is pretty funny. Anyhow, the *real* reason why I am calling is because . . . well, you know . . ."

"No I don't." Antonio said.

"The lunch date with Mrs. Simone Jackson?"

Antonio sat on his couch. It was OK."

"OK? That's it? Just OK?"

"Yes, just OK. We talked about business and stuff."

"What kind of business?"

"Greg, why are you trying to make something out of nothing? Man, I told you we just had lunch and that was it." Antonio paused. "And I asked if she wanted to go out."

"Aha!" Greg exclaimed. "I knew there was something else. That's my boy. So you asked her out. And her reply?"

Antonio hesitated. "Uh, she said yes."

"That's it my man! Now you're rocking it."

"Hold up, Greg! Who said anything about—" A buzz indicating a call waiting interrupted them.

"Greg, hold on a sec. Someone is on the other line."

"Yeah man." Greg said.

Antonio clicked over. "Hello?"

"Mmmmmmm . . . sexy . . . sexy . . ."

"OK, who the fuck is this?" Antonio said slowly and deliberately.

"Sexy . . . mothafuckin' sexy . . ."

Antonio's nostrils flared and his jaw clenched. He demanded, "I said, who the fuck is this?"

"Mmmmmm . . . sexy," she continued to repeat, until he felt like he was going to explode.

"FUCK OFF!" Antonio yelled, slamming the phone down. His phone rang again.

Antonio picked up. "Hello?"

"Guy, why did you hang up on me?" Greg said.

"Greg, I got that stupid annoying message again!"

"Again?"

"Yes, again, and quite frankly, it's seriously pissing me off. All I keep getting is 'sexy sexy,' and it's fuckin annoying."

"And you sure it's not Simone?"

"No, I asked her already. If I ever find out who is doing this I swear to God I am gonna pound their fucking face!"

"Maybe you should get your phone number changed." Greg said.

"Yeah, I thought of that, but why should I have to change my number?"

"Yeah, but Tony, you are getting harassed, and that's not cool."

Antonio sat back down on the couch, still furious. "And what pisses me off is that the number shows up as private, like it's all planned out."

"And it's a woman's voice?" Greg said.

"Yes, it's a woman's voice. This soft, older but panting seducing voice."

"Does it sound familiar?"

"No, I don't know who it is."

"Man, I don't know. That *is* pretty creepy."

"Like I said, Greg, whoever is doing this is fuckin' dead!"

Down the street from Antonio's apartment a police officer car pulled up behind a van. The police officer got out of his car, put on his hat, and walked over to the parked van.

The officer tapped on the window. "Excuse me sir, is everything alright?"

The window winded down. "Everything's fine, sir," the man with the deep voice answered.

The officer hesitated, but decided against taking any more action. "Very well, sir, have a good night."

The police officer got into his car and drove off. The man behind the wheel took out a cigarette, lit it, and puffed out smoke while staring into Antonio's apartment.

"Yeah officer, everything is just working out just fine."

CHAPTER TEN

Antonio walked past Lisa in the lobby.

"Tony, wait, you have two messages," Lisa said.

Antonio stopped and turned around. "Who?"

"One was a client. She didn't say her name properly so I forward that one to your voicemail. And Mrs. Jackson."

"Simone Jackson?" Antonio said.

"Yes, she called too." Lisa leaned over her desk. "So have you gone out with her yet?"

Antonio ignored her comment and turned toward his office. "Thanks Lisa."

"Hey, you never answered my question!" Lisa insisted.

"I didn't hear you ask one."

Lisa gave Antonio a knowing look.

Just as Antonio reached the elevator, Larry and Greg walked past Lisa.

"Hey, Larry and Curly! Come over here," Lisa beckoned.

Larry and Greg obeyed good-naturedly.

Lisa leaned in. "So . . . ?"

Larry shrugged his shoulder. "So . . . what?"

"So what is the scoop with Tony and this Jackson woman?"

Greg rolled his eyes. "Nothing of your concern."

"Greg shut up, you love me enough to tell me about Antonio."

Again Greg rolled his eyes.

Larry nudged Greg. "Yeah. So what is up with Tony and the old woman?"

"Old woman?" Lisa said.

"Yeah, the woman is like forty-two or something," Larry said.

Lisa stood back. "Mother of God, are you serious?"

Greg looked at Larry. "Man, why did you have to say that?"

Larry shrugged his shoulders. "What?"

"Antonio is going out with some who is fourteen years his senior? Lord have mercy. Jacqueline is gonna freak when she hears this."

Greg leaned in. "Alright, Lisa, what do you mean Jacqueline is gonna freak when she hears this? You couldn't keep a secret if your life depended on it."

"Correction . . . I can keep *my own* secrets. Others . . . I spread," Lisa coyly replied.

Greg shook his head. "Anyhow I've got things to do."

Lisa stopped him. "Greg can I ask you something?" She glanced at Larry. "In private?"

Larry was used to this kind of thing from Lisa. As he walked away, he responded, "I guess that is my cue to leave."

Greg laughed as Lisa leaned in. "So, what is it about this older woman that Antonio likes?"

"Lisa, why is this is so important to you?"

Lisa demurred. "Well, I just want to know."

"No, there is a reason why you want to know. What is it?"

Lisa started playing with her hands. "Well I kind of think Antonio is, you know . . . ?"

" A human being?"

"Shut up, Greg."

"Lisa, what is it?"

"OK fine . . . I think Antonio is kind of cute."

Greg's eyes widened playfully. "Oh really now?"

Lisa blushed. "Yes, I think he is kind of cute. The girls here at work have been harassing me to ask him out, but I guess I am too shy."

"You? Motor-mouth Lisa? Shy? That's a first."

Her guard was up again. "Oh, whatever, Greg."

"Well, if you are so interested in him why don't you ask him out?"

"Greg, I can't."

"Why?"

"Because I am scared too."

Greg laughed. "Scared. Ha! That's real funny."

"I'm serious, Greg."

"Lisa, if you like him that much, ask him out." Greg headed towards the elevator and turned around. "Maybe if you weren't such a gossip it wouldn't be so hard for you to do this."

Lisa stared at her feet as Greg walked away. "Gossiping," as Greg called it, was the only way she knew to actually talk about things she wanted to talk about. But maybe if she were actually serious with Antonio, he would see that she really liked him and would take her seriously.

The elevators doors opened and Greg walked in. Lisa stared at the elevator doors, sighed, and went back to work.

* * *

Antonio sat in his office gazing out the window. He was wondering if asking Simone out was really a good idea. Antonio admired her perseverance and her ability to stand up against all the turmoil that she had dealt with. Simone was also very attractive for her age. Initially, Antonio hadn't been attracted to Simone, but at lunch when she crossed her long, toned legs Antonio felt himself getting aroused. He remembered the way her honey eyes contrasted with her smooth, dark skin. Antonio shook his head. *Man, what I am doing? I can't be going out with a client. That's not right.* However, Simone was attractive and that was something Antonio could not deny. Greg's comment about older woman and their sexual peak came to mind and Antonio smiled. He turned to his computer monitor, and sighed. It was a while since Antonio had been intimate with a woman. The last time had been a one night stand. Yes, the sex was amazing, but that was about it. The girl ended up being a married woman whose husband was very abusive. Antonio did not want to commit himself to excess baggage, so he'd stopped calling her.

Antonio was typing when Greg came into his office.

"You don't knock, eh?" Antonio said.

"I did not know it was the golden rule."

Antonio got up from his seat. "What's up?"

"I need that Spencer and Spencer file from you. They said they wanted to look at Timothy's work."

Antonio nodded and found the file in a drawer. "You seem very happy today," he commented.

"I am." Greg said. "I have a hot date tonight."

Antonio raised an eyebrow. "With whom, that stripper from the night club last weekend?"

Greg didn't reply.

"You nasty bastard! You are going out with that chick?"

Again Greg didn't reply.

"Man. I knew you were desperate, but my God."

Greg grabbed the file from Antonio. "Just for your information, she is not a stripper. Grow up—she is an adult entertainer."

"Yeah, OK, buddy."

Greg started to walk towards the door but looked like he had something else to say.

"What?" Antonio asked.

"Huh? Nothing, It's not anything," Greg said turning around.

Antonio shrugged his shoulders. "Alright man, talk to you later."

"Yeah, later." Greg said.

Greg closed the door behind him.

"Nah," Greg said, shaking his head. "Make Lisa tell Antonio herself."

* * *

Lisa arrived at her apartment early that evening. All she kept thinking about was asking Antonio out, but the more she thought about it, the more embarrassed she became. What if Antonio said no? What if Antonio laughed at her? Lisa opened her bag and flung it on the sofa. She was tired from the day's work, yet her mind was energized thinking about Antonio. Lisa went into the kitchen and grabbed a drink. Her black tabby cat walked up to her feet and purred at her.

"How are you Mr. Whiskers?" Lisa said, picking up her pliant kitten.

Mr. Whiskers meowed and purred in response.

Lisa considered herself to be a helpless romantic but carried a strong self confidence about herself that made her likable by many. Her auburn red hair, dimples and green eyes were often complemented by men but she was often self conscious about her figure. Though Lisa worked out, she often was self conscious about her full figure and often wore large clothing to cover it. Lisa rubbed her face against Mr. Whiskers and placed him on the floor. He took off into the living room. Lisa followed towards her sofa, eager to rest after the long day. She kept thinking about Antonio and the idea of asking him out. The more she thought about him, the more agitated she felt.

"Yes, I'm tired, but I feel uneasy. Shit, I need to take a walk," Lisa grudgingly acknowledged.

Lisa had her hands in her jeans pockets as she walked along the sidewalk, her curly auburn hair bouncing on her shoulders and her usual socially acceptable smile painted on her face. Walking, she focused on how best to approach Antonio. She thought of coming up to him the first thing in the morning and asking him if he was interested in lunch.

Lisa turned the corner and bumped into an older lady.

"Oh my gosh.. I am so sorry." Lisa apologized, bending down and picking up the woman's purse.

The woman glared at her, wordlessly grabbed the purse from Lisa, and continued on her way.

"What the hell?" Lisa mumbled. "She couldn't even say excuse me or thank you?"

Lisa stared at her shoes as she walked, still thinking about Antonio. As she stepped on the road to cross, she quickly lifted her head as two beams of bright lights blinded her. Without any warning, Lisa felt a hard blow to her side that was so painful that it paralyzed and numbed her completely Lisa gasped as she felt herself slam against the concrete. The unknown vehicle drove off without stopping.

"Oh my God! Someone call 911!" a woman screamed from across the street.

Lisa's body lay splayed out on the cold concrete in a pool of blood.

CHAPTER ELEVEN

Simone sat behind a heavy oak desk in her luxurious office. The carpet was pearl white and spotless. The walls were covered with awards, media pictures, and plaques honoring the achievements of her late husband. Simone absently played with her pen as she stared at her laptop. Stroking her pen, she thought of Antonio: his chiseled face, slim athletic body, his chocolate eyes, and his smile. Simone shivered with delight, and she sank into her chair, closing her eyes.

A knock at the door interrupted her reverie.

"Yes?" Simone said.

"Mrs. Jackson, I have an Antonio on the phone?" the voice replied from behind the door.

Simone sat up. "Oh, put him through."

Simone's heart raced as she waited for her phone to ring. Simone picked after the first ring. "Hello?"

"Hey, it's Antonio, how are you?" Antonio said.

Simone smiled. "Fine, and yourself?"

"Doing good, thanks. Working late I see?"

"Yes, unfortunately."

"Well I just called to say hi."

Again, Simone closed her eyes. "Thank you. That was thoughtful. Excuse my boldness, but I don't understand how a man like you can possibly be without a girlfriend."

Antonio laughed. "It's called working long hours and not finding that perfect woman."

"Well I am sure you will find her," Simone answered.

Antonio took a deep breath. "Simone, I have a question."

"Yes?"

"I am just curious. Why do you want me to personally deliver that picture that you bought from the art gallery?"

Simone paused. "Well, I have my reasons."

"And the reasons would be . . . ?"

"You don't worry about that."

"Ok fine, be that way."

Simone laughed. "Do you always make people laugh?"

"No, but I've never had any complaints when I do."

"I'm sure you haven't."

Antonio paused, wondering if he should flirt with her. "Well anyhow, I should let you go. I am sure you're busy with work."

"Antonio, it's eight o'clock. I shouldn't be working this late, but I do have some stuff I have to do."

"Yeah, I know the feeling, I don't want to work right now either." Antonio decided to go for it. "Simone, do you want to go for coffee or something?"

Simone smiled brightly. "Sure, I'm up for that."

"Great, what time should I meet you?"

"How's this—meet me at eight thirty at the Gala Coffee shop."

"Sure."

"Great, I'll see you then," she replied, trying not to sound too excited.

Simone hung up. She sat in her chair, her hand on her jaw, and her eyes sparkling. She remembered her dream and wanted it to be him. Simone sighed, grabbed her things, and headed out the door. Just as she buckled her seatbelt in her car, she heard her cell phone ring.

She looked at the number, sighed, and answered. "Ronnie, what do you want?"

"I fucked up." Ronnie said.

"What do you mean you fucked up?"

"I fucked up."

"How?"

"Well you remember you wanted me to go take care of that business deal at the corner of 5th and Lakeside?"

"Yeah?"

"Yeah, well the bastard came up with nothing."

"Nothing? What did you do?"

"Well, I decided to take care of him myself."

Simone froze. "How?"

"Let's just say that he probably has some bullet holes in his car."

"Ronnie! What the hell is wrong with you! You're on parole. If the police catch you with a gun, then—"

"You and I will be arrested." Ronnie replied darkly.

Simone remained silent.

"Listen I am just telling you that the plan got fucked, alright? That's it."

"Whatever. Listen, I'm going out for a while. I will talk to you later. Oh, and tell Juan and Zeus that I need them tomorrow for a conference that I am going to."

"Alright, but wait, I should probably tell you . . ." Ronnie paused. "Never mind."

"Never mind what?"

"Forget it. I was gonna tell you something, but forget it."

"Whatever, Ronnie, bye."

Ronnie grunted and hung up the phone. Simone ran her fingers through her hair and cursed. "Fuck, I don't need this right now." She grinned. "What I need is Antonio." She sped off, leaving the whole conversation behind.

Antonio waited for Simone in front of the coffee shop. They both greeted each other and walked into the shop. They picked up right where they'd left off. They laughed and joked, and time passed quickly. Simone decided to turn the conversation a different direction.

"So Antonio . . . can I ask you what you like to do in bed?"

Antonio reddened, and he wondered if he'd imagined it. "I beg your pardon?"

"You heard me. What do you like to do in bed?" Her tone was light, but she seemed completely serious.

Antonio rubbed his eyebrows. "Um, stuff that I'd rather keep personal."

"Why, are you some kind of undercover freak?" Simone laughed.

Antonio was taken by surprised by the conversation, yet at the same time, he wanted it to continue. He licked the cream from his cappuccino off his lips. "I like to show, not to tell."

Simone's eyes widened. "Are you always this descriptive?"

Antonio laughed.

Simone reached over and placed her hand over Antonio's. "I still can't get over the fact that you are this single guy who does not have a girlfriend."

Antonio shrugged his shoulders. "Neither can I."

Antonio felt Simone's nails tracing patterns on his wrists. He closed his eyes.

"That's really relaxing," he admitted.

"I'm sure it is," Simone answered in a low voice.

Antonio and Simone stood outside the coffee shop laughing.

"Wow, I really didn't realize that it was so late. I should be heading back," Antonio said, looking at his watch.

Simone sighed. "Yeah, and I don't want to leave either, but I guess we have to."

"Well, I will see you tomorrow when I deliver the painting—when we have our actual dinner . . . date."

"That's right."

Antonio took out his car keys and started in the direction of his car. "I'll see you tomorrow."

Simone waved back. Antonio settled into his car and smiled. There was something so attractive about Simone, but he couldn't place it. He did know that it was something purely physical. He drove home thinking about the way she had scratched her nails on his palms.

When he got home, he saw his answering machine flashing. Antonio faced the machine. He didn't want to answer because he knew that if he heard that annoying message it would totally spoil his mood.

Antonio shook his head and walked into the kitchen. "I am not answering that goddamn machine." He grabbed a glass of water and sat on his couch, turning on the television.

The phone rang.

"Hello?"

There was silence.

"Hello?" Antonio said again.

No one replied.

Antonio raised his voice. "Listen, you have two seconds to say something or else I'm gonna hang up on you."

Again, no reply.

Antonio cursed and hung up the phone.

The phone rang again. Antonio immediately picked up the phone. "Hello?"

Again, no answer.

"HELLO?"

No answer.

Antonio hung up. "That's it, I am getting my phone number changed. This is ridiculous."

Simone sat in her car with her eyes closed. Janet Jackson's "Any time, Any place" mellowed from her speakers as she clutched her cell phone to her chest. She sighed, started her car, and drove off.

CHAPTER TWELVE

"Where the hell is Lisa?" Larry wondered out loud. "I need that report and she was supposed to send the Word document to me."

Greg shrugged his shoulders. "I dunno, man. It is unlike her not to show up to work like this."

Antonio walked in the office. Greg approached. "Hey Tony, have you seen Lisa?"

Antonio shrugged his shoulders. "No, why?"

"Because she's not here and it's really odd for her not to show up."

"Maybe she got lucky last night." Antonio said.

Larry and Greg both gave Antonio a doubtful look.

"OK, maybe she didn't."

"Alright, well I am gonna try to get this document myself. If she comes in, tell her I am looking for her," Larry said.

Antonio's cell phone rang. "Hello? Oh hi, Simone."

Greg started making faces at Antonio, mimicking his conversation with Simone.

"Yeah everything is cool . . . yes, I will be there with the painting at 2pm as promised. Alright, bye Simone."

"*OK, bye Simone,* " Greg said in a low voice, mimicking Antonio.

Antonio glared at Greg. "I should kick your ass for doing that you—"

William Huntingwood, the manager of the gallery, approached Antonio and Greg in a panic. "Guys, where is Lisa?"

They both shrugged their shoulders.

"That is so unlike her to not show up to work like that. I'm gonna call her house."

Greg turned to Antonio and leaned in. "Think she got laid?" Antonio shot a look. "Oh so when I ask that question, I get a strange look from you and Larry but now you ask me the same question?"

"Well now you have me thinking." Greg said. "So you think she did?"

Antonio shrugged his shoulders. "Who cares? Anyway, I have to jet. I have to drop off some stuff for one client, and then I have to drop off the painting at Simone's."

"Yes, we know." Greg teased.

Antonio shook his head and proceeded to the elevators.

Antonio arrived at Simone's house, stunned by its gold gates and beautiful, manicured lawn. The short roadway was lined with all sorts of flowers and perfectly trimmed bushes. Antonio reached to the entrance, where two large white pillars greeted him. A statue of a young lady rested peacefully on the doorsteps. Antonio hoisted his painting, walked up the stairs, and rang the doorbell. The doorbell chimed through the house as if it were a concert venue. There was brief pause before a short, bald gentleman answered the door.

"Yes, may I help you?" he inquired politely in a British accent.

"Oh. I am here to see Simone Jackson?"

"Yes, you must the painter boy, Antonio."

Painter boy Antonio? Antonio thought. *What has she been saying to people about me?*

"Right this way," the butler said, gesturing down the hallway. Large pillars lined the ceramic, mirrored hallway. A large painting of Mona Lisa hung on the wall next to a larger painting of slaves working in a crop field. Antonio's eyes widened as he walked down the hallway. Pearl white moldings emerged from the ceilings above, surrounding a huge skylight that poured the afternoon sun into the hallway. Simone emerged from around a corner dressed in black dress pants and a white blouse. Her hair was pulled up elegantly in a bun.

She smiled. "So you are here. Thank you so much."

Antonio rested the painting against a wall. "No problem. My God, your place is amazing."

"Oh, it's nothing."

"Nothing? The entrance looks like the house from The Fresh Prince of Bel-Air."

Simone looked at him quizzically and laughed. "Would you like a drink?"

"Yeah sure."

Antonio picked up the painting and followed Simone into her office. Simone locked the door.

"Sit," Simone said, pointing at the white leather sofa. Antonio sat while Simone went over and poured two Jack Daniels.

"Well, I am glad you found the place." Simone said.

"Well, as I said, you have a nice place." Antonio replied, looking around the living room that she called her "office." The living room seemed as large as a football field. Paintings and artwork hung from the ivory walls. To the far left was a stately grand piano. Towards the centre of the living room was a large statue of an obscure object that Antonio couldn't make out. Long, white silk drapes covered the windows.

"Thank you, Antonio." Simone sat down beside Antonio and gave him his drink. Simone and Antonio chatted for over an hour. Their conversation made it seemed like they had known each other for years. Simone placed her drink on the coffee table. "So Antonio, are you gonna tell me exactly what you like to do in bed?"

Antonio's eyes widened. "Should I remind you that we actually have a full date ahead of us this evening?"

Simone leaned in. "Why wait until this evening when we can start now?"

Antonio could not get over Simone's forwardness. He felt himself getting excited. He coughed. "Really? Well I mean it would be forward of me to . . ."

Simone placed her hand on Antonio's knee and leaned closer. "Antonio, remember I told you earlier that if I want something, I take it."

Antonio looked down at his hands and then back into Simone's eyes. He felt his neck burning. His lips twitched and his heart raced. "Yeah, but you know what they say. Good things come to those who wait."

Simone grabbed Antonio's hand and placed it on her thigh. "But not to those who wait too late."

Antonio drew himself closer to Simone and their lips met. Simone leaned back into the couch as Antonio moved his hand over her shoulder. Simone pulled him down to her, and they kissed, trembling at first, and then with increasing need. Simone grasped at Antonio's back, and her legs quivered as she sunk further into the sofa. Antonio moved his tongue from her mouth and started exploring Simone's neck and behind her ears. Simone whimpered as Antonio proceeded further. She moaned as Antonio reached her blouse. He looked up at Simone. Her heavy breathing and dreamy, pleased expression made Antonio more excited. He looked down, opened her blouse and greedily covered every inch of her chest with his eyes and his mouth. Simone moaned in excitement with closed eyes and clenched fists. Simone got up and aggressively pushed Antonio into the place she had been. She straddled his thighs, gazed into his eyes and moaned.

"I want you. I want you now," She whimpered.

Antonio felt as though his heart would beat out of his chest. Simone pushed him away, unbuttoned his shirt, and grabbed his hands. She wanted to take in every detail of his smooth, muscular chest—the way his muscles tensed with anticipation. She licked her lips, bent down and slowly, tantalizingly, and hungrily licked Antonio's chest. Antonio's eyes closed while Simone's tongue ravished his senses. He felt mesmerized, possessed, and weak, yet he knew her passion was right for him. Simone had reached Antonio's navel. Antonio pulled her again towards him and kissed her. Simone pulled away, stood up, and unbuckled Antonio's pants. Antonio unzipped Simone's pants, removed her top, and laid her on the couch. Antonio slowly placed his weight on top of her, and the sensation of his body, heavy and demanding, drove her insane. Her dream was now becoming a reality. Antonio's fingers trailed to Simone's breasts and towards her erect nipples. Simone flung her head back as Antonio dove in between her breasts and attacked them with his tongue. Sending Simone into a frenzy, Antonio's tongue trailed down between her breasts to her navel. Simone grabbed his head and pushed it down further. Simone moaned and shook as Antonio's tongue made its way between her thighs. He licked her slowly, up and down, as her hips pressed insistently toward his face Simone panted, and her moaning grew louder. Antonio continued.

"Oh my God . . . yes," Simone cried.

Slowly, Antonio moved his head upwards to Simone. She grabbed his hips and thrust them between her thighs. Antonio was overcome by the incredible warmth and wetness between Simone's thighs. Simone grabbed Antonio and kissed him while Antonio slowly teased her and reentered her. Simone groaned in ecstasy. Antonio and Simone were lost in a sea of passion. Their bodies attacked, wrestled, and pinned each other. Simone's body tensed and arched upward as Antonio thrust even deeper. Her nails dug into Antonio's muscular back, and he forcefully pulled her thighs over his shoulders. Simone's eyes were dazed, and she felt her whole body quiver with Antonio's thrusting. Her toes curled and she closed her eyes in deep pleasure as Antonio's body tensed and quivered.

Simone held on to Antonio's chest. "Oh my God . . . oh . . . my . . . yes . . ." Antonio didn't stop. He couldn't stop and he didn't want to. Simone's breathing was heavy on his neck, and she suddenly tensed as a ripple of unbelievable pleasure coursed through her body. Her whole body convulsed as Antonio let out a loud moan. Their bodies shook violently together. Antonio let out a sigh as he collapsed on top of Simone. Simone placed her hand on her chest as she sighed heavily. She opened her eyes and stared at Antonio's sweaty, naked, muscular body lying on top of her. Simone turned her head to the side, staring at Antonio's artwork. She bit her lip, closed her eyes, and smiled.

For a minute, they lay in complete silence.

"Simone, there is a gentleman here to see you," a voice suddenly interrupted from behind the door.

Simone jumped and opened her eyes. She got up from her office chair. "Oh, who is it?"

"It's Antonio. You were expecting him here with a painting."

Simone adjusted herself, took a deep breath, and smiled. "Send him in here."

* * *

Ronnie picked up the phone and dialed Simone's phone number. There was no response.

"Fuck, what the hell is she doing?" Ronnie wondered. "I hope she is not fucking that artist boy." Ronnie hung up the phone and stood in front of the mirror. He dabbed the cut over his eye with a Kleenex. His black T-shirt stuck on his large belly that over hung his black jeans. Ronnie's skin was smeared with sweat and oil. Ronnie opened the door and stepped into a dark, large room. He flipped on the light and stared at his dark blue van. Beside the van sat a bucket with water and a towel. Slowly, he walked over to the front of van with the bucket and water. He paused in front of the van, sighed, and began wiping away the blood-stains that were smeared on the chrome bumper.

CHAPTER THIRTEEN

Antonio stood in the hallway observing the paintings that hung on the white walls. Simone opened the door from the end of the hallway.

She smiled. "You're here." Her voice echoed down the hallway.

Antonio approached her. "Yes. You really have a great place here. It reminds me of the mansion in The Fresh Prince of Bel-Air."

Simone's heart raced. It was just like her dream. "That is so funny that you say that." Simone led Antonio into her office and closed the door behind her. She didn't lock the door.

* * *

Greg sat in his office reading through some files that he had to get ready for a meeting.

William Huntingwood barged in. "Greg, do you know where Monica is?"

Greg looked up. "No, why?"

William Huntingwood's voice shook. "I need her to come in and replace Lisa."

"Why, what happened to Lisa?"

"I just got a call from the hospital. Lisa was involved in a terrible hit-and-run accident. She was hit by a van that sped off, and the doctors say it's serious."

Greg dropped his pen. "Are you serious?"

"Yes, some of us were gonna visit her tonight. The doctors said she was hit really bad. She's in a coma."

Greg mouth widened. He slumped back in his seat. "Oh my God, that is terrible."

William Huntingwood nodded. "Well, I have sent out a general e-mail to everyone at work and we hope she pulls through. But now I need to track down Monica."

"Bill, if you need anything let me know."

William Huntingwood nodded and darted out of the office.

* * *

Antonio took a sip on his Jack Daniel's. "And then the girl says 'well, when the plane crashes, the first thing they are gonna look for is the black box.'"

Simone burst out laughing. "Antonio, that is a sick joke!"

Antonio laughed while pouring some ice into a glass. "Yeah, but you are laughing, aren't you?"

Simone nodded. "Yes, I am."

The two talked for an hour. Simone gazed into Antonio's eyes while he talked. She could not help but think about her daydreams. They were so real that they tormented her. She wanted to feel his body against hers. She wanted to experience the deep waves of passion and raw sexuality that were painted in her deepest thoughts. Even his voice made her sexually aroused. She slowly, seductively, and enticingly crossed her legs while Antonio yammered, blabbered, and chatted about the art gallery. She placed a hand on Antonio's knee. Antonio stopped talking. He lowered his head and then gazed up into her eyes. His lips twitched. Simone bit hers.

"You must be tired of you me babbling on like this." Antonio said. "I should be heading back—"

Simone grabbed his knee. "No, stay. I mean, if you want."

Antonio smiled. He knew he had to go back to the office, but he felt himself getting excited by Simone's invitation to stay.

"OK, I'll stay for a bit."

Simone smiled.

Just then, Antonio's phone rang. He looked at the phone and answered it.

"Greg, what's up?"

"Yo, Tony you would never believe what happened to Lisa."

Antonio sat up. "No, what happened to her?" Simone took her hand off Antonio's knee.

"She was hit by a van."

Antonio eyes widened. "What? Are you serious?"

"Yeah, and now she is in the hospital in serious condition."

"Well I hope she's going to be OK . . ."

"We are not too sure about her condition, honestly, Bill has reception covered. I will let you know later on if I hear anything. I will call you later, OK?"

"Yeah, later."

Simone leaned in. "Something wrong?"

"Yeah, a co-worker of mine was involved in some accident. Some van hit her."

Simone placed her hand on her chest. "Oh my gosh . . . that is awful."

"I know."

"Well, I hope she is doing alright."

"Yeah, I hope so too."

Antonio and Simone talked for another couple of minutes before Antonio got up to leave.

"You are such a good conversationalist," Simone said.

"Hey, we have a dinner date tonight so I don't want to ruin it."

Simone blushed. "Yes, you're right."

Antonio stood in front of the door. "Well, I should head back. I'll see you later on tonight."

Simone nodded. Antonio proceeded to the door, said goodbye, and left. Simone stood staring at the door as Antonio drove off. She ran her finger over her moist lips, sighed, grabbed her cell phone from her pocket and dialed.

"Yeah?" the voice answered.

"OK Ronnie, Antonio has left and he will be back later on this evening about 8pm. I will meet you at the corner of Missouri and Ontario. Please don't screw up this time."

Ronnie coughed. "Listen." He paused. "Are you sure this is all gonna work out?"

Simone laughed. "Ronnie, please. We discussed this already. Do I have to go over the plan with you again?"

"Dana, for crying out loud, do you really think this is gonna work? Frig, I am on parole for second degree murder on cases that you—"

Simone trembled. "Ronnie, shut the fuck up. First of all, don't you ever call me Dana again. Do you understand me?"

Ronnie did not reply.

"Answer me, goddamn it!"

Ronnie grunted.

"And second of all, I hired you as a hit man. You do what you're ordered to do. If you can't follow the orders, I have no problem going straight to the police and having you arrested for murdering—"

"Is that what you're gonna do, Dana? Blackmail me? Are you that fucking stupid? Listen, Dana, or Simone, or whatever your goddamn name is now. Don't fuck with me."

"Ronnie, shut the fuck up! Be here at 8 o'clock, and don't fuck it up this time." Simone hung up and sighed. "Stupid idiot." She licked her lips and took a deep breath. "I should get ready, I guess."

* * *

"So tonight is the big date, eh?" Larry said picking up his car keys from his desk.

Greg nodded. "Yep. My man Tony is gonna get some tonight."

Larry scratched his head. "You know, that name Simone Jackson rings a bell so much, and it bothers me that I can't remember."

"A past fling?" Greg said.

"Trust me, I would remember that Greg."

"Man you have to see her. She is a total knock-out for someone her age. Like, damn, she makes Tina Turner lose in any competition."

"Are you forgetting that Tina Turner is in her sixties and still looks good?"

Greg paused. "Yeah you're right, but still, she looks good."

Larry got up from his desk. "Anyhow man, it is Friday, and it's the weekend."

Greg nodded. "Any plans this weekend?"

"Well, since I am officially single, I guess I will visit the place where I can relax my mind and chill and reflect about life."

"Let me guess, the strip club?"

Larry nodded. "You know it."

Greg proceeded to the door. "Well, man, you have fun. I am gonna head out and relax. Maybe I should go visit Lisa and see how she's doing."

"I'd think that would be a great idea." Larry said.

Greg said goodbye to Larry, grabbed his belongings from his office, and left. Greg hopped into his black Acura and sped off. Greg had Groove Theory's "Tell Me" blasting from his speakers as the city lights and buildings buzzed by. The fresh air was warm, and a red sun hovered over the horizon.

Simone drove along Missouri Street and pulled over to the right shoulder behind a dark blue van. Putting on her sunglasses, she got out of her tinted white Mercedes and walked over the passenger side. Ronnie was passed out in the driver's seat. She tapped on the window. Ronnie woke up. He leaned over and opened the door.

"Took you long enough," he complained, yawning.

"Whatever, I don't have time to deal with you right now. Let's get this done and out of the way," Simone said, climbing into the passenger seat.

Greg hummed to the lyrics of Groove Theory's, "Tell Me."

He snapped his finger. "Shoot, I said I would go visit Lisa at the hospital." At the approaching street, Greg turned right onto Missouri

Street and headed south to the hospital. Greg thought about Lisa's crush on Antonio and smiled. He wondered if any of the other girls at the office had a crush on Antonio or even on himself, for that matter. He shook his head and headed towards Ontario Street.

Simone got out of the van with a black briefcase. She stared hard at Ronnie. "Remember what I told you."

Ronnie nodded.

"Hey, listen, I don't want to hear about any more screw ups."

"Dana, relax. I told you I took care of it already."

Simone answered between clenched teeth, "I told you, don't ever call me that again."

Ronnie gave her the finger.

Simone glared at him. "I'll see you later." Simone walked over to her car. Ronnie started his van and pulled out onto the street without checking his blind spot. As Simone got into her car she heard a screech from a car's tires and turned her head to see a panicked Greg behind the steering wheel, swerving his car away from the van. .

Greg got out of his car and started shouting at Ronnie. "What the fuck do you think you're doing, you fucking idiot?"

Ronnie rolled down his window. "Buddy, who the fuck do you think you are talking to?"

"You, you idiot. Check where you're going before pulling out into fucking traffic."

Ronnie got out of his car. "If I were you, I would get back in the car or else you will regret arguing with me."

"And if I were you, I would learn how to drive properly, you jackass."

Simone was frozen inside her car. Her hands trembled. She quickly slid the briefcase underneath the passenger seat, rubbed her face, and stormed out of the car. She approached Ronnie. "Um, excuse me sir, but I saw everything and this gentleman was right."

Greg turned around. "Oh my God, you are Mrs. Jackson, Antonio's girl . . . I mean client, right?"

Simone smiled. "Yes." She turned to Ronnie and gave him an innocent look. "I am sorry, sir. I hate to be a nuisance, but you were not looking at what you were doing. I do think this is your fault."

Ronnie understood Simone's act and played along. He folded his arms. "Listen, *madam*. I really think you should stay out of this."

Simone stepped in. "Well, I could always call the police and have them settle it right here."

Ronnie gave Simone an evil glare. "You know what? I don't have time for this." Ronnie got into his van and drove off.

Greg turned to Simone. "Wow, Simone, I don't know what to say but—"

"Greg, don't mention it. A friend of Antonio's is a friend of mine."

Greg smiled.

"Well, thanks. 'Thanks' doesn't really seem like enough, but . . ."

"Don't worry about it."

Simone's cell phone rang. "Listen, I have to go, but I guess I will see you another time."

Greg nodded. "Yes indeed, Mrs. Jackson .. um, or Simone."

Simone smiled and climbed in to her Mercedes. Greg adjusted his tie, settled in to his Acura, and drove off.

Simone answered her phone. "What?"

"What the fuck was that all about?"

"That was Antonio's friend, Greg."

"So?"

"So, I don't think that it would be a great idea to beat up Antonio's friend. Well, not yet, at least."

Ronnie paused. "What do you mean not yet?"

"Never mind. Anyway, stop calling me. I have to meet up with Antonio in two hours."

Ronnie hung up. Simone pulled out a briefcase from under the passenger seat. She rubbed her hands, smiled, and looked around to see if anyone was around. Cautiously, she opened the brief case, and her smile brightened. She picked up a thick band of $100 bills and fanned herself. She giggled and placed the money back in the briefcase. She then picked up a 9mm automatic gun from the briefcase and held it between her warm hands. She closed her eyes and started imaging Antonio in her bed satisfying her. She groaned and kissed it before placing the gun back in the suitcase.

"You are going to be helping me a lot," Simone said to it.

CHAPTER FOURTEEN

Antonio stood in front of his bedroom dabbing on his cologne. His stomach was in knots. He felt like a kid going on his first date. "God, Tony, stop acting like this," Antonio chastised himself.

The phone rang.

Antonio walked over and picked up the phone.

"Hello?"

No one replied.

"Hello?"

There was a pause.

"Hello!" Antonio shouted.

"Mmmmmm sexy . . . sexy . . ."

Antonio slammed the phone down and glared at his reflection in the mirror. He clenched his jaw until it hurt, picked up the phone, and dialed. Antonio sat on the couch, waiting for someone to answer.

A bubbly female's voice greeted him. "Hello, Abel Phone Company."

Antonio cleared his throat. "Yes, I'm looking to get my phone number changed. I am getting harassing calls on my phone."

* * *

Greg stood over Lisa's bed, looking down at her in shock. Lisa was unrecognizable. Her french vanilla complexion skin was all puffy, her lips were flaking, and her hair draped lifelessly on her shoulders. A plastic tube was taped inside her mouth. All kinds of other tubes and lines shot out from her body, making her seem trapped. Beeping and ticking noises were the only sounds that echoed in the cold, brightly-lit room.

Greg turned to a nurse that was observing. "Do you think she'll be alright?"

"It's hard to predict right now," the nurse responded. "She was hit really bad and suffered a major concussion. Only time will tell at this point."

Greg sighed and turned back to Lisa.

"Where's my baby! I've got to see my baby!" a female voice sobbed down the hallway.

Greg turned his head to the distressed voice. Her entreaties grew louder. A woman with grey curls and a red hat burst into the room and ran to Lisa.

"Oh my God, my baby!" she sobbed.

The nurse stepped in. "Ma'am, I am going to have to ask you not to disturb her. She is in serious condition right now."

"That's my baby!" shouted the woman. "Oh my God, that's my baby! How could someone do this to her?"

Greg watched helplessly.

"Madam, please, have a seat." The nurse said.

"Who did this to my baby? Who?" She turned to Greg. "Do you know who did this?"

Greg shrugged his shoulders. "Ma'am, I don't know. I am just her co-worker."

The woman let out a loud cry. "Lord have mercy. Lightning and brimstone to the wicked and evil person who has done such an awful thing to my daughter. Fire shall be dashed on his soul for destroying God's child."

Greg stood back. "Ma'am, maybe if you had a seat, you might—"

"NO!" screamed the woman. "I want my baby. I want that Lucifer's son to die in the flaming hells that surround his wicked soul."

Greg was overwhelmed. He turned and looked pleadingly at the nurse. She attempted to calm the woman by stroking her back.

"Madam, please listen to me. Your daughter is recuperating right now. Your carrying on like this is not going to make anything better," the nurse explained.

The woman glared at the nurse. "How dare you tell me how I should feel for my baby. That is my baby girl lying in that bed—that awful, wicked bed."

Three security men came into the room and took the woman gently by the arm.. "OK, Ma'am, we are gonna take you out to a room right now so you can calm down.

"NO! Let me go!" screamed the woman. She struggled weakly against the security guards as they escorted her outside.

"I WANT TO SEE MY BABY! LET ME GO! LET ME GO!"

Greg stood in the room, frozen and helpless.

* * *

Antonio sat in his car, staring through his rearview mirror. He adjusted his jacket and took a deep breath. His stomach turned. "God, Antonio, why are you feeling this way?" he asked himself. "This is not the first time you have gone out with her. He took a deep breath, got out of his car, and walked up to the front door. Simone waited on the other side of the door. Her long, black sequined dress shimmered with her silver earrings. She startled when Antonio rang the doorbell.

The butler walked in to the hallway and spotted Simone leaning against the door. "Madam, are you OK?" asked the butler.

"Yes, George, I am fine." Simone said.

The butler shrugged his shoulders and headed towards the kitchen. Simone took another deep breath and opened the door.

Antonio stood with a rose in his hand, smiling.

"Hey." He said.

Simone grinned. "Hey."

Antonio handed her the rose. "This is for you."

Simone took the rose and held it to her nose. "Oh this lovely. You didn't have to do this."

"Oh, it's nothing. I wanted to."

"Thank you. You are such a gentleman."

"Is your butler on holiday?"

Simone giggled. "Um, no, he's busy."

Antonio offered her his arm. "Shall we?"

Simone held on to him. "Oh yes, we shall."

They dined at Vito's Steak and Grill Restaurant in the classiest part of downtown. They sat on the patio with a candlelit dinner. Antonio mentioned the annoying call.

Sipping on her wine and staring down at her grilled salmon, Simone shook her head, saying, "I think that person is crazy."

"Tell me about it," Antonio said, carving into his steak and then into his steamed vegetables. Every so often, Simone would grab Antonio's hand and Antonio would stop what he was doing. Simone was destined to make her dreams a reality tonight no matter what it took. *Maybe if I can get him drunk enough, he will do whatever I say,* Simone thought to herself, but shook off the idea. After dinner, Antonio and Simone took a stroll down the promenade by the lake. The night air was warm. Simone held on to Antonio's hand as they talked.

Simone stopped him. "You know I had a great time this evening."

"So did I," Antonio said.

They stood in silence.

Simone leaned in. "How would you like to come over to my place and relax for a bit?"

Antonio felt himself get excited. "For sure." Antonio still felt uneasy dating one of his clients, but, he told himself, there was nothing long-term in their contract. They both headed to their cars and drove to Simone's house.

Larry arrived at his apartment and threw his keys on the kitchen counter. All he could think about was Simone Jackson and the familiarity of that name. He threw his jacket on the counter and sat down in front of his computer.

"I know I've heard of the name before. I just know it," Larry said to himself as he typed her name into Google. There were a number of "Simone Jackson's," but none were her. Larry scratched his forehead. He tried a few other entries with few results. He got up from his computer desk and went into the kitchen to grab a beer.

He sipped on his beer. " Jackson . . . Jackson. Wait? Harold Jackson? That company. We had some ties with them before." Larry left his beer on the counter and hopped in front of the computer. He Googled the named "Harold Jackson." Larry eyes widened as he saw the results. He then added the name "Simone" to the list. Larry grew excited by as more and more links appeared.

He clicked feverishly, reading biographies and news clips. "I knew it. I knew I heard that name somewhere." Larry then clicked on a picture of Simone and Harold. Larry's face dropped. He slowly brought his hands to his face in shock.

"Oh, my God. It can't be. It just can't be."

Antonio followed Simone inside her house. Simone proceeded to walk up her stairs.

Antonio stopped. "Um, where do you think you are going?"

Simone turned around. "Oh shut up, you sexy boy, and follow me."

Antonio laughed. "Um, well OK."

Simone led Antonio into her bedroom. Her bedroom was lit with fragrant candles.

Antonio adjusted his tie. "Simone, I really didn't think that . . ."

Simone grabbed Antonio and brought him to her face. "Antonio, from the first time I laid on eyes on you, I knew I wanted you."

Antonio's lips twitched. "Um wow, thanks. Simone, I confess I find you really attractive, too."

Simone leaned closer and whispered. "Then show me."

Antonio jolted as Simone pressed her lips firmly against Antonio's. His hand soon found its way onto Simone's shoulder and another caressed her back. His fingers trailed the bumps of her spine, making Simone moan. Antonio felt trapped. He didn't want to pursue anything, but Simone's sexual impulse was too much for him to resist. Antonio drew Simone's mouth to his and pressed his lips firmly to hers. Simone whimpered as her hands unbuttoned Antonio's jacket. She then stopped and gazed in his eyes. "Antonio, I want you."

Antonio nodded his head slowly, possessed. He pulled her to himself and kissed her passionately.

Larry continued, frantically clicking on links to other websites. Larry watched in horror as he saw the photos of Simone and Harold together.

"This has to be some kind of joke. This has to be . . . there is no way in hell . . . ."

Larry got up and paced around his apartment. His mind was spinning. He couldn't tell if he was dreaming or this was some kind of joke.

Larry stopped, walked over to the monitor and gazed at the photo.

He then grabbed his phone and dialed.

Simone's dress fell to the floor as Antonio picked her up and laid her on the bed. His tongue trailed all over her body, sending Simone into a frenzy. Antonio grabbed Simone's black silk underwear with his teeth and pulled them off. Simone forcefully grabbed his head and pushed it between her legs. Antonio ravished her with his tongue, making her legs quiver helplessly.

Simone repeated breathlessly, "Oh, my God, yes, yes . . ."

Antonio was relentless—he continued tonguing her, coaxing her legs open wider. Simone held on to Antonio, not wanting him to stop so that she could ensure that this was the real thing. Antonio pushed his head up, trailing up to her navel and to her breasts. Simone wrapped her legs around Antonio's back as he held onto her breasts and tantalized them with his tongue. Simone grabbed on to his back and flipped him over so that she was on top of him. She gazed into his eyes and started licking his smooth chest. Her tongue darted past his navel. Antonio's eyes shut as Simone's hand held onto him and she took him deep inside her mouth.

Antonio jolted. "Damn, you're some wild woman."

Simone smiled and continued devouring her dessert.

Larry paced around with the phone waiting for someone to pick up.

He grunted and finally hung up the phone. He walked past his computer monitor and stared at the photo of Simone. Her black hair draped over her navy blue business jacket. Her honey brown eyes shimmered through the flash of the camera. Her smooth coco skin seemed flawless.

Larry stormed into the kitchen and grabbed another drink. He then started dialing again.

Antonio rolled over on top of Simone and showered her with kisses. Simone's body felt helpless to Antonio's strong desire. She felt overpowered and it was too much for her handle. Antonio grabbed Simone's legs and wrapped them around his waist as he slowly, tantalizingly eased himself inside of her. Simone gasped. Antonio moaned. Simone's hands grasp Antonio's buttocks as Antonio started thrusting. The warmth and dampness between Simone's thighs was insatiable to Antonio and made him lose control as he thrust faster and faster.

Simone held on to her breasts as she started screaming profanity at Antonio. "Fuck me harder, Antonio, fuck me! Fuck me!"

Antonio grunted and moaned and thrust harder and faster, matching Simone's screams, yelps, and whimpers. Antonio's stiffness filled Simone and pleasured every nerve between her thighs. Simone felt her legs quiver as her whole body gyrated. Her eyes locked with Antonio's as he kept thrusting, enjoying the lust that overcame both of them. Simone gasped. She closed her eyes and her heart continued racing. She felt her body about to explode.

"Oh my God!" she panted. Her breathing was faster, Antonio was faster. Her heart pounded harder, Antonio went harder. Simone's legs quivered violently as she cried out. Her body convulsed as she screamed louder. Antonio couldn't hold on either. The wetness and warmth of Simone's thighs was too much and he too felt the wave. His hips bucked out of control as he let out a grunt as he felt himself release. Simone collapsed onto the bed, unable to move. Her breathing was shallow, and she lay motionless but content. Antonio's body shook violently as he collapsed on top of her. Sweat glistened from both of their naked bodies. Simone held on to Antonio's body tight, making sure this was not a dream. And it wasn't. It was Simone's reality. Simone opened her eyes, staring at the muscular chocolate body lying on top of her. She sighed in pleasure.

Larry sat by the phone. "Come on, pick up goddamn it!"

A woman's voice answered. "Hello?"

Larry sighed in relief. "Hey, it's me."

"Oh, Larry, how are you? Why are you calling?"

"Mom, no time for explanations. Listen, I need to talk to you."

There was a brief pause on the phone. "About what? God Larry, please don't tell me that tramp lady is cheating on you again. I told you—"

"No mom, listen to me carefully. This is really important."

"What is it?"

Larry paused, swallowed, and took a deep breath. "Mom, I found her. She's still alive."

There was no response on the other end of the phone.

CHAPTER FIFTEEN

Antonio's eyes fluttered as the morning sun stung his eyes. He squinted. He let out a yawn and rolled over. Simone had disappeared. Antonio rose, rubbed his eyes, and stretched. He slowly panned the room. The bedroom looked like a hurricane had passed through. Clothes were scattered everywhere. The bed sheets were ripped and soaked. A chair sat peacefully on its side by the window.

Antonio scratched his head. "Damn, what happened last night?" He grabbed a loose sheet from the bed and wrapped himself as he got out of the bed. Approaching the window, he squinted his eyes and pulled the lace curtains apart. He peered out across the large backyard that resembled a park. Simone was lying on a lawn chair in a white bathroom robe on with her sunglasses on. Antonio stood there by the window watching Simone. *"My God,"* Antonio thought to himself. *I can't believe I did this . . . I can't believe I actually had sex with Simone. And damn, I can't believe how good it was.* Antonio smiled.

Simone lay motionlessly on the lawn chair with her hands by her sides.

"Is this what you do to all your guys that you've had relationships with?" Antonio asked from the doorway.

Simone turned around. Antonio was standing by the patio door with a white robe on.

Simone removed her sunglasses and laughed. "No, I don't."

Antonio approached her, knelt down, and kissed her hand. "Good morning."

"Good morning." Simone replied, smiling.

There was a brief pause.

Antonio scratched his head. "Hey, Simone . . . um about last night. I really . . ."

"Antonio, you don't have to say anything, I will keep that our secret. I thought about it and I know that technically you should not be having a relationship with a client of yours and I totally respect that."

"That's not it Simone." Antonio stood up. "Simone, last night was . . . was . . ."

Simone sat up. "What?"

Antonio closed his eyes. "Simone, last night was amazing. I've never experienced that with another woman like I did . . ."

Simone got up and grabbed Antonio's hand. "Antonio, no, I should thank you. You showed me things last night that I thought I already knew."

Antonio laughed. "Oh really?"

Simone leaned. "Antonio, I think I woke up the butler, if not the whole neighborhood."

Antonio laughed again.

"I'm serious! I have never experienced such lust—such *orgasms*—before."

Her words made Antonio excited. "Well, what can I say?"

Simone squeezed Antonio's hand. "Please say that you can stay for breakfast."

"I'd love to, but I really should get going."

"Oh, before you leave. I am having a cocktail party Friday evening. Can you make it?"

"Yeah sure, I am free that evening."

"Oh, and you can bring your friend Greg and whoever else you want to bring."

"Great, thanks."

"When will I see you again?"

"Don't worry, you'll see me soon."

Simone sighed and smiled. "Are we going to get to repeat what happened last night?"

Antonio leaned. "If you are good, then maybe."

Simone laughed as she reached over and kissed Antonio. Their tongues swirled together as Antonio grabbed her closer to him.

Simone let out a purr. "You are so addicting, you know that?"

Antonio smiled slyly. "Maybe I am that perfect drug that you always wanted."

* * *

Antonio settled on his leather sofa. His mind was dazed. He couldn't believe what had happened last night. It was so sensual, raw, and animalistic that it was overwhelming. He kept thinking back to last night. Simone's legs wrapped around his waist, his hands caressing her firm breasts, her moans, and her screams . . .

There was a knock on the door.

Antonio stretched as walked to the door. When he opened it, Greg walked in and took off his jacket.

"Um, yeah, and good day to you too." Antonio grunted, shutting the door.

Greg grabbed a beer from the fridge, took his shoes off and sat on the couch. "OK man, details."

Antonio played stupid. "About what?"

"Oh don't give me that. I want details about what you and Simone did last night."

"What are you, Miss Gossip Queen or something?"

"Fuck off, Tony. You and I are friends, and if my friend is getting some poontang from an older woman, then fuck it. I deserve the right to hear it."

Antonio shook his head. "I can't believe you."

"Enough with the chitchat. Tell me what happened."

Antonio paused. "We went out for dinner. We had a lot to talk about. We went to that expensive restaurant by— "

"Yeah, yeah, whatever. Let's cut the small talk here. Did you bang her?"

Antonio screwed up his face. "Greg, what the fuck is wrong with you?"

"Oh, don't give me that. I want to know—did you rock her boat?"

Antonio didn't reply.

"You slammed her, didn't you? Didn't you, Tony?"

Antonio got up and went into the kitchen to grab a drink.

"I knew it! I knew it. I knew you would hit it. You are the man!" Greg followed Antonio into the kitchen. "So was it like riding the waves?"

Antonio turned around. "Man, you are too much—not to mention a desperate fool. And what makes you think I slept with her in the first place?"

"Because I see that big ol' love bite on your neck." Greg said, pointing at Antonio's neck.

Antonio laughed. "Whatever man, that does not mean a thing."

Greg followed Antonio into the living room. "*And* you're still wearing the same clothes you did last night."

"Whatever, Sherlock Holmes."

"Antonio, why are you hiding the fact that you got some pussy last night?"

"And why are you so goddamn interested if I did or not?"

"Because we are best friends and best friends share stuff like this."

"No they don't."

"I tell you who I had sex with."

"Yeah, but I don't ask you. You just tell me, and half the time I don't want to know."

"You are such a prude. Good Lord, Tony, why are you acting as if I'm asking you for your life savings? All I am asking is if you got some punana last night. It's a simple question between two guys that can easily be shared."

Antonio glared at Greg and shook his head.

"Uh did it ever occurred to you that I might have gone to church this morning, and that's why I'm wearing a suit?"

Greg rolled his eyes. "On a Saturday?" Come on, be honest with me. Was it wild?"

Antonio slouched in the couch and gave in. "Yes, it was good."

"How good?"

"What kind of question is that?"

"A smart question. How good was it?"

Antonio rubbed his hands over his face. His eyes darted at the ceiling before he looked at Greg. "I think we woke the neighbors."

Greg leaned in. "What? What kind of freaky shit did you guys do?"

"Greg, please. We didn't even do anything kinky. It's just she is very sexual woman."

". . . because she is an older woman. See, Tony?"

Antonio gulped his drink. "Man, it was phenomenal. Like we did things that were just out of control."

"Such as?"

Antonio laughed. "Guy, we did it everywhere in her bedroom. On the dresser, on the bed, on the floor—everywhere."

"Man, Tony." Greg said. "You don't get any for so long, and when you finally got it, you really attacked it."

Antonio laughed. "Whatever, man. You know, I am really feeling this woman."

"Say what?"

"Yeah, I mean our conversation is great, and the sex—well, the sex is stupendous."

"Stupendous?"

"Yes, illiterate one, stupendous. Grand, magnificent."

Greg got up and headed to the kitchen. "Man, she has you whipped now."

"Huh?"

"She has you whipped."

"I am not whipped."

Greg rolled his eyes.

"Alright, you are confusing me here."

"How so?"

"One minute you want me to brag about how I spreaded it and conquered it and now that I tell you it was the bomb because I kind of like her . . . now I am whipped?"

Greg patted Antonio's shoulder. "Tony, you just have to remember that when you get a real good pussy you have to maintain your manhood. Some pussy will make you lose control and become subordinate."

Antonio brushed off Greg. "Greg, get lost."

"Tony, I am serious."

"Whatever man, now you're just talking bullshit. Oh, and Greg, I forgot. She told me about this cocktail party she's having on Friday night. She wants me to invite you too."

"Cool," Greg said. "I guess that's her way of making up of for what happened the other evening."

Antonio stopped. "The other evening?"

"Yeah, she didn't tell you?"

"No, what happened?"

"I was driving on my way to visit Lisa at the hospital—which I will tell you about in a bit—but anyhow I was driving, and this stupid fuckin' idiot in his blue van pulls out from the side and nearly hits me."

"Really?"

"Yeah, well ironically, Simone was parked behind him. She got out of her car and basically said the guy was at fault, too. The guy was trying to act all macho and shit and I was like 'whatever dude.' Anyhow, she threatened the guy that she would call the police and the guy took off."

"Really? She never mentioned that to me."

"No biggy. I am sure you guys were too busy knocking the boots."

Antonio paused at the thought. "Maybe she forgot."

"Tony. Really and truly you had the bombest sex with her last night. I am sure she forgot after you gave her the Tony Thunder."

Antonio laughed. "Man, you are just too much."

* * *

The weekend flew by without a trace. Antonio kept thinking about Simone and their intimate night together. Monday morning rolled around and everyone at work was dragging in the office. Antonio passed Monica at the receptionist's desk, waved to her, and headed to his office. Antonio noticed there were three messages on his machine.

"Who the hell would call me on the weekend?"

Antonio played his messages.:

Beep: "Hey Antonio, it's Simone. I tried to call your home number but your number is no longer in service. I think you forgot to give me your new number. Anyhow, sexy, give me a call."

Antonio smiled.

Beep: "Ooooh yeah . . . sexy . . . mmm, sexy."

Antonio dropped his briefcase on the floor. "This is fucking driving me crazy. Who the fuck is doing this?!"

The voice continued. "I know where you live, I know what you do, and I want you. I need you. I breathe you."

Antonio screwed up his face. "What the fuck?"

The message ended. Antonio stood dazed in front of his answering machine. He was determined to put at an end to this, but how could he?

Larry came into the office. "Hey Mr. STUD, how are you?"

Antonio turned around. "Oh, hi Larry, what's up?"

"Nothing much, and yourself, you STUD?"

Antonio glared at Larry. "Greg told you, didn't he?"

Larry closed the door behind him. "Well, yes."

"God, Greg is worse than a ten-year old girl."

Larry laughed. "So man, spill the beans." Antonio told Larry about the evening, only briefly mentioning their intimacy.

"You lucky bastard," Larry said forcing a smile. The thought of him being intimate with Simone actually terrified him.

"Whatever." Antonio said. "Oh, Simone is having a cocktail party. She invited me and wanted me to come and invite some people. Wanna reach?"

Larry froze. His hands trembled. "Um, well . . . I, um . . ."

"Guy, what's wrong with you? I am asking you to go to party, not answer the million-dollar question."

Larry cleared his throat abruptly. "Um, yeah sure man. You mind giving me the address?"

"Actually, Simone is quite picky about me giving her address, so she'd rather you guys follow me."

Larry raised his eyebrow. "Really?"

"Yeah, don't ask me." Antonio laughed. "Maybe she has the Feds after her."

Larry didn't reply.

"So you're coming, right?"

"Yeah man, for sure."

"Alright man, well I'd better get back to work here."

Larry proceeded to the door. "OK, I'll talk to you later."

Antonio closed the door behind him. He stared at the answering machine. "This is too freaky. " He tried to clear his head and sat down to begin his work.

Once outside the door, Larry stood and wondered what to make of his encounter with Simone. He adjusted his tie and headed off down the hallway.

* * *

Antonio got home from work. He threw his jacket on the counter, grabbed his cell phone, and dialed.

Simone picked up. "Hello?"

"Hey, Simone."

"Hi, Antonio. How are you doing this evening?"

Antonio kicked off his shoes and sat on the couch. "Fine, and yourself?"

"I'm doing good."

"I was wondering if you were free this evening," Antonio asked.

Simone paused. "What for?"

Antonio paused. "Simone, I am gonna be up front with you. All I have been thinking about is Friday night."

Simone sighed. "So have I."

"And . . . not to be forward, but I wouldn't mind continuing that evening. I mean, not the sex part. I mean just spending some time with you, you know?"

Simone stumbled on her words too. "I know, Antonio, I don't really know what to say either. Yes, I'd like to see you."

Antonio felt his heart pound. "Do you want to come over to my place?"

"Sure," Simone said. Antonio gave her his address and phone number.

"OK, I'll see you soon."

"Most definitely."

Antonio hung up. His hands trembled. He looked at his watch, dashed upstairs, and took a shower.

Simone sat behind her desk. She stared at the black briefcase that was leaning against the wall. "Yes, Antonio, I want to relive that night again."

CHAPTER SIXTEEN

Simone knocked on the door.

Antonio answered. "Hey."

Simone's white top and blue tight jeans hugged her in all the right places. "Hey," Simone replied. They both sat down on the sofa As soon as they began chatting, Antonio instantly started discussing the phone call.

"Simone, it's really weird. I don't know who is calling me, but it's starting to freak me out."

"I am sure a strong man like you can handle it." Simone said.

"Simone, I am serious. It's really freaky. The person claimed that they knew where I live and what I do and said how they want me and everything. What am I supposed to think about all of that?"

Simone paused. She placed her finger on his lips. "I say you call the police."

"Simone, I am not gonna call the police. They can't do anything."

Simone half-smiled. "Yeah, I guess not."

"Hey you never told me that you met up with Greg the other night."

Simone jolted in her seat. "Oh . . . yeah, I did. Sorry, I forgot."

Antonio grabbed her hand. "No worries. Who cares—he's just a friend." He released her hand. "Simone, what am I gonna do about these phone calls?"

Simone shrugged her shoulders. "I don't know, but there is something that I want to do." Simone hands slid into Antonio's pants, and she fondled him. She felt his erection grow in her palm.

Antonio grunted. He couldn't resist her. "I think we can take care of that."

* * *

Antonio got out of his car and adjusted his tie. Greg exited from the passenger's side, trying to smooth his dress shirt.

Antonio looked at Greg. "You know, you really need to go back to fashion school, man. Why do you always choose to wear the most off-colour stuff?"

Greg brushed off his black polka-dotted shirt as he put his black jacket on. "Man, *this is* fashion."

"Yeah, back in 1989 when it was all about Heavy D and Kid 'N Play," Antonio said.

Greg ignored him.

"Does Larry know how to get here?"

"Well, he is gonna have to. I left the directions on his cell phone. Not to sure why he wanted to go by himself, but whatever."

They walked up the house. A few guests were smoking and drinking on the front porch. Antonio pushed the door opened. Voices echoed throughout the hallways and smooth jazzed hummed from the living room.

The butler approached Antonio and Greg. "Mr. Madison, great to see you."

"Great to see you too, George." Antonio said, shaking his hand.

Greg gave Antonio a look. "She has a butler?"

Antonio nudged Greg. "Man, shut up and behave yourself."

Antonio walked down the hallway towards the living room. The partygoers were all dressed casually and were talking amongst themselves. Greg's eyes panned the entire place.

"Fuck, this place is huge." Greg said as he marched over to the appetizer table.

Antonio looked around, hoping to find Simone. He felt a hand grab his buttocks. He turned around. Simone stood behind him wearing a pink top and black pants. Diamond studs sparkled on her high heels.

"Hey you," Antonio said, delighted. He kissed her on the cheek.

Simone grabbed his hand. "Hey listen, let me introduce you to some people." Simone tugged Antonio away and they both disappeared in the crowd. Greg stood by the table nibbling on a piece of cheese and a biscuit as he panned the place. He caught the glance of a taller woman with short, black braids in her hair. She wore black lipstick and had dark chocolate skin, which contrasted with the white dress that caressed her well-endowed behind.

"Is that biscuit that good?" a voice said from behind Greg.

Greg turned around. Larry stood behind him smiling.

"Man, do you get a kick out of staring at people eating?" Greg said.

Larry didn't reply.

"What was the delay, man?" Greg said, switching to his glass of white wine.

Larry paused. "Oh, I had some stuff that I had take care of."

Greg nodded. "Well you just missed Simone. She is somewhere with Antonio, I think. I saw them last together a couple of minutes ago. Who knows where they are. Maybe humping up in her bedroom."

Larry rolled his eyes and looked away.

"What, did I say something offensive?"

Larry shook his head. "No, man. Sorry, just been thinking about stuff."

Greg sighed. "Larry. GET OVER HER."

"Man, it's not her. I've just been thinking about stuff."

"Such as?"

Larry thought up of a lie. "I don't know. Finances, shit like that."

"Larry you're thirty-seven, not forty-seven, so stop your midlife crisis bullshit and enjoy yourself." Greg shoved a glass of wine in Larry's face. "Drink."

Larry rolled his eyes and took a sip. Greg then pointed out two brunettes sitting on the couch. "Now Larry, check those two out. Now according to my woman radar, the one on the left likes to play hard to get, and the one on the right likes to play hard enough, you know what I'm saying?"

Greg chuckled, but Larry's face remain motionless. "Maybe it could be the other way around?"

Greg placed his wine glass on the table. "God, don't tell me you're getting this "lonely man syndrome" shit. First it was Tony, now you . . . who's next?"

Larry looked at Greg.

"Oh hell no, not me. I am not gonna be like that."

Larry shook his head. "Man, I am going for a walk."

"OK, wait, I'll come with you." Greg said, grabbing another biscuit.

Simone and Antonio were busy throughout the night mingling and socializing with everyone. Greg was busy mingling and socializing, too, while Larry just stood in a corner and watched everyone else having fun. When Larry finally spotted Simone, he felt everything in his body stopped and a sharp pain penetrating him like a knife stabbing him. It was her. Larry could not believe it. It was her! His suspicions about Simone Jackson were true. The horrid thoughts, chilling memories and the pain were all coming back. He tried so hard to control himself from ripping her into pieces but the locks on Pandora's box felt like they were gonna break any moment. He watched Simone as she interacted with everyone. Every so often she would grab Antonio's hand and bring him close to her. It made Larry sick to his stomach. Larry gulped down his wine, wiped his mouth, and headed towards the back of the room. He stood against a wall looking up at the maroon ceiling. He felt a tap on his shoulder and turned around.

"Where have you been?" Antonio asked.

"I've been here, but you, Mr. Social Butterfly, have been busy."

Antonio smiled. "Sorry man, it's just . . ."

"No problem, man."

"Actually, hold on. Grab Greg, will you? Let me introduce Simone to you and Greg formally."

Larry coughed. "Oh, no, I . . ."

"Oh, stop your nonsense and come on." Antonio grabbed Larry's arm and jerked him inside. Greg was talking with a slim lady with long black hair.

"Hey Greg, follow me. I wanted to formally introduce you guys to Simone."

Greg nodded, told the woman he would return, and followed Larry and Antonio. Antonio spotted Simone on the stairwell laughing with some people.

"Simone." Antonio said.

Simone turned around and spotted Greg and Antonio. She walked over.

"Hey, what's up?" she asked.

"I wanted to formally introduce you to my friends."

Simone smiled at Greg. "Well, we've met before."

Greg nodded. "Yes, we have."

Antonio turned around, trying to find Larry. He beckoned him, and Larry walked through the thick crowd.

"Simone, I want you to meet Larry. He also works with me."

Simone turned around and looked at Larry. Her smile dropped. Her eyes widened and her hands shook.

Larry froze as he stared at her.

Simone's voice croaked. "Oh my . . . hi . . ."

Larry had his hand out. "Good evening, Dana. How are you?"

CHAPTER SEVENTEEN

Simone's hands shook. Larry stood silently, awaiting a response, while Antonio and Greg stood awkwardly.

"Dana? Who's Dana?" Antonio said.

Simone coughed abruptly. She shoved her sweaty hands into her pockets.

Larry's eyes pierced into Simone's, which were frigid and uncommunicative. "You remember me, don't you Dana?"

Greg turned to Larry. "Um, buddy, this is Simone Jackson. You must be confused."

Larry didn't reply.

Simone grabbed Antonio's hand firmly. "Dana? I'm sorry, I think you have me mixed up with someone else." She turned to leave, but Larry grabbed her arm. Simone struggled.

"Let me go."

Antonio stepped in. "Larry, what the hell is wrong with you? Get off of her."

Larry shoved Antonio to the side and kept his grip on Simone's arm. He pulled her towards him. "Dana, stop lying to everyone here."

Antonio pushed Larry away. "Dude, what the hell is wrong with you?"

Simone crossed her arms protectively. "Antonio, I don't who this man is, but can you please escort your *friend* out of here?"

Antonio turned to Larry. Larry clenched his fists and snarled. "You bitch! You fuckin' lying bitch!" Larry's arm flung in the air aiming to strike Simone in the face, but Greg caught it.

The commotion had caused a number of people to gather around.

Simone turned to Antonio. "Antonio, escort him out of here right now!"

Antonio stood and grabbed Larry's shoulder.

Larry jolted. "Let go of me, man!"

"No, man, what the hell is wrong with you?!"

"She's a fuckin bitch, she's a—" The twin towers Juan and Zeus had sprung out of nowhere and knocked the wind out of Larry, pinning him to the ground.

The onlookers gasped. Simone ran her fingers through her hair, fidgeting. Greg's eyes widened and Antonio froze. Juan and Zeus picked up Larry and escorted him outside.

Antonio turned to Simone. "Simone, I am so sorry. I don't what the . . ."

But Simone had darted upstairs. Everyone milled about, unsure of what to do. Antonio paused and then headed outside, following Greg. When Antonio arrived outside, Zeus had Larry in a headlock. Juan stood, grabbing Larry's face.

Juan spoke with a thick Spanish accent. "Do I make myself clear, motherfucker?"

Larry nodded sheepishly. Zeus released Larry and they both wiped their hands and headed back to the front entrance.

Zeus passed Antonio. He stopped and tipped his sunglasses. "Yo. Control your friend next time." He adjusted his sunglasses and proceeded to walk inside.

Antonio ran to Larry, who was crouching on the floor. "Larry, what the hell is wrong with you?"

Greg kneeled to help Larry up. Larry looked up at Antonio. "Tony, stay away from her."

"Why?"

"Because she is bad news. That's why."

"And you know her?"

Larry paused. "Yes."

Greg leaned back. "Really, how?"

Larry turned to Greg. "Man, I don't want to talk about it."

Antonio stood in front of Larry. "Hold on. No—wait. How do you know her? And why were you calling her Dana?"

Larry felt torn. He desperately wanted to tell Antonio about Simone and her secret life but was afraid that Antonio might accuse him of being jealous or would simply not believe him. Larry also knew that if Antonio did not know the truth that matters could get worse, extremely worse. Larry already made an ass out of himself at the party and did not want to make an ass out of himself again.

Larry leaned. "Listen, all I am gonna tell you is just stay away from her . . . as far as possible. She's poison."

"Larry, why?"

Larry looked down. "Forget it. I don't want to talk about it."

Larry turned around but Antonio grabbed his shoulder. "No, fuck it. I want to hear this, man. What the fuck is going on?"

Larry jolted away. "I said forget about it."

"For fuck sake's, Larry, you were just about to slap Simone!"

Larry growled. "Her name is Dana."

"Dana? Who is Dana? " Antonio threw his hands up in the air. "Fuck, what the hell is going on here?"

"So her real name is Dana?" Greg said.

Larry didn't reply.

"You know what? You are fuckin' drunk. Who do you think she is, anyway?" Antonio said, bewildered.

"I'm not fucking drunk!"

"Then explain to me what the fuck just happened in there, Larry?" Antonio said.

"Tony. Listen, As a co-worker and a friend, let me just tell you this. Stay away from her. OK? Just stay away from her. She's sick!"

Again Antonio threw his hands up in the air. "You know what? Forget this shit. I am going back in to see if Simone is OK. " Antonio turned to Greg. "You coming, Greg?"

Greg shrugged his shoulders.

"Fine, I am going inside, I'll see you guys later." Antonio marched back towards the house. Larry and Greg stood watching from behind.

Greg turned to Larry. "Man, what was that all about?"

Larry spat and wiped his forehead. He turned to Greg. "Someone who is gonna get fucked over big time."

*　*　*

Antonio watched the afternoon sunlight shift through the blinds on his office window. Antonio had spent a full day in the gallery, but all he wanted to do was put his head down and sleep. He slumped in his office chair and rested his head on his desk. His memories cascaded to last night. *What the hell was that? Why did Larry act like that? And Simone? Why was he calling her Dana?* Simone had excused herself for half of the evening. When Antonio approached her, she claimed that everything was fine, but Antonio kept remembering her eyes and how apprehensive they were. Was her real name Dana? And if it was, what did she do to Larry to make him say that to her? And how did Larry know Simone in the first place? All these questions flooded Antonio's mind. Antonio felt he was hung-over from being mentally drunk; he had too many thoughts and events going through his mind, and his body was not able to process them properly.

Someone knocked on the door.

"Leave me alone," Antonio grumbled.

The person knocked again.

"I said, leave me alone."

The person continued knocking. Antonio got up from his seat and walked over to door. "I told you to leave me—" Antonio opened the door. Simone was standing there , taking off dark shades. She wore a black dress pants and a black blouse with a white scarf wrapped around her neck.

"Hey, I was just—"

"Antonio," Simone said as she closed the door behind her. "Listen, I just wanted to apologize for the way I acted last night."

Antonio screwed up his face. "Apologize? Simone, it was Larry who acted the fool last night, not you."

Simone removed her glasses. "I know, but . . . it's just—"

Antonio leaned against his desk. "Simone, is there something that I should know about?"

"No. Nothing."

"Why was he calling you Dana?"

Simone folded and unfolded her hands. She then sighed. "OK, fine, you got me."

Antonio scratched his head. "Huh?"

"Me and Larry had a thing in the past, and I lied to him and told him my name was Dana. Well, things didn't work out, and I broke up with him."

"Why would you tell him your name was Dana?"

Simone scratched her eyebrow. "Because I don't know, women do these things to fool men. Besides, Larry was a little bit creepy."

"So is your real name Simone? Or is it something like Takesha or Bonquisha?"

Simone laughed. "No, my name is Simone."

Antonio stared at Simone, studying her facial expressions. Simone felt apprehensive. She didn't know if Antonio was seeing through her. Antonio approached her, grabbed her hand, and started laughing.

"Um, what's so funny?"

"I'm sorry, but Larry is such an ass sometimes."

"Why?"

"The man has had women problems for as long as I can remember. His last girlfriend cheated on him with a co-worker from here. And now I hear that you had a fling with him in the past and you had to lie about your name because he was creepy. The man has women issues."

Simone smirked. "Really?"

"Yeah, he's been having a lot of trouble recently. That's probably why he lashed out like that. What a loser."

Simone chuckled nervously. "Yeah, what a loser."

"But Simone, why didn't you say anything at the party?"

"Antonio, come on. Like I am gonna say to you , 'yeah I actually dated your good friend and co-worker for a while' in front of everyone."

Antonio nodded.

"Does it make sense to you?" Simone said.

"Yeah." Antonio grabbed Simone's hips and pulled her close to him. "Listen, I apologize for my friend acting that way."

Simone kissed him on the cheek. "No problem. Anyhow, I have to go. I have some stuff I have to care of. I'll talk to you later." Antonio kissed Simone and she left.

Antonio sat in his chair chuckling to himself. "Oh man, Larry."

Simone hopped in her car. She took out her phone and dialed.

"Yeah?" answered Ronnie.

"Alright, I've taken care of the problem."

"You really know how to play with fire, don't you?"

Simone rolled her eyes. "Ronnie, I don't want to talk about it. God, what are the odds that Larry would know Antonio?"

Ronnie belched on the other end.

"You are so disgusting, you know that?"

Ronnie didn't reply.

"Anyhow, I just thought you should know."

"What did you tell your new lover boy?"

Simone rolled her eyes as she played with her keys. "I told Antonio that Larry and I were a couple, and I called myself Dana because I thought Larry was a creep."

Ronnie burst out laughing. "Nice one."

"Whatever, Ronnie. I'll talk to you later. Bye." Simone hung up her phone and stared at herself in the rearview mirror. She smirked, started her car, and drove off.

* * *

"I still don't get it," Greg said, lifting his dumbbell.

Antonio sat up from the workout bench. "Man, I dunno. All I know is that Larry's got issues."

"Are you sure it's him and not her?" Greg said.

"Why would it be her?"

"I don't know. I am just playing devil's advocate. I mean, I know Larry can be out of control sometimes with his relationships, but the way he was carrying on the other night didn't look like a joke."

Antonio grabbed a barbell from the rack. "Greg, listen. I don't want to talk about it. What is done is done."

"Have you talked to Larry?"

"Not since that incident."

"You avoiding him?"

"No, but I do wonder if he is avoiding me."

"We should talk to him."

"Why should *we* talk to him?"

"Because we are all good co-workers and we talk."

Antonio paused. "Yeah, well I kind of find it strange that he never mentioned Simone."

Greg snapped his fingers. "A-ha! It all makes sense now."

"What?"

"You remember how Larry kept saying he'd heard that name somewhere?"

"Yeah?"

"Well, he probably found out after the fact that her real name was Simone Jackson, It wasn't until he saw at her party that he realized who she was."

"Man, I don't know, but I all I can say is that what they had was in the past."

Greg nodded. "So how are things with you and the special woman in your life?"

Antonio rolled his eyes. "Oh shut up, man. She is not the 'woman of my life.' We are not even an item. We are just casually dating."

"And getting a little bump and grind at the same time?" Greg said.

Antonio didn't reply.

"Hey man, did you find her G-spot yet? I heard that shit is the bomb."

Antonio screwed his face. "Greg, really though, are you that desperate?"

"Dude, I am serious. The G-spot is the bomb. I was with this one girl, and I hit her spot, and the girl, like, soaked the sheets."

Antonio stood back. "And you feel that is necessary to tell me this in the middle of the gym on a quiet evening with these innocent people just trying to work out?"

Greg ignored his last comment. "Dude I am serious. That is what you need to do. The girl will call you big daddy and scream your name and beg for that candy rain when you hit that spot."

Antonio grasped the barbell and starting lifting it over his head. He stopped and turned to Greg. "OK, first of all, you have issues. And second of all, 'call me big daddy and scream my name?' And 'she is gonna beg for my candy rain?' Which song did you get that from?"

"Dude, I am telling you, you need to hit that spot."

"And what you need to do is stop giving me advice on women when you can't even get one yourself."

Greg stood back. "Whatever, man. When it comes to girls, I rock the show."

Antonio rolled his eyes. He then glanced over by the clock on the wall. "Shit, is it after 9 already? I gotta go." Greg nodded goodbye to Antonio and they both took off.

Antonio felt lethargic as he dragged his feet towards his apartment door. All he wanted to do was sleep. He wondered how he'd had the energy to go to the gym that evening. As he approached his door, he noticed a white envelope, unaddressed and sealed, lying outside his door. Antonio picked it up and opened the door. When he got inside he threw his gym bag on the floor, kicked off his shoes, grabbed a sports drink from the fridge, and plopped on the couch with the letter in his hand. He opened the envelope and read the letter:

> I know where you live, sexy. I want you, sexy. Can I have you forever . . . sexy? Mmm . . . sexy. You can't hide or run away from me. I am watching you.

Antonio crumpled up the letter and threw it on the ground. "WHAT THE FUCK IS GOING ON?" he shouted. He kicked the coffee table, got up and started pacing.

Outside in the hallway, the smell of cigarette smoke hung in the air. A cigarette butt dropped on the floor and was crushed by a black heel.

Leaning against the wall, the shadowy figure took out another cigarette and lit it. The long black trench coat brushed against the floor as the person turned around and headed toward the elevator. As the doors opened, the person stepped in chuckled, and reached into a pocket and grabbed a white envelope. The chuckle echoed down the hallway as the elevator doors shut closed.

CHAPTER EIGHTEEN

Larry sat in front of his computer monitor with a half-full glass of vodka. He yawned, rubbed his eyes, and took a sip from his drink.

He slammed his drink on his desk. "Fuck!" he swore sharply. He got up, ran his hands over his head, and paced up and down the living room. He couldn't believe that he had seen Dana, alive and in the flesh. The more he thought about it, the more he wanted to see her suffer. His mind flashed back to the party. Seeing her and Antonio together made him upset. He thought of the chances of Antonio finding out everything from Dana, but his hopes and dreams easily shattered when he realized that Dana would come up with some kind of lie to protect her reputation and avoid revealing her past. Larry felt betrayed, and seeing the past before his eyes that night haunted, terrified, and exasperated him. He walked over to his bedroom and grabbed a photo album from the closet. He sat on his bed and began listlessly flipping through the album pages. He stopped at an older photo of a group picture at a dinner table. Larry was on one side with his parents with his curly brown dark brown hair still dripping from the hair gel he had used earlier that day. Dana sat beside them with a younger man. The sun reflected off the younger man's bald, smooth head, and the smile on his face conveyed a warm sense of content. Larry stared at the photo. His hands trembled and his nose flared. Unexpected tears rolled down his cheeks.

He threw the album across the bed and screamed. "Killer!" He rubbed his face with his hands and broke down crying.

The phone rang.

Larry wiped his face, walked over to the phone, and picked it up. He cleared his throat. "Hello?"

"Yo, L., it's Greg. I need a favor from you."

Larry sat on the edge of his bed. "What?"

"Remember that file that you have for me from this afternoon?"

"Yeah."

"Well, I need it tonight because I have some shit I have to look up. Can you drop it off at my place?"

Larry sighed. "Can you come and pick up here?"

Greg paused. "Yeah, fine. I'll come over and get it."

"I'll see in you in few, then."

Greg hung up. Larry stared at phone. He pondered if he should tell Greg about Dana, but that would also mean betraying Antonio. He shook his head.

"Fuck it, I am telling everything." Larry said.

* * *

The police officer scribbled on his notepad. "Is there anything else beside the letter and the phone calls, Mr. Madison?"

"No, that is it." Antonio said. "I find this quite annoying, is there anything that I can do about this?"

The police officer cleared his throat. "Well, right now, nothing. The only thing I can say right now is that you should save all messages and notices. You said that this has been going on for a couple of weeks now?"

Antonio nodded.

"Had any bad relationships lately with anybody?"

Antonio shook his head. "No, why?"

The officer took off his hat and rubbed his grey moustache. "Well, we get a lot of domestic calls from women or men who have an ex-partner who constantly harass them for whatever reason. Most of the time it's harmless, but you do get the few that are kind of *psycho*."

Antonio chuckled. "Well maybe that is what happening with me."

The police officer shrugged his shoulders. "Who knows, Mr. Madison. There is nothing much that I can do right now, and this letter does not really lead us to anything. Just keep it, in any case."

Antonio nodded and the police officer proceeded through the door. "Have a nice evening."

Antonio shut the door and stared at the door. He sighed and shook his head. "Who the hell would be doing this? It makes no sense." Antonio shrugged his shoulders and went upstairs to shower.

Greg knocked on Larry's door.

Larry answered the door. "Hey man what's up?"

Greg stepped through the door. "Nothing, man. Do you have the file?"

Larry grabbed the files from the kitchen counter and handed it to him. "Hey Greg, do you have a couple of minutes?"

"Yeah, sure, why?"

"I need to talk to you."

Larry closed the door and sat on the living room sofa. "Have you spoken to Antonio?"

Greg nodded. "Yeah. Is this about what happened at Simone's?"

Larry rolled his eyes. "Dude, we need to talk."

"And why aren't you talking to Antonio?"

"Because I don't know if he wants to hear this yet."

Greg raised his eyebrow. "What?"

"Listen, that chick that Antonio knows—I know her."

Greg sat down across from him. "Yeah, I kind of figured. How do you know Simone?"

Larry sighed. His voice croaked. "Well, first of all, her real name is not Simone. It's Dana Robinson."

Greg leaned in. "Dana Robinson?"

Larry nodded.

"And you know this because . . . ."

Larry cleared his throat. "She was married to my brother."

Greg leaned back. "You had a brother? You never mentioned this to anyone."

"I know. I really didn't want to tell anyone."

"Why?"

Larry took a deep breath and closed his eyes. "My brother was partner at a computer software company. He and Dana were business partners. Apparently they had an affair and fell in love. My folks and other family members totally disapproved of it because of Dana was fifty-three years old."

Greg leaned in. "Fifty-three years old?" Antonio said that Simone was forty-two."

Larry nodded. "Another flat-out lie from that bitch."

Greg froze. "Wait? How long ago did this occur?"

"Five years ago."

Greg leaned back appauled. "So wait! If she was fifty-three five years ago . . . that makes her fifty-eight!"

Larry nodded in glee of Greg's reaction. Greg scratched his temple. "Larry, my man. What is really going on here?"

Larry got up and went to his bedroom. He returned with the photo album. He opened the page, gave it to Greg, and pointed to the picture of his brother.

Larry continued. "Greg, my brother was in love with this girl. Well, there were some business problems that fell through, and Dana—or Simone, or whatever the fuck you want to call her—tried to take over the company from my brother. When my brother refused, she figured the only way she could get a piece of the pie would be if they had signed some agreement saying that if anything happened, then she would get it. "

Greg shook his head. "Wait, Antonio told me she was married to some dude name Harold."

"That's Dana's second husband."

"Second husband?"

"Yeah, I will get into that later on. She and my brother got married. Three weeks later, he dies."

Greg sunk in his seat. "Oh man. How did he die?"

Larry paused. "Apparently, in a car accident."

Greg and Larry continued talking, and Greg absorbed everything he said. Greg kept shaking his head as each new detail emerged.

"So what makes you think that she had something to with this?"

Larry rubbed his face. "My brother phoned one night, upset. He told me that he and Dana had a huge fight. She said that she was the only person in his life and she knew that he couldn't live without her. My brother told her that she was psycho and needed help. He then said that one night he overheard her talking quietly to someone about 'accidents' and business deals. When he told me this part, I was of course taken by surprise. Then three weeks later, he dies. I know she had something to do with it, I know."

"So why did she pick Antonio as her next victim?"

"Greg, think about it. Antonio pulls so much money for Mahogany and our art gallery has been in the top ten best money earning business for three years in a row. Everyone is still surprised how an art gallery business like us has made so much profit. You don't think that bitch realizes that Antonio is good money and wants some of it?"

"The same kind of high profit deals you were telling me about with Harold and your brother?"

"Exactly."

Greg sat shaking his head. "Holy fuck, this is some serious shit. And you haven't told Antonio any of this?"

Larry shook his head. "Man, how I am gonna talk to Antonio about this when the man probably thinks I am fool?"

Greg shrugged his shoulders. "I don't know man, but you should tell him."

Larry laughed. "Antonio thinks that I am probably making this shit up. I am sure that Simone has already fed some bullshit to him."

Greg darted his eyes away.

Larry got up. "What did she say to him?"

Greg sighed and swallowed hard. "Apparently, Simone told him that you and her were an item, and that you are psycho."

Larry made a fist. "That fuckin' bitch. See what the fuck I am talking about?"

"Man, this is some fucked up shit. You should talk to—" Greg's cell phone rang before he could finish. Greg answered. "Hello?"

"Hey Greg, it's Tony," Antonio said.

Greg eyes widened as he turned to Larry. "Oh hey, Tony, what's up?"

Larry sat down and ran his hands over his head stressed.

"Man, we need to talk. I just got another fucked up message."

"What?"

"I am serious. This time it was a written message: 'I know where you live, and I know who you are sexy, sexy, sexy, etc.'"

Greg shook his head. "Man that is some serious stuff. Look, can I call you back in a bit?"

"Yeah man, but you should come over so you can see this thing."

"I'll call in you five minutes."

"Alright, later."

"Later, man."

Greg hung up and looked at Larry. "Man, Antonio's got a stalker on his hands. Someone keeps leaving messages on his work and voicemail saying how he is sexy. Now he just received a letter at his place from some anonymous person."

Larry didn't reply.

"Man, you really should tell Tony this. I mean does he really know what he is getting himself involved with?"

Again Larry didn't reply.

Antonio sat up from his seat. "See I told you I have a stalker."

Greg looked at the letter. "Yeah, you do."

"Fucked up, huh?"

Greg nodded. He wanted to tell Antonio what Larry had told him, but now he felt that he couldn't find a way to say it.

"So what did the police say?"

"Well, they can't do anything right now. They just said to keep all the evidence, and if anything else happens, they might be able to build a case."

Greg didn't reply. He thought of the possibility of Simone doing all of this. Larry's story seemed surreal, but he did seem like he was telling the truth.

Greg got up. "Antonio, I should probably go. I promised this one client tomorrow morning that I would show them Mike's work."

Antonio nodded and followed Greg to the door. "Alright man, I'll talk to you later.

"Later," Greg said as he left.

Antonio still felt frustrated and tense over what was going on. He picked up his phone and dialed.

Simone yawned as she answered. "Hello?"

"Hey, sorry to wake you up."

"No worries, what's up, sexy?"

Antonio smiled. "It has gotten worse."

"Huh?"

"I got another message."

"I thought you changed your number?"

"Simone, they mailed me a letter to me this time. The letter said that they knew where I lived and stuff."

Simone paused. "I hope you called the police."

"Actually, I did. They said they can't do anything yet but just collected evidence."

Simone paused. "Well I hope they catch the person."

"So do I."

Simone purred. "You know Antonio, hearing your voice now makes me kind of excited."

"Oh really?"

Simone teased. "You know if you want, you can come by my place or I could visit your place for a little while."

"Well, if you really want it, why don't you come over and get it?"

Simone hung up. Within twenty minutes, she had arrived at Antonio's place. She wore only a long trench coat. When Antonio opened it, she revealed her red lingerie.

Antonio felt an erection growing. He pointed to his shorts. "You see what you are causing?"

Simone approached him and cupped his erection. "But you know you want it."

Antonio leaned in to Simone. His tongue trailed over neck, and she moaned in deep pleasure. Antonio grabbed her by her hands and led her into the bedroom. He pulled her panties off and immediately lost himself inside her, needing to find all of her pleasure spots. Their bodies and the bed sheets became soaked with sweat, heat, and passion.

* * *

Antonio and Simone laid on a torn sheet, panting and staring at the ceiling.

"You know, you are really some woman." Antonio said.

Simone smiled in a daze. "Antonio, I've never felt that before."

Antonio leaned over and kissed her. "Yeah, right."

"I am serious Antonio. I've never experienced an orgasm like that before. Where did you learn to do that?"

Antonio laughed. "I don't know."

Simone glanced over at the clock radio. "Shit, it's 3:30am? Fuck, I should be going."

Antonio sat up and rubbed his eyes. "Shit, I have a meeting at 8am. You know you are more than welcome to sleep here for the night."

Simone got up. "Trust me, I'd love to, but I can't." Simone got dressed and headed towards the door. Antonio stood behind her in his boxers. They kissed. The scent of raw sex was still pungent in the air, and Antonio could still smell it on her.

"I'll talk to you tomorrow," Simone said, opening the door.

"Likewise." He shut the door behind him and smiled.

Moments later, his cell phone rang.

He picked up the phone. "Did you forget something?"

There was no reply.

"Hello?"

Again, no reply.

"OK whoever the fuck this is, fuck off and stop bothering me. I've contacted the police." Antonio hung up and threw his cell phone on the sofa.

His cell phone rang again. Antonio looked at the display: "restricted caller." He hesitated for a moment and decided to let his voicemail pick it up.

Again, the phone rang: "restricted caller."

Antonio clenched his fists as he grabbed the phone. He then dropped it and waited for a voicemail to appear on his phone.

No message was left.

Antonio decided to turn off his phone.

As he headed towards his bed, a heavy pounding on his door startled him.

He looked at the clock. "Who the fuck is knocking on my door at 4am?"

The pounding got louder.

Antonio quickly rushed to the door and opened it.

No one was there.

Antonio looked around and saw another envelope with a letter stuffed inside. Antonio quickly scooped up the letter, dashed inside and locked the door. His hands trembled. He was apprehensive to read what psychotic message might have been written. He opened the envelope and unfolded the letter.

Nothing was written.

* * *

Simone jumped in her car. She checked her rearview mirror. Her hair was tangled, her make up smudged, and red marks spotted her neck. She giggled, smiled and started her car. She felt sexually satisfied from Antonio but always yearned for more. Simone drove down 7th Avenue before making a quick left turn onto Broadview Street and then onto Simcoe Drive.

So did the tinted red Mustang that followed her.

CHAPTER NINETEEN

Simone yawned as she got out of bed. Her eyelids felt heavy, but she was contented. She looked up at Antonio's painting and blew it a kiss. She smiled and went into the bathroom. Simone was rather quiet this morning. She was on a cloud with her new relationship, but she was dumbfounded by the reappearance of Larry. Every time she thought about the incident at the party, she shivered. It haunted her. Was Larry there to torture her? Was he purposely there to bring up the past?

As Simone got ready to leave, her butler called from down the hallway.

"Simone, someone is here to see you."

"Fine, George, but I can only see them for five minutes."

Simone turned the corner and Ronnie stood leaning against the wall. Simone rolled her eyes. "Oh, it's you."

"Yeppers."

"What do you want?"

"I'm here for my money, Simone. You promised me my money if I took care of those assignments for you."

Simone rubbed her forehead. "Ronnie, I'll give you your cut. How many times do I have to tell you this? God, you drive me up the wall."

Ronnie narrowed his eyes at Simone. "So you fucked the artist boy again last night?"

Simone didn't reply.

"You can't get enough of that artist boy's dick, can you?"

Simone gave Ronnie a dirty look. "Ronnie, seriously. Fuck off."

Ronnie smiled. "You know, Simone, I've always found you very attractive. Too bad you can't handle me."

"Ronnie, you're an overweight, hairy grease ball. When you shave your back, lose some weight, and stop bragging to me about your huge Italian sausage, then maybe, just *maybe* we might have had something physical. In the meantime, forget it."

Ronnie smoothed Simone's hair. "You see, that is why I am so into black women. Their fierce attitudes just get to a guido man like me."

Simone stood back. "Well go watch a rap video on BET and fulfill your fantasy. But right now you are working for me, and you will do what I tell you to do. If I tell you you'll get paid when *I get the money*, then I mean it. End of discussion."

Ronnie whistled and cracked his knuckles. "You know, if I was really that bad, I could go to police and tell them *everything*. I mean, what do I have to lose? I've already spent five years in jail, and I'm on parole now. "

"Ronnie, don't waste your breath. You can go to them if you want. They will never believe you."

"And are they gonna believe that your name is Simone Jackson or Dana Robinson?"

Simone's hands shook. "Ronnie, fuck you."

"I love you too, babe."

Simone grabbed her keys. "Look, horny fucker, I have to go to a couple of meetings. I will meet you tonight with your 'stuff,' OK?"

Ronnie grinned. "Yes, Dana."

Simone glared at Ronnie.

Simone followed Ronnie outside. Ronnie got into his van and drove off. Simone sat there in her car playing with her keys.

"Everything will soon come into play and we will soon see who will be laughing last." Simone started her car and drove off.

* * *

Antonio left early from work. He needed to escape and his only way of escaping was to paint. Antonio arrived home before 2pm and changed into his track pants and white, stained T-shirt. He grabbed his materials for painting, placed an empty canvas on the easel, and started painting. Antonio could not stop. He kept painting and painting. There was a possessive, insane motor inside of Antonio affecting each powerful, emotional stroke. He felt compelled not to stop. Objects and shapes that were at one time lifeless transformed into lifelike, vivid images. It was finally after 10pm, and Antonio felt his heavy eyelids droop. He sighed and stared at his art work. A fire-engine red background provided the scenery. A devil woman stood on top of a mountain with her pitchfork at her side. Her long hair waved in the air as the hands of men stretched from below to trying to reach her. Her eyes were dark and cold and her red lipstick matched her red PVC suit. Flames flickered in the background, and she stared at the viewer, licking her lips and smiling. The painting had at first seemed purely artistic, but now it began to take on a special meaning, a meaning that Antonio found haunting. The more he stared at the painting, the more he found it disturbing and cold. His eyes remained fixed on the devil woman and her face, her smile and her lips. Antonio wasn't just looking at just any woman, he was looking at a woman that he knew and met. He was looking at Simone.

CHAPTER TWENTY

Larry stood by Antonio's office door. He hadn't spoken to Antonio for almost a week and most times tried to avoid him. However, Larry knew that he should tell Antonio everything if Greg hadn't done so already.

Larry took two deep breaths before knocking on the door.

"The door is open." Antonio yelled.

Slowly, Larry walked through.

Antonio paused. "Oh, hey."

"Hey."

"What's up?"

"Nothing much, you?"

"Nothing."

Larry closed the door behind him. "Um, Tony look I need to talk to you."

Antonio got up from his desk. "Look, if it's about last week, man, don't worry about it. Just let bygones be bygones."

"No, Tony listen. You have to hear me out."

"About what? Simone told me already. Y'all use to go out and she thought you were creepy." Antonio laughed. "Which I kind of believe at times considering the stuff you told me about your dating life."

Larry sat down. "Listen, Tony. What she said to you was a lie."

Antonio continued laughing. "Oh really, and why is that? Why would she make that up?"

Larry paused. He took a deep breath. "Because she is psychotic killer."

Antonio's laughter stopped. He raised his eyebrows and rubbed his chin. "Oh really now? And who told you that gibberish?"

Larry leaned in. "Man, listen I am not bullshitting you. Simone Jackson is not really her name. It's Dana Robinson."

Antonio sat down. His face grew serious. "OK, Larry, you are starting to scare me here. What the hell is going?"

Larry cracked his knuckles. "Antonio I never told you this but—"

Antonio's phone rang. "Fuck, who is it now?" Antonio grabbed the phone. "Hello? Yes, OK . . . OK, I'll be there in a few." Antonio hung up the phone. "Larry, can we continue this another time? I have a client downstairs who is interested in one of my paintings."

Larry shrugged his shoulders. "Yeah, if you have to go, I suppose so."

"Larry, listen. I am not mad at you or anything. We are still friends and you don't have to go through all this to prove anything. Anyhow, man, I have a meeting I have to go. Talk to you later?"

Larry got up and headed towards the door. "Yeah, fine. I'll talk to you later." Larry opened the door and left.

Antonio stared at the door, shook his head, grabbed his stuff, and headed out.

"Oh really?" Greg said, munching on his sandwich.

Antonio guzzled down his iced tea. "Yeah, he was gonna tell me why, but I got a call and couldn't bother continuing."

Greg looked to the side. "Yeah I see. Do you think there is any truth to what he is saying?"

Antonio shook his head. "Man, I don't know, and quite frankly I don't care. As I said, Simone told me what the 411 was, and I am sure Larry feels like shit for what has happened."

Greg rolled his eyes. "Yeah . . . well I still find it odd that he would call her a killer, no?"

Antonio paused, and then scratched his chin. "Yeah, but like I said, obviously Simone and him had it going on that he went all crazy and shit."

Greg leaned back. "Tony give me a break. Why would anyone just call anyone a killer like that?"

Again Antonio scratched his chin. Greg had a good point. Why would Larry go this far? The more Antonio thought about it, the more it became peculiar. Antonio took a bite of his sandwich. "Man, I don't want to think about it right now. All I know is that I am with someone who is really good in bed."

Greg laughed. "Oh so that what is now eh? All about the sex."

Antonio screwed up his face. "Excuse me—you are the one to talk, Mr. 'Call me big daddy and scream my name, make her beg for my candy rain.' How come all of a sudden you've become the more emotional, sentimental type?"

Greg laughed. "Whatever man."

Antonio laughed, and then stopped. "Greg. Did Larry talk to you?"

Greg choked on his drink. "Um, why?"

"Because I am asking you."

"Um, not really. Um . . . why?"

"I wanted to know if he told you why he acted that way that night."

Greg cleared his throat and darted his eyes away. "Um, no he didn't."

"You're lying."

"I am not lying."

"Yes you are. Tell me what he told you."

Greg sighed as he took another drink of his Sprite. "Listen, he just told me what he told you."

"Yeah, but he never told me the full story."

Again Greg sighed. He leaned in. "Larry thinks Simone killed his brother."

Antonio leaned back. "What?"

"Yeah."

"Since when did Larry have a brother?"

Greg sighed.

"And what is his proof?"

"He doesn't have any."

Antonio laughed. "Give me a fuckin' break, is this some kind of joke?"

Greg shrugged his shoulders. "Man, I don't know."

Antonio shook his head. "This is so fucked. This has to be some kind of joke—and a bad one, too. I don't know what Simone or Dana or whatever

Larry wants to refer her has done to him, but this is too funny. Sounds like to me that Larry got pussy-whipped by Simone."

Greg didn't reply.

* * *

"Thank you for coming over, Antonio. I really appreciate this," Simone said, sipping her wine.

Antonio nodded. "Not a problem. You know, Simone, this is just too wild. I mean we've only known each other for just a short while and already there is such a huge physical attraction between us."

Simone smiled.

"I know I have said this so many times but I have never had such great . . . such incredible . . ."

Simone placed her finger over Antonio's lips. "I know. Trust me, I know."

Antonio smiled.

Simone removed her fingers and seductively licked them.

Antonio got excited. "You are such a tease, you know that?"

Simone purred. "I know."

Antonio leaned back in his seat. "Simone, listen I gotta ask you something. I feel so weird asking you this."

"Shoot."

"I know this is none of my business, and I know you already told me about the relationship you had with Larry, but I wanted to know out of curiosity—was it good? Was it bad? Was it weird?"

Simone grabbed her fork and dug into her pasta. "Why do you ask?"

"Larry came into my office and we had a chat."

Simone stopped eating. "Really? About what?"

"Well we never got into a huge discussion. I honestly think you must have put a spell on that boy because I think he really feels bad for doing what he did."

Simone half-smiled. "Oh, I guess."

"I mean the fact that he would call you a killer, too."

Simone froze.

"Simone, why would he call you a killer? I mean isn't that psycho? I mean, I know why you told him why your name is Dana, but man. A killer?"

Simone grabbed her fork and played with her pasta. "Larry is crazy. I stuck him with the crazy glue and now he will do anything to get me back."

Antonio laughed. "Really?"

Simone smiled. "Yes."

Antonio got up and approached Simone. He slowly caressed her neck and his hand slid underneath her blouse and fondled her stiff breasts. His hands then slid further down. "Can I have some of that crazy glue?"

Simone moaned. "Only if you are good."

Antonio grabbed Simone and carried her to the couch. His cell phone rang.

"Oh for fuck's sake, every time I try to—"

Simone grabbed his face. "Ignore it."

Antonio looked into Simone's eyes. He lowered himself onto her, pressing his lips against hers.

Antonio's cell phone rang again.

Antonio got up. "Fuck it, Simone, can I at least turn it off?"

Simone nodded as she unbuttoned her blouse.

Antonio grabbed his phone and noticed that he'd received a text message. "Who sent me a text message?"

Antonio opened and read the message. His body shook.

I know who you sexy are . . . mmm . . . sexy . . . mmmm sexy.

"Who the fuck *is* this?" Antonio threw his phone across the room.

Simone sat up from the couch. "Antonio, what's wrong?"

"I got another message, but this time through a text."

Simone held her hand to her chest. "Are you serious?"

"Yes, this is fucked . . . this has got to stop. Who the fuck is doing this? And why are doing this to me?"

The red tinted mustang sat by the corner of Missouri and Ontario streets. Laugher erupted from the driver seat as the driver sat staring at a cell phone.

CHAPTER TWENTY-ONE

Simone grabbed her phone. "Hello?"
"Dana, I'm waiting for you."
"Who is this?"
"Don't give me that bullshit. You know who this is."
"No I don't, now tell me who this is?"
"Don't fuck with me, Dana," the voice menaced. "You know who this is."
Simone didn't reply.
"Did you tell Antonio the truth?"
"How the fuck did you get my cell phone number? Freak?"
"Answer me. Did you tell Antonio the truth?"
Simone didn't reply.
"Dana, did you tell him how you killed my brother? Did you tell him how you killed your husband? Did you tell him that you are fucking insane?"
Simone's hands trembled. "Fuck off!"
"Did you tell Antonio that the only reason why you are fucking him is so you can do the same thing that you did with my brother and your husband? Take over some of the business with your drug money and then have them killed for bait?"
Simone eyes burned with tears. "Fuck you! You understand me? Fuck you! Don't you ever call me again! You understand me, you sick fucker!? Don't ever call me!"
"Dana, the only sick fucker out there is you. You are the sick fucker! You are the killer!"

Simone screamed. "Fuck off!" She threw her cell phone on the car seat.

"Um, excuse me. Is everything OK?" the freckled red hair boy asked from behind the drive-through window.

Simone adjusted herself. "Um, yes, sorry. How much was it again?"

"Your total is $8.04."

Simone paid the freckle-faced teenager, grabbed her sandwich and drink, and drove off.

CHAPTER TWENTY-TWO

Antonio stared at his devil woman painting. It spoke to him with meaning that scared him. What compelled to him to paint such a thing? What was the driving force? The more Antonio stared at that painting, the more freaked out he became. His painting told him something that he did not want to hear and was too afraid to admit. Antonio went over to the phone and dialed.

"Um, hello?" answered a muffled a voice.

"Larry? Hey it's Antonio. Listen, can I come by your place?"

Larry paused. "Uh . . . sure, why?"

"Larry, I want to finish discussing what we were talking about the other day."

Larry paused. "Yeah, for sure. When can you come over?"

"I'll be over in fifteen minutes. Something has been bothering me and I need to ask you about it."

"Sure, I'll be home."

* * *

Fluorescent lights stung Lisa's eyes as she blinked. The cold, damp air brushed against her dry, chapped skin.

"Oh my God, she is waking up! My baby is waking up!" yelped Lisa's mother. Greg rushed over the bedside. Lisa's eyes flickered and her fingers moved. A nurse ran into the room, grabbing the stethoscope from her neck.

The nurse smiled. "Great! This is just what we want to see."

"Oh my baby, my baby!" Lisa's mother said as she held on to Lisa's arm.

"Madam, please. I would ask you to refrain from touching and disturbing her. She is coming out of a serious coma and it's best if she can take it easy."

Lisa's mother glared at the nurse. "Excuse me, this is MY DAUGHTER you are dealing with here."

Greg intervened. "I think the nurse is right."

Lisa's mother sighed as the nurse observed Lisa.

A tall ball headed doctor walked into the room with a clipboard. "I see we have progress here."

The nurse nodded. "Yes, there is. Her BP right now is 125 over 83; her heart rate is about 74."

The doctor bent over Lisa. "Honey, do you know where you are?"

Lisa slowly shook her head.

The doctor smiled. "You are in the intensive care unit at the hospital."

Lisa didn't reply.

"You were in a coma for about three weeks now. You were involved in a serious car accident, but everything is fine now."

Lisa nodded.

Lisa's mother hovered over her. "Oh Lisa, are you OK? You alright, darling?"

Lisa smiled.

Greg leaned over. "Hey Lisa, hope you are doing OK."

Lisa opened her mouth. Her voice was hoarse. "Where's Antonio?"

Greg smiled. "Antonio couldn't make it today. He will visit you tomorrow."

Lisa smiled.

Lisa's mother leaned towards Greg. "Who is Antonio?"

"Oh, a co-worker of ours."

Lisa's mother rolled her eyes. "Oh really now, some new boyfriend?"

Greg bit his lip. "Um, no, just a co-worker, ma'am."

Antonio stood in the entryway of Larry's apartment and buzzed the entry code.

No one answered.

Antonio buzzed again.

Again, no answered.

"What the heck, I tell the man that I will be here, and he isn't?" Antonio said.

Antonio grabbed his cell phone and dialed Larry's number. The phone rang five times before his voicemail came on.

Antonio hung up. "Fuck," he said, and decided to wait a couple of minutes. Antonio headed back to his car, sat down, and turned on the stereo.

* * *

Simone parked her car in her driveway and sat there staring out at the sky. Her blood was boiling. She was fuming. Everything that she had been planning for was starting to crumble . . . all because of Larry.

"That fucking asshole!" Simone yelled. What were the odds of Antonio knowing Larry? What were the odds that Larry would work for the same place as Antonio? Why didn't she dig up Larry's info to find this out? All these questions raced through her mind.

There was a tap on the driver's window.

Simone looked up. Ronnie stood there with a grin.

She spoke through the window. "What do you want?"

Ronnie motioned her to wind down the window. Simone ignored him.

"I wanted to let you know that Ben Lee was looking for you last night. He wanted to know about that 'deal' you guys have."

Simone opened the window. "Tell Ben Lee that I will call him back."

Ronnie studied the expression on her face. "What's your problem?"

Simone sighed. "Larry's told Antonio everything."

Ronnie laughed.

"And you find this so funny?"

Ronnie leaned in the window. "And you weren't expecting this?"

"Ronnie, please, the last thing I need is to be nagged by you, OK?"

"Dana, don't give me that. From the time you told me you that Antonio invited Larry to your party I knew that the game was over."

Simone got out of her car, "Well good for you Sherlock. I am glad you figured that out."

"Dana, why don't you just give it up?"

"Why don't you just follow my orders and shut the hell up OK?"

Again, Ronnie laughed. "Geesh, you are a tough bitch. Oh, and another question?"

"I told you already, Ronnie. I am not sleeping with your sorry ass."

Ronnie rolled his eyes. "Whatever. My question is when are you gonna make your next move. You know, suggest to Antonio that you and him should be doing a business deal. Next thing you know, he is wrapped around your finger, and then low and behold, you are holding onto his job title and a piece of the company, and the only thing he will be holding onto is his life support?"

Simone glared at Ronnie. She knew that her attraction to Antonio was something that neither she nor Ronnie had ever expected, making it a major obstacle in their plan. Antonio was more than just a decoy in her plan; he almost became an obsession for her. Every time she needed a sexual release or felt sexual tension, she needed to call Antonio. She had never experienced the kind of pleasure that she had felt with Antonio. Antonio was almost lethal to her plan, and that confused her the most.

"Ronnie, please. Leave me alone in peace. I've got a lot on my plate, and the last thing I need is to have you interrogate me with your stupid questions right now."

"Ha! *Stupid?* Why is it stupid? The only thing that is stupid is you, Dana."

Simone stretched her hand out her car window and forcefully grabbed Ronnie's crotch.

Ronnie let out a yelp.

She looked deep in his eyes. "Ronnie, listen to me and listen to me clearly. I call the shots and I ask the questions. Not you. I will say this once, and I will not say this again. You do not ever—and I repeat, *ever*—address me as Dana again. It is Simone. Do I make myself clear?" Simone released him.

Ronnie grabbed his crotch and bent over in excruciating pain. "You are a fuckin' bitch, and that fuckin' hurts."

"Yeah, and remember, I am cold-hearted bitch, too. Remember that, bastard."

* * *

Twenty minutes passed, and Antonio had lost his patience. He rolled his eyes and started his car.

"This is bullshit. Why did I even come over?" Antonio wondered. Antonio reversed out into the parking lot and accelerated back to his place.

When he arrived, he noticed Greg's car in the parking lot. He grabbed his cell phone and dialed Greg's number.

"Hey where are you?" Greg said.

"I just came back from Larry's place."

Greg paused. "Oh . . . what did you guys talk about?"

"Nothing—the man wasn't even home. In any case, I am coming upstairs; I'll let you in the lobby."

Greg followed Antonio into his apartment.

"So, she is finally out of the coma, eh?" Antonio said, throwing his jacket on the sofa.

"Yeah man, isn't that great?"

"Yeah, it is."

"So Larry wasn't at his place?"

"Nope."

"Why were you going over there?"

"Because I needed to talk to him."

"Let me guess—about Simone, right?"

Antonio darted his eyes towards the floor. "Yes, and now the man is not there."

"Maybe he stepped out."

"Or maybe he feels like chicken shit and does not want to confront me."

"Um, I highly doubt it. Remember that this is the same guy who punched out two guys for fucking his ex-girl, remember?"

Antonio laughed. "True, you do have a point."

"So what are you gonna do?"

"I guess I'll talk to him tomorrow."

Antonio's cell phone rang. He picked it up. "Hello?"

"Mmmmmm sexy . . . . sexy . . . mmmmmm."

Antonio hung up the phone instantly.

"Tony, what's wrong?" Greg said.

Antonio paced. "That same fucking annoying message, man."

"Guy, this is getting out of hand. Did you contact the police officer about the text message?"

"No, I didn't. I've been really busy with shit and—"

Antonio's cell phone rang again. He gave it Greg. "Man, you answer it."

"Tony I am not going to—"

"Man, just answer it." Antonio said.

Greg picked up the phone. "Hello?"

Greg paused as he listened to the voice. "Oh. Hold on." He handed the phone to Antonio. "It's for you."

"Who is it?"

"I dunno, some guy."

Antonio grabbed the phone. "Hello?"

Greg went into the kitchen and grabbed a drink. His mind drifted to Simone and the uneasy feeling he had of her. Greg took a sip out of his beer before slamming it on the kitchen counter.

Antonio walked in.

"Tony, everything cool?"

"Oh it's the officer. He wants me to come in sometime this week to review the situation."

"You gonna tell him about the recent stuff?"

"Yeah, I have to. Greg this is just plain sick. Why would someone do this to me? Is there someone out there really that psychotic that is obsessed with me?"

CHAPTER TWENTY-THREE

Simone stared at Antonio's painting in her bedroom. She stared at the two lovers whose bodies intertwined in their lovemaking. She placed her fingers to her lips and shook her head.

"Antonio, you drive me crazy sometimes, you know that?" she said to herself. She picked up her phone and dialed Antonio's number.

The call went straight to Antonio's voicemail. Simone hesitated to leave a message, and she hung up right before the beep. She walked over to bed, kneeled down, and pulled out her briefcase. She opened it and stared at the wrapped bills and the 9mm automatic. She picked up the gun and kissed it. "In due time, Dana, in due time. You can't get so carried away like this. Pretty soon everything will fall into place and you will be able to achieve another piece of that pie."

Her phone rang. She answered. "Hello?"

"I didn't find anything at the place you sent me and my crew to," answered a voice with a hoarse Chinese accent.

Simone adjusted her voice. "Oh you didn't? Shit. That boy told me he had it there and must have been lying to me. I know he has at least thirty grams of that stuff stashed somewhere."

Ben interrupted. "Listen I don't have time to talk right now, I am meeting you at our usual place?"

"Yes, Ben. Oh and remember to bring that thing I want."

Ben laughed. "My Nubian sister, you know I would do anything for you."

Simone rolled her eyes as she walked to her closet. "All you Chinese guys say that now?"

Again Ben laughed. "Well you know what they say, once you go black you never go back."

Simone shook her head as she grabbed a skirt from her closet. "Real cute, Ben. I'll see you in few minutes."

Simone hung up the phone. She stood in front of the mirror and smiled.

"Thank you Ben, you've solved one of my problems. Now I just have to solve my other problem." She turned and stared at the painting and laughed.

* * *

Antonio could not concentrate. His mind was all over the place. One minute he was thinking about the disturbing messages, and the next minute he would think about Simone and their sexual rampages. Then the next minute, he would think about Larry and his explanations as to why he made those accusations. Larry was away from the office today, which Antonio found quite odd. Ironically, no one really noticed his absence because Larry always worked from home and did a lot traveling to meetings across town. However, Antonio knew his schedule. Antonio got up from his desk and headed towards the door. When he opened the door, Simone appeared outside.

"Simone, what are you doing——"

"Ssshhhh, please be quiet," Simone said, pushing her way inside the office. "I snuck past the secretary's desk to the elevators."

Antonio laughed. "What are you, a secret agent or something?"

Simone closed the door behind her and grabbed Antonio's hand. "So, how are you?"

Antonio sighed. "OK, I guess." He drew his hand away. "No, I am not OK."

Simone stroked Antonio's forehead. "Why?"

"Simone, it's just too weird. I know Larry well and I just don't understand why he would call you a killer like that."

Simone stopped. "I told you—Larry has issues." Simone cleared her throat. "Listen, I really think there is nothing to talk about. Larry and I are history. You shouldn't dwell on that. Larry needs to get over it."

Antonio took a deep breath. "Ok, fine. I'll ignore it."

Simone smiled. "Good. Anyhow the real reason why I came here is because I brought this." Simone grabbed a yellow legal-sized envelope from her coat jacket and handed it to Antonio.

Antonio stared at it. "What is this?"

"Listen, I don't want you to look at it yet. I want you to wait until the end of this week."

Antonio raised his eyebrow. "OK, Simone, now you've got me. What is this?"

Simone placed her fingers on Antonio's lips. "Hush. Open it on Friday."

Antonio shivered to the touch of Simone's finger on his lips. He nodded.

Simone turned around and headed towards the door. "Listen, I gotta go. Call me tonight OK?"

"Yeah, sure." Antonio said. Simone opened the door and left. Antonio stared at the yellow envelope.

* * *

"Tell Ben to come up here," Simone said.

The twin towers left the room. Moments later they returned with Ben, a 5'8 muscular Chinese man with jet-black hair. He wore a black T-shirt, black blazer, and black slacks with black shoes. A deep scar ran across his cheek.

"Good to see you again, Ben," Simone said.

Ben sat before her at her desk. "So do we have everything finalized?"

Simone leaned in. "Yes we do. I have your briefcase, but I wanted to know if I can keep the gun."

Ben laughed. "For what? You have your guys to take care of any dealings like that."

Simone laughed. "No Ben, see I need a gun so I can handle my own."

Ben licked his lips. "Dana, you are so seductive. You know that?"

Simone sat back. "Dana? Excuse me?"

Ben sat up and adjusted himself. "Oh, sorry. You don't like be called that?"

"Who told you my name was Dana?"

Ben leaned back in his seat. "Who the fuck cares? I came here to do business, not play name games."

"Ben, answer me, who you told my name is Dana?"

Ben smiled. "A little bird told me."

Simone sneered. "Whatever. OK, let's talk."

Antonio sat by his desk staring at the yellow envelope. His curiosity got the better of him. After a long, depressing day at work, he got home and couldn't resist opening the envelope. He ran into the kitchen and tore it open. Inside appeared a cheque addressed to Antonio for one million dollars. Antonio gasped and shook his head.

"Holy shit, what is this?"

Antonio turned over the cheque to examine if anything else was on it. He grabbed his cell phone and started dialing.

Simone picked up. "Hello?"

"A cheque for a million dollars?" Antonio said.

Simone chuckled. "So you broke my promise?"

Antonio ignored Simone's question. "Simone what is this for?"

"Well since you already opened the envelope and revealed my surprise to you, I would like to discuss this matter over lunch tomorrow if that is OK with you?"

"Why, is this a business deal?"

Again Simone chuckled. 'You are too much. Tomorrow at 1pm. Can you make it?"

Antonio nodded. "Um, yeah. Sure. 1pm tomorrow."

"Good."

Antonio ended the conversation quickly and hung up. Nothing made any sense. Why was Simone giving him a cheque for one million dollars? Antonio's phone rang. He answered it.

"Hello?"

No one answered.

Antonio cleared his throat. "Hello?"

Again no answer.

"I said hello, who is this?"

There was a brief pause. Suddenly there was a loud scream in the background, followed by a huge slam.

Antonio held onto the phone. "Hello? Hello? What the hell is going on? Who is that? Is there anybody there?"

The screaming got louder, followed by three short loud bangs. Then the phone disconnected.

CHAPTER TWENTY-FOUR

Simone's eyes widened. "You heard what?"

Antonio stared at his empty wine glass. "I heard a scream and then three loud bangs."

"And you didn't call the police?"

"The officer or detective or whatever his name is wasn't there. I left a message."

"Was it a woman's scream or a man's scream?"

"I couldn't tell . . . it sounded androgynous . . . it almost sounded like a recording of some sort . . . like it had come from a movie."

"Strange."

"Well, what I find strange is that the only people who have my new number besides you and my parents are Greg and Larry."

Simone stared down at her plate. "Mmm ,strange indeed."

Antonio looked up at Simone. "Simone, you didn't give any new potential clients my number, did you?"

Simone shook her head.

Antonio scratched his chin. "Simone this is just too freaky. All too freaky. It's almost like I am being cursed or something."

Simone held his hand. "Well hopefully you will feel better when I say what I am about to tell you."

"Which is what?"

Simone leaned in. "That cheque I wrote. I want to offer $1 million dollars for you to start working for me."

Antonio froze. "Um, Simone . . . I don't know what to say, but . . ."

Simone squeezed his hand harder. "Say yes."

"But Simone, I mean that money sounds great, but what kind of business would you have me doing if . . . ."

"Antonio I have your position lined up. You will be co-owner of my company. I was also thinking that it might be possible to strike up some business deal with your work."

"And that would be what?"

"I am willing to buy Mahagony."

Antonio gasped. "Hold up . . . what?"

"You heard me."

"Um, Simone. First of all, I don't owe that company. I am just an artist and an executive sales guy. Yes, I do quite well in what I do, but if you are looking for that kind of business deal, you are gonna have to talk to William Huntingwood."

Simone grabbed his hand and held it to her lips. She kissed it softly. "Well what if I offered you two million dollars to leave that gala and come work for me?"

Antonio paused. He did not know what to think. "Simone, I have to think about it."

Simone released his hand. "Fine, but I am only giving you a week to decide."

"A week? That's it?"

"Why, do you need more time?"

"Uh, yes."

"Antonio, don't be stupid. I am offering you two million dollars here. What is there to think about?"

Antonio leaned in. "Like I said, give me more time to think about it."

Simone leaned in. Their noses touched. "Fine, two weeks and no more."

Antonio smiled and leaned back. "Deal."

* * *

Greg walked through the door. "OK, Tony, what is it you have to show me that you can't tell me over the phone?"

Antonio shut the door and sat on the couch. He showed him the envelope. "Open it."

Greg followed Antonio's instructions. He pulled out the cheque and stared at his. His eyes widened. "Holy shit! Who wrote you this?"

"Guess?"

"No fucking way!"

"Yep."

"For what?"

Antonio laughed. "Get this, man. She wants to offer me a million dollars to start working for her. Oh and get this! She said she wants to purchase Mahagony."

Greg froze.

"And now she said she's willing to offer me two million dollars to leave and start working for her."

The cheque dropped out of Greg's hand.

"Man, you are acting like she is offering *you* the job and not me. Isn't that wild?"

Greg's stomach knotted. He instantly remembered what Larry had told him before and everything started to make sense. What if Simone really was a killer? What if she tried to kill Antonio? What if she really killed Larry's brother and her husband?

Greg took a deep breath. "Man, I really think you should think this through."

"I know Greg, but come on . . . I mean this money I know is legit. I mean two mil? You can't go wrong with that. Plus, you know I would invest at least half of it."

Greg felt a lump in his throat. "And exactly what will you be doing for her?"

Antonio scratched his head. "Um, to be quite honest with you, I am not sure. But she said she had a job lined up for me."

Greg felt the lump in his throat grow. He felt like a complete coward. "I just seriously think you should think about it first."

Antonio got up. "You know what my true answer is going to be, but I am more inclined to take this offer. I mean come on. Simone and I have been going out for some time. I trust her, and the woman has a lot of connections."

Greg sat up. "Hold on a second. Weren't you the same one who said earlier on that you don't mix business with pleasure?"

Antonio smiled. "Yeah but dude for two million? Come on now."

Greg smiled nervously. "You know, since you've been going out with Simone you've changed a bit, and it's all good. But right now, dude, I really don't think you're thinking clearly."

"Oh bullshit, Greg. You know what I am thinking. I should be taking this offer, shouldn't I?"

"Well, um, I . . ."

Antonio frowned. "Wait. Maybe I should really think about this before I jump the gun."

Greg smiled. "Yeah you should."

Antonio sat back down. "Yeah you are right. I'll think about this clearly before I make any drastic decisions."

* * *

The large half-moon hung in the crisp night air, while the howls of owls and the chirping of crickets echoed throughout the quite suburb neighborhood. An old man with fuzzy hair and liver spots dotting his face walked along the sidewalk with his golden retriever. The old man looked around, staring at the houses along the sidewalk. He crossed the street and walked into Farina Park. Lamp posts shined their lights on the paved walkway. Whistling "Born Free," the old man continued walking his dog. As they approached a bushy forest area, the dog started sniffing and pulling on his leash.

"Woah, Charlie, control yourself there boy," The old man said as he tugged on the leash. Charlie got more excited and started dragging the man towards a secluded area.

"Charlie, what is wrong with you? What are you sniffing?"

Charlie stopped at a large bush and started barking. It was dark and the old man did not know what Charlie was barking at. The old man grabbed a key chain with a light on it and pointed it at the area. Charlie continued barking.

"Charlie what did you find?"

The old man pulled away the bushes and found a large sheet that wrapped a large hump. Charlie barked some more as he sniffed the object and then whimpered at his owner.

The old man screwed up his face. Cautiously, he pulled aside the sheet. He was stunned. He held his hand to his chest. He couldn't believe what he was seeing. Charlie continued barking.

The old man fainted.

CHAPTER TWENTY-FIVE

Greg got home to his apartment. All day he had been trying to contact Larry and could not get in touch with him. Greg grew apprehensive as he thought about what Simone's plans might be. *Simone wants to kill Antonio*, Greg kept thinking. The more he thought about it, the more it horrified and haunted him. Those slick, seductive moves, cunningly sayings, and flirtations were all a game— an evil game that she ended up winning and some loser ended up . . . dying. Greg grabbed his cell phone and dialed Larry's phone number.

No answer.

"Where the hell is this guy?" Greg muttered to himself. He decided to head towards Larry's apartment.

* * *

Antonio stared at the cheque. He wasn't sure what to do. One part of him wanted him to jump the gun and go ahead with this deal because it seemed like the opportunity of a lifetime. The other half of him suggested he should walk away. He had a stable job, and there was no telling what would happen if he went with Simone. Antonio laughed. A couple of months ago he couldn't find himself a woman—he was a loner and a workaholic. Now, he'd found himself an older, attractive lady who had sexuality oozing out of her pores. AND she was offering him two million dollars for a job. Antonio simply couldn't decide what to do.

"This is just my luck," he said, shaking his head.

He grabbed the cheque and held it in front of his face.

* * *

Greg arrived at Larry's apartment. He ran up to the lobby door and buzzed Larry's number.

No answer.

Greg buzzed again.

Again, no answer.

"Where the hell did this guy go?" Greg said to himself.

Greg buzzed again. and still no answer.

A younger lady came out of the elevator and opened the door. She smiled at Greg. "Do you need to get in?"

Greg smiled. "Thank you." He held the door open for the lady and rushed to the elevator.

Greg got off on the twelfth floor and marched down to Larry's apartment. He knocked on the door.

No one answered.

Greg knocked on it again, this time harder. Again, no reply. As Greg prepared to knock again, he noticed that the door was unlocked. He slowly opened the door.

"Hello? Larry, are you here? It's Greg. Anyone here?"

Greg stood in astonishment. Furniture and bookshelves were turned over. Clothes, plates, and pieces of furniture scattered all over the place.

Greg mouth gaped. "What the . . ." He looked down the hallway. Black, oily finger prints smeared the white walls, and more books and furniture had been strewn on the floor.

Greg couldn't believe what he was seeing.

He croaked, "Larry, are you here?"

His voice reverberated against the walls of the empty, terrorized apartment. Greg turned around and hurried out the apartment. He grabbed his cell phone as he open pushed the elevator button and starting dialing.

Antonio yawned. "Hello?"

"Tony, dude. You have to hear me."

"Greg, what's wrong?"

"I just went over to Larry's place."

"And?"

"Man, his place has been trashed and vandalized."

"What?"

Greg stepped into the elevator. "I'm serious. Someone came into his apartment and trashed the whole place."

"Is he there?"

Greg pushed the ground-level button on the elevator. "No, he isn't. Have you heard or seen him lately?"

"No. I wanted to speak to him, but I haven't seen him in like days."

Greg's hands trembled. "Guy, this is really strange. "

The elevator doors opened. Greg sprung out. As he turned the corner, he bumped into someone. The person ignored Greg and kept walking.

Greg turned around. "Hey, watch it."

Greg continued his conversation as he walked outside towards his car. "Do you think something bad has happened to him?"

"I don't know," Antonio said. "Greg, I—oh, hold on, someone's buzzing on my next line."

"I'll hold on," Greg said as he entered his car. Greg sat staring at the parking lot. He tried to figure out why and who would trash Larry's apartment. Greg turned his head and noticed a red Mustang parked out by the lobby entrance. As he sat there waiting for Antonio, he noticed the person he'd hit that day hopping into the driver's seat. The Mustang started, and the driver pulled away slowly and sped off.

Antonio clicked on the next line. "Hey, I'm back."

"Listen," Greg began, "I'm heading over your place."

* * *

Simone lay sprawled out naked on her bed. Her hands were trailing her ample breasts as she stared at Antonio's painting. She felt a shiver go through her body as she closed her eyes. She placed her finger between her breasts as she trailed it down past her navel to between her thighs. Simone let out a moan when her cell phone rang.

She sighed as she reached for the phone. "Yes?"

"I've delivered that suitcase for you," answered a muffled, coarse voice.

Simone let out a sigh. "Good. Tell Ronnie everything is fine and that you and him are to meet up with me tomorrow at 11am sharp."

"Alright. You know Dana, I really don't feel comfortable going through with all of this."

"Listen to me. I don't want to hear that kind of crap. You'll do as you're told."

"But—"

"I don't want to hear anymore." Simone hung up the phone and closed her eyes. She ran her cell phone between her breasts. The cold feeling left her with goose bumps.

She smiled. "All I need Antonio to do is to take my deal and everything will fall into place."

Greg arrived at Antonio's place. Antonio offered Greg a seat, but he was too nervous to sit. Everything had started to make sense to Greg about Simone. With each of the men she had dated, she had signed some form of contract with them, and after, they ended up dead. But why? Was she cursed? Was she a woman scorned?

Antonio loudly cleared this throat. "I said, would you like a drink?"

Greg shook his head. "Oh, sorry man. I'm fine, thanks."

"You seem all nervous." Antonio said.

Tell him. Greg thought to himself. *Tell him what you think the deal is.* Greg took a deep breath. "Tony, I think you should stay away from Simone."

Antonio leaned back in his seat. "And why is that?"

"Because I get this weird vibe from her, man. Like she is bad news."

"Is that what Larry has been feeding you?"

"No man, I am serious. I really kind of get this weird vibe from her now."

"You didn't at first—why now?"

Greg sat down. "What did Larry tell you about Simone?"

"Well, nothing as yet."

"So he never told you why his brother died?"

"No, how did he die?"

Greg held his breath. "Larry thinks Simone killed him."

Antonio broke out laughing. "You are kidding me right?"

"Dude I am serious."

"How did Simone kill him?"

"Well, that's just it. Larry doesn't know for sure, but he said he was positive that she did it."

Antonio shook his head. "Oh come on, that is complete bullshit, man."

"Well, hear this. Larry told me that his brother and Simone's husband both signed business deals with her. Within a number of weeks they were both dead."

Antonio felt nervous, but he tried not to show it. "Yeah, OK there, buddy. Where does Larry get this stuff?"

"Man, why would Larry make this up?"

"I don't know, but this whole thing does not rub me the right way, and I don't think Larry would ever lie about a thing like this." Antonio's cell phone ring punctuated their conversation. He picked it up, walking into the kitchen. "Hello?"

Greg sat back down with his hand on his jaw. Deep down, he knew that Larry had to be right, and the more he thought about it, the more justified it sounded.

There was a crash in the kitchen.

Greg got up and rushed to the kitchen. Antonio stood there with his mouth opened, his eyes wide, and his face pale. Broken pieces of glass had scattered all over the kitchen floor.

"What happened?"

Antonio started shaking his head slowly. "Greg, that was the police."

"For what?"

"Larry."

"Where the hell is he?"

Antonio paused. "They found him at Farina park. Larry's dead."

CHAPTER TWENTY SIX

Weeks had passed and everything around Antonio seemed surreal. Larry's death remained a complete mystery to everyone. No one could figure out why someone would kill him. Every time he thought about it, chills ran down Antonio's spine. But when Antonio felt stressed, Simone seemed to be there for him, regardless. Their passion grew stronger each time they met. At times their sexual encounter became completely animalistic; they tore into each other's flesh, devouring and conquering each other, night after night. Simone had often asked about the deal she'd proposed, but Antonio wouldn't give her an answer. He couldn't make deals, especially at a time like this.

Friday night after work, Antonio walked through the parking lot to his car. As he approached his car, he noticed shattered pieces of glass from the driver's side. Antonio panicked. As he rushed to the door, he found that the driver's side window had been smashed. Antonio's eyes filled with exasperation and heat. He ground his teeth and cursed. Stepping away from his car, he noticed that his tires had been slashed and a large scratch had been made along the side of his car.

"What the fuck!" he yelled. Nothing had been stolen; however, a white envelope lay on the driver's seat. Antonio's hands shook. He had seen these envelopes before and knew what was in them. He was afraid to come across yet another one, and yet he felt compelled to open it:

> I know who you are sexy . . . I know where you live sexy . . . And all I know is that I want you, sexy motherfucker . . . I need you . . . I need you.

Antonio ripped the paper in shreds and threw them at his feet. His eyes filled with hot tears. He felt like exploding.

The officer took off his hat. "This certainly *is* serious. However, you should not have ripped the letter."

Antonio sat up in his seat. "Officer, please. This is getting out of hand. Can't you guys do something about this? I mean, for the past couple of months I have had harassing calls to my work, home, and cell number, I have had these psycho letters dropped off at my place anonymously, and now I have had my car vandalized, with another letter put in there. And you're telling me that I shouldn't have gotten a little upset when I got that letter again?"

The officer cleared his throat. "What I said is that you should not have ripped the letter. Listen, we are obviously going to have to hand this over to one of our special investigators because this does sound like a serious problem."

"Too little, too late" Antonio muttered.

* * *

Antonio watched as the tow-truck drove off with his black Nissan. Staring up into the cloudy night sky he shook his head, cursed loudly before picking up the phone and dialing.

Simone answered cheerfully. "Hey, sexy, how are you?"

"Not that great."

"Why?"

"Someone vandalized my car."

"What?"

"You heard me. "

"That is awful."

"I know."

"What are you going to do?"

Antonio sighed. "I spoke with the police. They are so useless."

"I know . . . Did you want to come over?"

Antonio smiled. "Actually that is why I'm calling. Can you come by and give me a lift? I'm so stressed out now."

"Of course I will babe."

"Thanks."

"No problem."

"So I guess you will be here in about fifteen minutes, then?"

"For sure."

Antonio hung up, and smiled. Simone hung up, smiled, laughed quietly, and got ready.

Antonio fell on the bed, exhausted and sweaty. Simone fell on top of him, panting heavily.

Antonio laughed. "I really wasn't expecting this, I swear. I was just hoping that we would just talk and . . ."

Simone giggled. "Antonio, please. You really expected to come here and just talk? Come on, you know you wanted some nookie."

"Whatever," Antonio said. "That was not my intention."

Simone licked her lips. "Whatever you say, artist boy. Listen, I hate to switch subjects here, but I am wondering if you . . ."

"If I what?"

Simone sat up. "Did you have a chance to think about that deal?"

Antonio played with his hands. "Um, actually yeah I have."

Simone's eyes widened. "Really? OK, and the answer is . . . ?"

Antonio got up and gazed at Simone. "Simone, first, I want to thank you for this offer. It's amazing . . . but I am gonna have to decline it."

Simone's smile dropped.

"Simone, I know this might sound silly but I am quite comfortable where I am, and I know that I will expand in what I am doing. Plus I don't think William would be pleased to hear of me leaving. He would be really upset."

Simone didn't respond.

Antonio kissed Simone on her forehead. "I hope you understand that."

Simone folded her arms and cleared her throat.

"You are pissed, aren't you?" Antonio said.

"No, I am not pissed. I am actually happy for you. It's just that I would have hoped that you would have said yes." Simone moved her head below Antonio's navel and then gazed up. "Is there anything I can do to change your mind?"

Antonio looked down. "Simone I really honestly think that—" Antonio let out a moan as Simone started licking him up and down.

"Simone, really I do . . ." Antonio let out a louder moan as Simone used her tongue to lick the tip. Simone hummed as she took the whole shaft in her mouth. Simone's hot, wet mouth and tongue made Antonio squirm.

Antonio looked down and smiled. "You never take no for an answer, do you?"

* * *

Antonio arrived at the office late in the morning. Despite what had occurred to him, he felt a little better than usual. He was preparing some information for clients when his phone rang.

"Hello?"

"Hey, William wants you to see him in his office ASAP." Monica said.

"OK."

Antonio got up and left his office. As he walked down the hallway, a couple of employees saw him and gave him peculiar looks. Antonio ignored them and knocked on the office door.

"It's open," William Huntingwood shouted.

Antonio entered. William sat at his desk. On each side were two other directors.

"Have a seat," William Huntingwood said.

Antonio felt uneasy and sat down. He adjusted his tie. "How are you?"

William Huntingwood took off his glasses. "I don't know, you tell me."

"Um, no problems."

"No problems? Can you explain this to me?" William Huntingwood handed Antonio a fax sheet.

"What is this?" Antonio asked.

"That's what I want to know."

Antonio read the fax sheet. His eyes widened. "Hold on one second. I did not write this!"

"Well it has your signature on it, Antonio."

Antonio scratched his head. "No, wait, this is a mistake. Why would I sign something like this?"

William shook his head. "Then if it's not the case, explain this to me." William handed him another fax form. Antonio read it.

His hands shook. "What the hell is this?"

"I don't know, Antonio. First I get a faxed letter of resignation from you. Then I get another faxed letter from another company telling me that you are willing to sign a deal to congregate and join partnership—without discussing any of this with me?"

* * *

Simone picked up the phone. "Hello?"

"Simone what the hell is wrong with you?" Antonio said.

"Excuse me?"

"You heard me, what the hell is wrong with you?"

"What are you talking about?"

"You faxing a memo to my boss that I plan to leave, and also faxing him a memo saying that I was interested in partnering with 'another company?'"

Simone laughed. "Oh please, Antonio. From what I remember last night, you said yes. So I decided to jump the gun."

"Simone I didn't say yes to anything! And now you fax my boss a letter of resignation and a proposal for a merger?"

"And the problem with that would be?"

"Um, that I should have been the one who told him if I had said yes."

"You did."

"Simone, I am going to lose my job now because of this."

"Antonio, God, stop whining! You are not losing your job. As far as I am concerned, you are resigning."

"Listen, Simone, you can't just do that. Especially like that. It's so unprofessional, it's so . . ."

"Excuse me, Mr. Antonio Madison, are you calling me unprofessional?"

Antonio paused. "Considering what you have just done, yes."

Simone remained silent.

"Look Simone, I know you are trying to help but—"

"Trying? I wasn't trying. I *was* helping Antonio. And let me just remind you that the job that you would be doing would pay you a lot more than what you're currently making."

"Simone, you forged my signature on that application, for Christ's sake!"

"For your own benefit, Antonio."

Antonio let out a sigh. "Look, Simone. Seriously, I think you jumped the gun a little."

Again Simone remained silent.

"I think you should have let me handle it first."

"Fine, be that way." Simone hung up the phone.

* * *

Ronnie picked up the phone. "Hello?"

"Ronnie, listen. I need you to do a couple of things for me," Simone responded.

"What?"

"I need you to watch and follow Antonio."

"Um haven't I already been doing that?"

"Yes, but I want you to keep a guard on him all the time."

"And what do you think I was doing all this time? Picking my nose?"

"Listen, Ronnie. I have a lot of work to do here, and I don't have time for your dilly-dallying shit. What I want you to do is follow him. I don't want him to catch on."

"Dana, how long is this gonna go on for? Usually at this point in the game you would have gotten the guy engaged and stuff. You are starting to lose your touch here."

Simone didn't reply.

"Oh and I wanted to add another thing. You keep encouraging Antonio to go to the police. Why on God's earth would you encourage him to do that? Won't that eventually lead to us?"

"Ronnie, listen. No one has found me out in years and no one will unless someone blabbers his mouth. I know what I want and I will get it."

"Yeah, if anything I would keep an eye on Antonio's friend there."

"Who. Greg?"

A smile spread across Ronnie's face. "Yeah, him. I think that guy knows what's going on. Larry must have told him the whole story."

"And what makes you think that?"

"Oh come on, Dana. Larry knew Antonio and Greg. You don't think he didn't tell either of them? Considering Antonio does not know the full story, I am sure he must have told Greg."

Simone paused. "So what are you saying?"

"I am saying that he would be the one who might blow our cover. Dana, what are we going to about him?"

"Well, we are gonna have to take care of him."

"How?"

Simone paused, and then took a deep breath. "Ronnie, you know what to do."

CHAPTER TWENTY-SEVEN

Antonio sat by the phone. He wanted to talk to Simone but he was also upset about what she'd done. Why would Simone do such a thing? He admitted that after their wild sex together Antonio did say he would think about it and would more likely agree, but he didn't fully say yes. Maybe she had misinterpreted him? Maybe she had deliberated on this? Antonio didn't know. All he wanted to do was reconcile with Simone. Antonio shook his head thinking about how wild everything had been since he'd met Simone. He found himself purposely scheduling his time so that he could can accommodate Simone anyway, anyhow. Even if it was a quick night "rendezvous," Antonio had somehow managed to schedule her into his time. Was he falling in love with her, or was he infatuated with the hot sex they had together? He scratched his head and raised his eyebrows thinking about the weird phone calls and Simone. Was this all too coincidental? Was there someone out there who knew about them and was pissed? Antonio briefly considered the idea of Larry's involvement. Simone did say they were in a previous relationship. Or were they? Antonio got up and went into the kitchen and grabbed himself a glass of water.

There was a knock on the door.

"Who is it?" Antonio shouted.

"Special delivery," replied the muffled the voice behind the door.

"Special delivery? Who the heck is making a special delivery?" Antonio approached the door and cautiously, slowly, and nervously opened it.

A man wearing dark shades, khaki pants, and a white t-shirt stood in front of the door with a large red box wrapped with a white bow.

Antonio stood back. "Um . . . who is this for?"

"This for you, sir." said the man.

"From whom?"

The man shrugged his shoulders. "Not too sure, sir."

"Is there anything for me to sign?"

"Nope."

Antonio reluctantly reached for the gift.

"Have a nice night, sir," the man said. He spun around and headed towards the elevator.

Antonio shut the door. He walked in the living room and placed the gift on the coffee table. Antonio raised his eyebrow before he opened the gift. A white sheet of paper was folded perfectly in the middle. Antonio's hands shook. He was apprehensive to read the letter. Antonio closed his eyes before grabbing the paper, opening it, and reading it. Antonio opened his eyes and read.

Go to the window.

Antonio scratched his head. He didn't know what to think. Cautiously, he edged towards the window. He stared outside to see anything he might recognize. He then looked down. At the bottom of the street corner stood Simone in front of her white Mercedes, wearing a fur coat and sunglasses. In her hand, she held a long-stemmed red rose. Antonio rolled his eyes and smiled.

His cell phone rang. He picked up. "Hello?"

"Would you care for a little drive?" Simone asked.

Antonio sighed. "Yeah sure, give me about fifteen minutes then, OK?"

"For sure."

Within fifteen minutes, Antonio had walked out of the lobby of his apartment in dark jeans, a grey blazer, a white shirt, and brown shoes. Simone smiled.

Antonio got inside her car. "And may I ask why you went to all of this trouble to have a delivery guy send that message?"

Simone squeezed his hand. "Shut up and let me drive you somewhere."

Antonio smiled. "OK, Miss."

Simone started the car and hung a right down Broadway Avenue.

Ronnie followed them in his dark blue van.

* * *

Antonio and Simone arrived at Schneider's Steak and Grillhouse, an expensive restaurant uptown. They sat in an exclusive booth in the back corner of the dim, quiet restaurant.

Simone grabbed Antonio's hand. "Listen, Antonio. I do want to apologize for what I did. I know I jumped the gun and . . ."

"Simone, don't worry about it. Obviously you did this because you cared and wanted the best for me. Quite frankly, I find that quite . . . quite . . . cool."

Simone smiled. "I like to care of the people I trust."

Antonio's face gleamed. "That is sweet of you to say that. I mean, we have to admit, Simone, our relationship has mainly been physical, and . . ."

Simone squeezed Antonio's hand harder. "Antonio, look. From the first day I laid eyes on you at the art gallery, I knew there was some form of chemistry—some form electricity between us. I don't know if you felt it, but I definitely felt it that day. And as much as I do enjoy your art work, the real reason why I buy your paintings is so I can get closer to you, think about you, get next to you when you are not around."

Antonio leaned back with widened eyes. "Oh wow. Um, that is really . . . wow," Antonio said. "Simone that is really deep. I never had anyone say that before."

"Well, that is why I brought you this." Simone said, digging out her pocket. She placed a small white box on the table.

"What is this?"

"Open it."

Antonio opened the box. He was blinded by the shimmering light bouncing off the studs of a diamond ring that nested in the middle of the box.

Antonio looked up at Simone. "Um . . . what is this?"

Simone leaned in. "It's a friendship ring. I want you to wear it. It's something that can remind you of me and our blossoming relationship."

* * *

"Friendship ring? Blossoming relationship?" Greg said pushing the weights above his head.

"Yeah I know. Wild, huh?" Antonio said, finishing his last sit-up.

Greg shook his head. He did not like what he was hearing. Larry's story was making so much sense that what was happening to Antonio was becoming predictable.

Greg dropped his weights. "So let me get this straight. She gets a delivery guy to deliver a special box to your place. You open it, and there's a letter sending you to look out the window. You look, and she is out there with a rose in her hand. You follow her now to this Schneider's restaurant, y'all talk, and she presents you with a friendship ring?"

Antonio nodded.

Greg rolled his eyes. "This girl is a bit much."

Antonio frowned. "Why do you say that?"

Greg shrugged his shoulders. "I don't know, man. I mean this seemed all cool at first, but it almost seems like . . . well, like she is using you as her sex kitten."

Antonio got up from the mat and broke out laughing. "Sex kitten? Dear God Greg, give me a break."

"No, I am serious. I mean, I know that I was all up for this, but I don't know, man."

Antonio sighed. "Listen, Greg. I know what Larry told us was kind of freaky. But look. I can take care of myself, and I can tell when something is not right."

"Tony, the girl faxed a letter to Bill saying that you wanted to resign and that you wanted to have a joint business partnership? Like what the fuck is that?" Greg said.

"Greg I know, I know. But hey, she said she jumped the gun and I forgave her. And I already concluded that she did that because she wanted to look out for me."

Greg rolled his eyes. "Man, that woman has you whipped."

Antonio leaned back. "Excuse me? No, man, the girl does not have me whipped. Having me whipped would mean that she would have me at her beck and call. Being whipped would mean that every time she needed a favor that was *non-sexual*, might I add, I would have been there. Being whipped means that she can dominate me whenever she pleases. That, my friend, is being whipped. And that is something that I am not."

"Yeah whatever, you know best."

"That's right, I do." He tried to calm down. "Anyway, speaking about the resignation. I wanted to talk to you about that."

"Yeah, what about it?"

"Yeah, so Simone and I were talking about this again last night. She kept insisting on it, and I told her that I would think about it, but I told her that where I am currently is fine for me."

"Good."

"So then we talked more and more, and after talking for God knows how long . . . Greg, I am resigning."

Greg dropped the weights, causing them to smash against the gym equipment. "You're what?"

"On Monday, I am going to give them an official resignation letter."

"Please tell me you are joking."

Antonio shook his head. "No man, honestly, I thought about this, and I honestly think that will be a good step for me."

Greg's face paled. His heart thumped. His mind went delusional. *Larry was right.* He thought to himself. *She is a killer.*

CHAPTER TWENTY-EIGHT

"That can't be so! Are you serious, officer?" Greg asked.

The officer nodded. "Yes about thirty grams were found in his apartment." Antonio and Greg were sitting at the police station at the corner of Fifth and Broadway Avenue. The police had contacted Antonio because they found his name on some work documents in Larry's vandalized apartment and wanted more information about Larry. They both sat in a dimly lit room with a rusty light hanging from the chipped tiled ceiling. A brown-bearded, beefy officer stood at the head of the table.

Antonio shook his head slowly. "That can't be right. We've known Larry for years. The man never told us that he did cocaine. I think this is an honest mistake, officer."

"Most coke users don't advertise that stuff to their friends unless those friends are part of that environment."

Antonio and Greg both shook their heads. "We don't do that shit."

The officer leaned in. "Well, my point taken. If you guys don't do it, then he might have not mentioned it to you guys."

Greg got up from his seat. "Officer, so exactly what are you trying to say here—that foul play might have been involved?"

"Could be. The evidence is quite clear. There was cocaine found in his place, his place was vandalized, and he ends up dead in park ten kilometers away from his house. To me, it sounds like some people came into his place for a drug deal, the deal did not work out for some reason, and so they decided to kill him."

Antonio placed his hands over his head and continued shaking it "no." "Man, this is so fucked. I feel like I am in *The Twilight Zone*. I still can't believe Larry would do such a thing. That makes no sense. I know Larry does not do drugs."

The officer cleared his throat. "I know it's hard to believe, but we get a lot of cases like these, and usually we end up finding out information about someone that family or friends never knew."

Antonio raised his hand. "Officer I have a question. So if cocaine was found in his place, why are you just now coming forward with this information? It's been weeks now since Larry died and now we are just hearing about this drug thing?"

The officer cleared his throat. "Mr. Madison, we discovered this when we first arrived at the place but we did not disclose this to you because we were looking into other factors.

Greg sighed. "Man, this is too much."

"Do you know if Larry had been going to any wild parties?" the officer said.

"Nope," replied Antonio.

The officer started writing. "Do you know if Larry had any enemies or 'friends' that might do such a thing?"

Greg froze. He immediately thought of Simone. His gut instinct said that he should tell the officer that Larry did have enemy and her name was Dana Robinson. But was there proof? And how would Antonio react to this? Greg swallowed. "Um, nope. Not that I aware of."

Antonio got up. "Is there anything else, officer?"

"Nope, not unless you have any further questions."

"No, we don't, but thank you officer."

Antonio and Greg left the police station and stood outside.

"Man that sounds so fucked. This makes no sense," Greg said. "I never knew Larry did coke. That seems impossible."

"Yeah man, I agree. I honestly think that it was a set-up or something."

Greg turned to Antonio. "Tony, I know you are gonna hate me for saying this but . . . do you think Simone might . . . might know about this?"

"Greg, if you are asking if Simone had anything do with this, the answer is no, and I can't believe you would be so fuckin' stupid to suggest such a thing."

"Hey, chill! All I said is if she had known about Larry's cocaine habit. I wasn't suggesting that she was the one who killed him."

Antonio stared at Greg. "You really don't like her, do you?"

Greg rolled his eyes. "Guy, I didn't say that, but . . ."

"No, answer the question. You don't like her. You've said it before that you felt this weird vibe from her. Tell me the truth."

"Man you are blowing this out of proportion."

"You know what your problem is, man? You're jealous. That's what the problem is."

Greg stood back. "I beg your pardon?"

"You heard me. You are jealous. You are jealous because I've got someone and you are still single and you got nobody."

Greg laughed. "Tony, you sound like a fucking immature girl. You've got to be kidding me. Why the fuck would be jealous of you? You're this wide-eyed, 'you want me to do *what*? In bed' kind of kid losing his shit over some woman. You know, if anything you should be happy that I gave you some tips on how to treat her like a lady."

Antonio stood back even further. "Hold up one fuckin' second. Since when did you start schooling me on how to treat her like a lady? What, find her G-spot and make her call me big daddy and scream my name? Yeah that is fuckin' treating a lady alright. And yeah, I maybe I'm too conservative, and I *am* shy, but look where I ended up, Greg. I am with an attractive, mature lady who—quite frankly—is hotter in bed than any girl either of us has been with, and she fulfills me both sexually and intellectually. So you can stand there and act like you're all that, but at the end of the day, it's *this* man who has a woman on his side, not you!"

"You think you got a real lady, huh? You honestly think you do? Well get this. If she is such a real lady, I double dare you to check her driver's license."

"And what does that have to do with anything?"

"That night I went to Larry's place, there were a couple of things that he told me that I never told you."

Antonio folded his arms. "What the fuck are you babbling about?"

Greg glared at Antonio. "First of all Simone's not forty-two, she's fifty-eight."

Antonio rolled his eyes. "Oh fuck off, that is such bullshit. What proof do you have of that? And even if she's fifty-eight, big fuckin' deal. What woman do you know who tells her real age?"

Greg leaned in. "Well she seemed all high and mighty and proud of the fact that she was forty-two, didn't she? And I also recall, didn't she say some bullshit about how she is always up-front and honest? Well, she wasn't honest about that."

"That's bullshit."

"Bullshit? You think so? Well try this on for size, Tony. Larry's brother who died, remember that? Did Larry tell you that his brother was married to Simone?"

Antonio froze. "What?"

"Yeah, Tony. It was Larry's brother who involved with Simone, not Larry—contrary to what Simone made you believe."

"No man, that is all lies. That is all fuckin' lies!"

"Fuckin' lies, Tony? Fuckin' lies? Tony, Larry told me that his brother married Simone after they got into a little business deal, similar to what she has now with you. Things didn't go right, so weeks after, he died in a car accident."

"Car accident?"

"Yes, Tony, a car accident. Larry's brother Shane died in a car accident. Apparently the brakes failed to work or some shit like that, and his car ended up hitting a tree."

Antonio felt paralyzed. He couldn't believe what he was hearing. *No, that can't be true. Shane? That is the Shane she was referring to?*

"And her husband Harold? Yeah, well Simone or Dana or whatever her name is killed him too—same process, same bullshit."

Antonio grew angrier as he made his fist. His fist flew in the air and slammed against Greg's jaw causing him to fall over onto the ground.

Greg got up, holding his jaw. "What the fuck is wrong with you, man?"

"You are fucking liar. I can't believe you would make up that fuckin' bullshit."

Greg got up and threw a punch at Antonio, sending him flying backwards.

Antonio got up. "You fuckin' prick!"

Antonio threw another punch, but Greg blocked it. The two wrestled on the concrete, creating a commotion amongst on lookers. Three officers ran out of the doors, pulling the two apart.

"You are fuckin' jealous, man. That's what your problem is!" Antonio screamed as two officers held him down.

"And you are fucking blind! Simone has got you pussy-whipped man, fucking pussy-whipped." Greg yelled, trying to free himself from the one officer.

Antonio pushed the officers aside and tackled Greg onto the floor. Punches flew as the two fought each other furiously. Two more officers rushed out, pulling the two apart.

Antonio was dragged inside kicking and struggling by the officers. "You fucking asshole!"

Greg struggled to free himself from the other officers. "This is your own fault now, Tony!!! Don't come to me when she fucking takes everything you have!"

The tinted red Mustang sat across the street. The windows wound down and a cigarette butt was thrown out. The red Mustang started and veered down the street.

CHAPTER TWENTY-NINE

Antonio slammed the door when he entered his apartment. A painting from the living room fell off the wall, cracking down the center hitting the floor.

"I fucking can't believe that asshole!" Antonio muttered as he threw himself on the couch. Antonio felt like ripping Greg's heart out of his chest. His anger fueled him, and the more he thought about Greg's comments, the angrier he became. He needed to calm down, he needed comfort, he needed to ease his mind . . . he needed Simone. Antonio reached over the phone and dialed.

"Hello?" Simone answered.

Antonio sighed. "Hey."

"Hey, sexy, how are you?"

"I'm fucking fuming!"

"Don't tell me you got another message?"

"No, Simone. Greg and I got into a huge fight."

Simone paused. "Oh?"

"Yes, we got into a fist-fight."

"Oh, what happened?"

"He was saying bullshit about you that pissed me off. "

"What do you mean he was saying stuff about me?"

Antonio got up and grabbed a drink from the kitchen. "Some shit that Larry told him."

Simone, who had been sitting at her desk, got up and sat on her sofa. "What did he say?"

Antonio took a deep breath to calm down. He sat back down on his sofa. "Oh, some bullshit about your age and stuff. Simone, I am so pissed right now. I don't even know if it's even worth mentioning to you."

"No, no. I want to know what Greg said."

"Well for starters, apparently Larry told him that you are not forty-two, you're fifty-eight . . . and Greg actually believes him. Would you believe that shit?"

Simone felt a chill go down her spine. "Huh? That's what he said?"

"Yeah, it was. I mean even if you were fifty-eight, would you ever tell me? What girl do you know that tells a man her real age?" Antonio paused and remembered what Greg had said about Simone being proud of her age and not caring. "Simone, how old *are* you?"

Simone felt a lump in her throat. "Antonio, I told you already. Do you believe Greg—who obviously believes everything Larry tells him—or do you believe me?"

Antonio sighed as he ran his hand over his face. "Simone, this is messed up. And then there was some other shit that he told me. Listen, Simone, would you mind coming over to my place? I'd rather talk about this in person than over the phone."

"Yeah, for sure. I won't be over there for about an hour. Is that OK with you?"

"Yeah that's fine."

Simone hung up and Antonio sat staring through his window. He was still fuming. He still could not get over what Greg had said to him. Antonio kept replaying the questions over and over. His stomach turned. He started sweating. The questions were starting to make sense. If Simone was proud of her age and said she has no problem discussing it, why would she lie? *But who cares, right? But fifty-eight years old?* Antonio squirmed in his seat. *I'm sleeping with a fifty-eight year old woman? Someone old enough to be my mother?* Antonio felt sick to his stomach. Images of Larry popped in Antonio's head. *Larry had a brother? A brother named Shane? Was this the same Shane that was married to Simone?* Antonio's hands trembled when he grabbed his drink. No. Something was definitely wrong, and he couldn't keep ignoring it to be with Simone. Could Greg be right? Again Antonio shook his head and gulped down his drink.

There was a knock on the door.

"Who is it? Antonio yelled.

No one answered.

Antonio raised his voice. "I said, who is it?"

Antonio got up and marched over the door. When he opened it, he saw Greg standing there with his hands in his pockets.

"What the hell do you want?" Antonio said.

Greg stood still. "Look man, I did not come here to fight. I've come here because I want to clear up some things."

"There is nothing to clear up," Antonio said. "You have your opinion, I have mine. End of discussion." Antonio attempted to push the door closed.

Greg stopped it midway. "Hold up a second. No man, wait. It's not about my opinion. It's about reasoning and facts. Have you really stopped and thought about the whole situation?"

"Yes I have, Greg, and I have concluded that you are delusional and wrong. I don't know what Larry said, to you but you've obviously misinterpreted it."

"Oh give me a fuckin' break, Tony. Why would Larry make shit up and why would I make this shit up? You know I'm not jealous of you. Come on, think, Antonio."

Antonio shook his head and rolled his eyes. He knew he should listen to Greg, but he just couldn't give up Simone so easily. "I have to go, Greg. I have a guest coming."

Greg glared at Antonio. "Fine." Greg stood back and let the door slam. He stood in the hallway shaking his head.

"I can't believe how fucked he is." Greg said turning around to the elevator. As he got to the elevator, the doors opened and Simone walked out. Greg froze and stared at Simone. She glared at Greg. She stood up straighter, smirked, and headed towards Antonio's apartment door. Greg gave her the finger as she walked away and stepped into the elevator. Greg got off on the lobby floor, got back in his car, and veered off down the road. The tinted red Mustang that was parked across the street followed him.

Antonio answered the door. "Wow, you are fast."

Simone smiled. "Whenever you call me I'm here in a hurry."

Antonio screwed up his face and laughed. "Isn't that a lyric from a song?"

Simone laughed. "No, honey, I make up my own sayings."

Antonio smiled and closed the door behind Simone as she walked in. The two sat on the sofa. Antonio started from the beginning about how he and Greg ended up at the police station. Simone seemed less interested in the fact that cocaine had been found in Larry's apartment.

Antonio sat back in his seat and rubbed his hands. "OK, Simone, I want you be up front and honest with me."

"Yeah, sure." Simone said. She felt her stomach turn.

"What was the name of your second husband?"

Simone paused. She wanted to make up a fake name but knew that would not get her far. "Shane."

Antonio took a deep breath. "Was Shane related to Larry?"

Simone sat up. "No, no he wasn't. But I will tell you this."

Antonio sat up. "What?"

"Larry and Shane did know each other very well. They were good friends, like brothers. From what Shane use to tell me, Larry was always jealous of him. "

Antonio leaned back. "Really? Larry didn't seem like the jealous type."

"Oh yes he was . . . I never told you this, but when Larry and I use to date . . . um . . . he use to . . ."

"Used to what?"

Simone's eyes watered. "He used to abuse me."

"Are you serious?"

Simone wiped a tear from her eye. "Yes, he used to a do a lot of drugs, too, which is why when you told me about the cocaine found at his apartment, it really didn't shock me."

Antonio shook his head.

"I know," Simone said. "So, I dumped Larry, and shortly after, me and Shane started dating—until he died."

Antonio squeezed Simone's hand. "As I said before, Simone, you are a very strong woman."

Simone grinned. "You know, every time you say that you make me blush."

"It's true, Simone, and I'm not going to stop telling you that." Antonio said.

Simone grimaced slightly. "Thank you."

"However," Antonio said raising his eyebrow, "I still don't understand this whole story. I mean, the dating, the abuse . . . and going out with his friend who I guess he claimed was his brother. This is so messed up. Why would Larry make all this up?"

Simone leaned in. "Because he was sick, Antonio. He had issues. He might have appeared normal at first, but he was hiding from all of us."

Antonio gazed at Simone. As much as he felt she was sincere, Antonio still had a hard time believing all of this about Larry.

Greg arrived at his apartment.

"I can't believe Tony." He said as he walked through the door. "He is so fucking whipped that it's disgusting." Greg plopped on his sofa and turned on the television. He flipped through the channels, but he still couldn't clear his mind. Every image, every word, and every sound seemed to circle back to his fight with Antonio. "What else can I do, though? Does Tony know how he is being fucked over? Does he?"

A pair of binoculars pointed at Greg's living room window peeped through the red Mustang parked across the street from below. The driver coughed and lit a cigarette.

Greg poured himself a scotch and sat back down on the sofa, still shaking his head. His phone rang and he reached over to pick it up.

"Hello?"

There was silence.

"Hello? Who is this?"

Again, no answer. Greg hung up the phone and continued watching TV.

The phone rang again. Greg answered. "Hello?"

No answer.

"Hello?"

Again, no answer.

"OK, who the fuck is this?" Greg said. Greg waited for an answer before hanging up the phone. Five minutes later, the phone rang again. Greg replied with an attitude. "Look, if you call me one more time—"

"If I were you, I would keep quiet," muffled the voice.

"Excuse me?" Greg said.

The person hung up.

Greg looked at the phone's display: a private number. Greg sat there staring at the phone. "OK, what the fuck was that?"

The driver parked the red mustang at the corner of Greg's apartment closed his cell phone and laughed.

* * *

Simone nuzzled on Antonio's sweaty chest. "Antonio, you know that you are a better lover when you are upset?"

Antonio laughed. "Please, Simone, I don't need compliments right now. I am upset, remember?"

"Oh yeah, you are upset alright. You are so upset that you ripped my clothes off, bent me over and . . ."

Antonio placed his two fingers over Simone's mouth. "Woman, watch your mouth."

Simone bit at Antonio's finger. "But it's true."

Antonio rolled over onto Simone and nibbled on her neck. Simone let out a giggle.

"And you are really forty-two, right?" Antonio cooed.

"Antonio, will you stop asking me that silly question?" Simone said.

"Yes," Antonio said. He then started trailing his tongue between her breasts.

* * *

Greg zipped up his jacket and closed his apartment door behind him. He couldn't think and needed to clear his mind. He left his house and walked down Davey Street. His hands in his pockets, his eyes focused ahead and his mind still cluttered, Greg walked along.

Simone screamed as Antonio thrust and lost control. They both gasped as they reached deep, intense orgasm and collapsed naked on Antonio's sofa.

"Oh my God," Simone panted. "I can't feel my legs."

Antonio let out a gasping laugh. "Neither can I."

Simone laughed. "Where did you learn how to do that, Antonio?"

Antonio shrugged his shoulders. "Like I said before, hidden talent."

"Man, what else are you hiding?" Simone held Antonio's hand and placed it on her breast. "Antonio, I think I am falling in love with you."

Antonio paused. His stomach knotted and his heart thumped. He leaned in. "Simone, I think I'm falling in love with you, too."

They embraced each other and kissed.

Greg turned the corner onto Sixth Avenue. He clenched his hands in his pockets and started at the concrete ahead. Greg couldn't help getting so upset. His frustration and anger overwhelmed him. He suddenly stopped and looked ahead, staring into the distance.

"That's a nice jacket you got there," replied a raspy voice behind him.

Greg turned around to reply when he felt a huge blow on his head. He collapsed onto the cold concrete.

The figure stood over Greg's body and chuckled.

CHAPTER THIRTY

Simone kissed Antonio gently on his cheek as she tiptoed out of his apartment. When she stepped outside, the morning sun blinded her. She felt like a teenager all over again sneaking back from a boyfriend's house in the early morning, hoping she wouldn't get caught. Simone had just reached her car when the phone rang. She looked at the number and saw Ronnie was calling. She rolled her eyes, ignored the call, and started her car. Her phone rang again. She sighed before picking it up.

"What took you so long to answer?" Ronnie grouched.

"Ronnie, what do you want?"

"Thought I'd let you know that I have been watching Antonio as followed."

Again Simone rolled her eyes. "Let me guess, and you are going to make some comment, aren't you?"

"Why would I do such a thing?" Ronnie said.

"Because I know you, Ronnie."

"Well whatever, Dana, I am just letting you know."

"Fine, Ronnie, I'll talk to you later."

Ronnie didn't have a chance to say goodbye before Simone hung up. Ronnie stared at the phone and shook his head.

* * *

"So you really are leaving us?" William Huntingwood said, squinting his eyes as he tried to sip his scalding-hot coffee.

Antonio sat in front of him at his desk, his back straight, arms resting on the chair's arms. "Yes, Bill, I've thought about it, and I really think that this is going to be a good opportunity for me."

William Huntingwood took of his glasses and rubbed an eyebrow. "You know, you have a lot of great artwork in this place. Being gone will really leave this gallery pretty empty."

Antonio sighed. He felt guilty leaving because he knew that his artwork had generated a lot of revenue for the company. "I guess so, but I am sure you will do fine."

William got up and patted Antonio on his shoulder. "You know, Antonio, I usually don't make this kind of offer, but I am willing to keep this position open for you if you ever decide to come back."

Antonio smiled. "I really appreciate that. And you know what? I promise I will keep you in mind."

"I hope you do Antonio. I don't think we will be able to replace someone like you. You're a good kid."

Antonio's heart pounded and his face flushed. It felt weird hearing this from William Huntingwood—the same man who, a couple of days ago, was scolding and belittling him. Now he was talking to Antonio as if he were his son. "Um, thank you sir. Thank you very much."

After his discussion with William Huntingwood, Antonio went back to his office, threw his jacket on his desk, and sighed as he stared through the window. He wondered if he'd actually made the right decision and if this was going to work. He felt his stomach knot as he reconsidered what he'd just said to William. Then he thought of Simone, closed his eyes, smiled, and sat down behind his desk.

His phone rang. "Hello?"

"Hey, babe, how are you?" Simone asked.

"Um, a bit nervous, but OK."

"Why are you nervous?"

Antonio took a deep breath. "Well Simone, consider your dream a reality."

"What you are talking about?"

"You now have a new business partner."

Simone screamed in delight. "Are you serious? Thank you so much! Antonio I knew you made the right decision. You are not going to regret this."

Antonio smiled nervously on the other end. "I am sure I won't."

"Well you know, this calls for a celebration."

"Really? And where are you treating me?"

Simone laughed. "Anywhere you want."

Antonio paused. "OK, let's do Stanley's Steakhouse on Park Avenue at seven this evening."

"Fine, I'll see you then." Simone said. They both said goodbye and hung up. Simone sat in her Mercedes Benz with Luther Vandross's "Power of Love" blaring from her car stereo. She bit her lip closed, and her eyes.

"Perfect. Just perfect." Simone muttered. She started her car and veered down Avenue Rd.

* * *

Antonio dropped his fork. "You know, if you keep doing that, you are gonna regret it later on."

Simone laughed as she continued rubbing her feet up Antonio's leg. "No one can see what I'm doing."

"Yeah, that's just the problem." Antonio said squirming in his seat.

Simone leaned in and purred. "Antonio, am I too much to handle?"

Antonio stared deep into her eyes. "I can handle anything."

Simone licked her lips. "You know that is why I like you so much. You are so . . . wild."

Antonio grinned. "It's always the quiet ones." He then cleared his throat. "So, as we were discussing, exactly when do you want me to start?"

Simone leaned back. "Tomorrow."

Antonio blinked. "Um, sorry . . . what?"

"You heard me, tomorrow."

Antonio raised his eyebrow. "Don't you think that's way too soon? I need to give the art gallery at least . . ."

Simone jumped in. "Nonsense. Listen, I want to get you up to speed as soon as possible."

" . . . which is my next question. Exactly what is my job title, and what will I be doing?"

Simone sipped her white wine. "You are going to be director in sales and management." She squeezed Antonio's hand. "You'll also be working very closely with the CEO."

Antonio smirked. "Is that so?"

"Yes, and if everything runs smoothly, you'll be part CEO as well."

Antonio's hands trembled.

"Baby, is there something wrong?" Simone said.

Antonio sighed. "Um, Simone, that's kind of a big leap, no?"

"Antonio, you are such a baby. Wake up and sniff the cocaine."

Antonio leaned back. "That's not very funny."

Simone laughed. "Lighten up, I was just trying to get you to smile. Listen, you have a lot of potential."

"Simone I am glad you think that way, but I am not much of a sales person. Besides, do you remember what my degree is in?"

"Antonio, a lot of people get degrees that they rarely use in their real jobs."

"I just hope that I'm not jumping the gun here."

"Are you saying that you don't trust me?"

"No, but . . ."

"End of discussion."

Antonio laughed. "Simone, hear me out. I am not saying doing this is a bad thing. I am just hoping that I don't move too fast here."

"What do you mean?"

"I mean I am hoping that I am joining your partnership because I am interested in the partnership, not because . . . I have a strong lust for you."

"Do you honestly think that?"

"Simone, honestly, you have me addicted."

Simone blushed. "I beg your pardon?"

Antonio sipped his white wine. "You heard me. You have me hooked, and I have you hooked too. We've been seeing each other for months now and quite frankly the passion between us is scary sometimes."

Simone smiled. "Antonio, that is very nice for you—"

Antonio grabbed Simone's hand. "Look, all I am saying is that I don't want our relationship to get in the way of the business side of this. I am happy to work for you, but I don't want things to get messy. You know what I mean?"

Simone didn't reply.

"I obviously said something to upset you."

Simone cleared her throat. "No, it's just you are so goddamn sexy."

Antonio rolled his eyes. "Maybe you should work in sales. I'll just do all the paperwork in the business."

Simone pouted her lips. "You don't worry about what I do."

Antonio smirked. "You really are looking for some trouble tonight."

Simone licked her lips. "In fact, I am." Simone rubbed her foot up between Antonio's thighs. "Care to start any trouble, Mr. Bedroom bully?"

Antonio felt himself get excited. "Only if you can handle it."

* * *

Lisa limped to the fridge door to grab a glass of orange juice.

"Baby, no, let me get that." Lisa's mother said, rushing into the kitchen.

"Mom, I am fine. Please . . ." Lisa said.

Lisa moaned as she tugged on the fridge door.

Her mother intervened, opening the door and grabbing the carton of orange juice from the fridge. "Child, what is wrong with you? You are still ill."

"Mom I am fine. The doctor said that in a matter of weeks I can be back at work."

Lisa's mother placed her hands on her hips. "Yeah, when you recover from your broken hip."

"Mom, the doctor said I didn't break my hip—I dislocated it, and I am fine, so please!"

"Child, you could have died," Lisa mother sighed, clenching her hand towards her chest. "I don't what I would have done if . . ."

Lisa poured herself a glass of orange juice. "Mom, seriously, I am fine. Please. Ever since you became a 'born again' Christian, you've been too much."

Lisa's mother's eyes widened. "I beg your pardon? And what is that supposed to mean?"

Lisa shook her head. "Never mind. It's not worth it."

Lisa' s mother rolled her eyes and headed towards the living room. She sat down and grabbed an *Elle* magazine that lay on the glass coffee table. "So you still have a crush on that Antonio boy?"

Lisa reddened. "I beg your pardon?"

"You heard me. Antonio."

"What about him?"

"Do you still have a crush on him?"

Mr. Whiskers trotted along and curled up next to Lisa's mother at the foot of the coffee table.

"Why would you think that? And who told you about anything Antonio?"

"So you're having some kind of memory lapse aren't you? At the hospital you were asking for Antonio. Antonio this and Antonio that."

Lisa's face reddened. "Mom, stop."

"Lisa, don't give me that. Who is he?"

Lisa eased herself onto the sofa. "A guy from work."

"I know he's a guy from work, but I want to know about him. Does he go to church? Is he a faithful man?"

Lisa laughed. "Mom, you are making it sound like I am trying to hunt the man down for him to be my future husband."

"Listen, a mother knows these things." Lisa mother said. She moved beside Lisa and leaned in. "Is he cute?"

Lisa giggled. "Yes, mom, he's cute."

"Single?"

"Yes."

"Any children?"

"No."

"Educated?"

"He has a degree."

"Independent?"

"Yes, he lives on his own."

Lisa's mother smiled. "So what the heck is stopping you from snatching him up?"

"I don't think he's interested in me."

"Lord, please tell me you don't pick your nose in front of him or something like that. If not, there's no reason he wouldn't be interested. "

"I don't know. He never pays any attention to me. Maybe he's shy."

Lisa's mother shrugged her shoulders. "Honey, there are more fish in the sea. I admit, though, from the sound of this guy, he's a good catch."

Lisa grinned. "Mom he is handsome and just has everything going for him. He's intelligent, respectful, everybody likes him, He's a hard worker, he's . . ."

"Your future husband." Lisa's mother said.

Lisa bit her lip. "Yeah, I wish."

CHAPTER THIRTY-ONE

"Where the hell is that man? He was supposed to have that file for me this morning!" William Huntingwood yelled frantically. He stormed into Antonio's half-vacant office. He paused and sighed as he watched Antonio slowly packing his stuff.

He coughed to get Antonio's attention.

Antonio turned around. "Oh hi, Mr. Huntingwood."

William Huntingwood nodded. "How's everything?"

Antonio smiled. "Good, good."

William Huntingwood sighed. "That's good to hear."

Antonio sensed his agitation. "Um, so . . . have you been looking for my replacement?"

William Huntingwood scratched his temple. "Um, no, Antonio, I haven't."

Antonio slowly nodded. "Oh, I see."

"Antonio, listen. I want you to be honest with me." William Huntingwood said closing the door behind him. He turned around. "Do you think I treat you like shit?"

"I beg your pardon?"

"You heard me, do I treat you like shit?"

"If you did, I would have left a long time ago."

"But you are leaving now."

"Mr. Huntingwood, yes, I'm leaving, but it's not because of you. As I mentioned, I am taking on this opportunity because I think it might be good for me. It has nothing to do with you. Why would you think that?"

William Huntingwood sighed. "Because my reputation is on the line."

Antonio raised his eyebrow. "Um, on what line?"

"Antonio, we are very successful here at what we do. Not only do we sell art, but we also run a business that distributes all kinds of expensive work and supplies. We have a gallery . . . a company like ours is unique. When word gets out that one of my best people is leaving for some 'opportunity,' it leaves a sour taste in everyone's mouth. They question why he would leave, and they start to think maybe the company was the reason. Maybe the boss was an asshole or something."

"So let me get this straight," Antonio said. "The reason why you are concerned about me leaving this gallery is to protect your reputation?"

William Huntingwood looked like he wanted to backtrack.

There was a knock on the door.

"Come in," Antonio said.

Monica stood at the door. Her tight black dress hugged her curves. "Antonio, have you seen Greg?"

Antonio rolled his eyes. "Nope."

William Huntingwood turned around. "I've been looking for that goddamn man all day. Where the hell is he?"

"Probably in the arms of some slut." Antonio snarled.

Monica looked at him with distaste. "Antonio, that's not really appropriate."

Antonio didn't reply.

William Huntingwood turned to Antonio. "Well? Where is he?"

Antonio shrugged his shoulders. "I dunno, why are you asking me?"

"Um because the two of you are like best friends," Monica said.

William Huntingwood cleared this throat. "Listen, I need him now. He has an important file for me, and I need it by 1pm this afternoon. If I don't see his midget ass here by 1pm with the file, I swear to God he is going to be up shit's creek."

William Huntingwood stormed out the door. He then turned around to Antonio. "We'll talk another time."

"Yeah . . . for sure."

William Huntingwood marched off.

Monica started laughing as she entered. "The man has issues."

Antonio rolled his eyes. "Tell me about it."

The pungent smell of marijuana and stale air filled the empty graffiti-covered room. Crumpled newspapers, empty plastic bags, used coffee cups, and dirty paper towels were strewn across the yellow cold linoleum floor. The sound of muffled arguments made its way through the thick, dirty walls.

"You bitch! Get back here!" screamed a deep, hoarse voice.

"Get away, you fucking bastard, or I will kill you with this goddamn knife, I swear!" screeched a hysterical woman.

A rusty, bright light hung from the chipped tiled ceiling. It swayed back and forth as heavy footsteps pounded from the apartment above. Pipes creaked behind the wall, and a heavy door slammed from above. Police and fire truck sirens blared from the busy city streets below.

The door flung open. The incandescent lights from the hallway illuminated the cracks and holes in the dilapidated room. A tall man stood at the threshold with a beer can in his hand and a cigarette in another. His tight black T-shirt stuffed in his black jeans overemphasized his beer belly.

He belched. "Hey faggot, are you up yet?"

Greg lay in the corner of the room with his head resting on a wooden stool. He moaned in pain.

The man smiled. "I really wopped you good." He threw his cigarette out and marched over towards Greg.

Excruciating pain shot through Greg's neck when he lifted his head, seeing only the tall man's stained yellow teeth.

Greg moaned. "Who are you?"

The man kneeled towards Greg. "Never mind who I am. The question I have is who are *you*?"

Greg raised his eyes brows. "Huh? What are you talking—"

The man grabbed Greg by the shoulder and pulled him towards his face. "Don't fuck with me."

Greg shook his head. "Man, I don't know what—"

The man punched Greg in the stomach. "Stop pretending that you don't know what the fuck is going on. You and I know what the deal is here!"

Greg laid with his hands open in agony. "Honestly, I don't know who you are or what you are talking about."

"Then do you know this?" The man grabbed a photo from his pocket and shoved it in Greg's face. Greg looked up and stared at the photo.

His eyes widened. "Hey that's Larry."

"Yes, there's poor Larry," the man said.

Greg squinted. "How do you know him?"

The man smiled. "Because I do."

Footsteps echoed down the hallway and approach the room. Greg was confused and dizzy. Everything was a blur to him.

The man turned around to the shadowy figured that appeared at the entrance. "Yo, Jazz, he's still alive," the tall man said.

Jazz walked in. A shiny stud on his right nostril flared from the little light that was in the room. A large fresh scar resembling a dried-up river ran across the side of his cheek. He wore all black—black jeans, a black shirt, and a black leather jacket. His pitiless black eyes took in the tall man and Greg at once, and his hands clenched as he marched over to Greg.

"Mr. Greg. Just the person we wanted to see."

Greg shook his head. "Why? Who are you?"

Jazz grabbed Greg's face, sinking his nails into his cheeks. "You are a dumb motherfucker, and you are getting in our way."

Greg squirmed in pain. Jazz threw him on the floor and started to pace around the room. "You see, dear friend Greg. The problem is that you know too much."

Greg blinked his eyes trying to understand Jazz. "I don't understand what you mean."

"Oh you will, buddy, you will. You see, you have a friend name Antonio, right?"

Greg froze.

"And he is going out with Dana—or "Simone," as you guys call her?"

Greg felt his heart jump out of his chest. His leg trembled.

Jazz walked over and kneeled down towards Greg. "See, we like to play a game of elimination here. When we play our game and something gets in our away, we get rid of it."

Sweat dripped down Greg's face.

"And you see, my friend, that's what happened to poor Larry. He got in our way, and we had to get rid of him." Jazz reached into his pocket and grabbed a 9mm gun, pointing it at Greg's head. Greg's lips twitched as he closed his eyes tightly.

"You see, Greg, you are getting in our way and we have to take care of that."

Greg whimpered and clenched his teeth. With a burst of anger, Greg spat in Jazz's face. "Fuck you," he managed to get out.

Jazz smiled, wiped the spit off his face, and punched Greg in the stomach, sending his body sliding across the floor. Greg lay motionless.

CHAPTER THIRTY-TWO

Antonio awoke to the ring of his phone. Yawning, he answered.

"Hey Tony, sorry to bother you, but this is Monica."

Antonio sat up. "Hey, what's up? It's a little early for a phone call, isn't it?"

"Yes, well the reason I'm calling is that we haven't seen Greg for days at work, and we're all becoming a concerned.

Antonio furrowed his brow. "Maybe he decided to go on vacation and not tell anyone."

"Antonio, I'm serious." Monica said. "This is not like him. And with everything that happened to Larry, everyone is starting to think the worst. You haven't spoken to him?"

Antonio cleared his throat. "Um, no . . . just been busy. Haven't spoken in days."

"Wow that is not like the two of you. Aren't you guys like best friends? You haven't heard anything? When was the last time you saw Greg?"

Antonio reflected back to when Greg came to his door and Antonio had shunned him off. "Um, a couple of days ago, I think."

"This is just too freaky." Monica said. "I have someone on the next line. Antonio, let's talk later."

"OK, later." Antonio got up and went into the kitchen.

The phone rang again.

Antonio sighed when answering. "Yes, hello?"

"Antonio, this William Huntingwood."

Antonio raised his eyebrow. "Oh, hi Mr. Huntingwood, how are you?"

"Good, Antonio. I am just going to make this short. Have you seen Greg?"

Antonio shook his head in disbelief. "No . . . Monica just called me not even a minute ago for him, but no, I haven't seen him."

"Antonio this is serious business. Greg hasn't been to work in a number of days and we're growing concern. You haven't heard from him?"

"No, I haven't. Have you tired contacting his family?"

"No answer."

"Well listen, I don't know where he is. I'm sorry."

"Very well then." William Huntingwood hung up.

Antonio scratched his head. Antonio wanted to phone Greg, but his pride held him back. Getting up from the couch, he went into the kitchen and grabbed a glass of water.

His cell phone rang.

Who is it now, he wondered. "Hello?"

There was silence.

"Hello?" Antonio shouted into the phone.

Again, no response.

Just as Antonio was about to hang up he heard a muffled voice on the other end. He placed the phone to his ear.

"Who the hell is this?"

A crackling noise interfered with the muffled voice on the other end before the call was disconnected.

Antonio stared at his phone trying to see who had called him.

He shook his head. "Go figure, private number."

Antonio returned to his easel and started on a blank canvas. He was due for a new painting, but the last couple of days had left him completely uncreative. He wasn't sure where he should start. Everything just seemed so bizarre. The more he thought about what Greg had said about Simone, the more he felt uncomfortable. Antonio let out a sigh, grabbed his cell phone from the coffee table and started dialing Greg's number.

"This shit is bothering me and I have to get this off my chest." Antonio said to himself.

Greg's voicemail picked up. Antonio hung up.

Antonio dialed Greg's cell number. Greg's voicemail automatically played.

Antonio hung up. "Where the hell is he?"

* * *

Simone sipped on her wine. "Ronnie, I know this is going to work to my advantage. Just shut the fuck up and let a woman take charge of what she knows."

Ronnie rolled his eyes. "Yeah whatever, Dana. You're the boss, but listen. If something fucks up—"

"Ronnie, it won't, and stop saying that."

Again Ronnie rolled his eyes. "This doesn't make any goddamn sense."

"What are you talking about?"

"OK, let's just back this up. You get involved with this Antonio guy because he is a successful artist and sales rep for Mahogany, an international well known art gallery business. It is also by fluke that Antonio is good friends and works with Larry, your now ex deceased brother in law. Mahogany has money come out their assess and you being the greedy bitch want Antonio to leave his company so you can turn around and buy it. But it seems like that the only thing you are benefiting is getting your legs spread by him. Is getting a hard cock up your pussy worth screwing this over Dana? I thought that your objective was to take over his profits, have them amalgamated with yours, and then when you were ready, you would get rid of him like when you got rid of . . . well, you know."

"Ronnie, please. Things will come into play."

"Come into play? Dana, you are fucking falling in love with this guy and it's screwing up everything for us. This was not supposed to happen. This fucking Antonio guy is working you over and has you dripping wet like a old faucet."

Simone ignored Ronnie's comment and tousled her hair. "Ronnie, just do what I tell you do and do not question it."

"Dana, you are fucking up it up!! What are you going to gain if this all fails? Then what?"

Simone closed her eyes. "Something that I've always needed."

* * *

Antonio stood outside and pounded on Greg's door.

No one answered.

Antonio pounded harder. "Greg, open up. It's Tony."

Again, no answer.

Antonio shrugged his shoulders and headed back downstairs. "Where the hell is he?"

Just as he stepped into his car, his cell phone rang. He smiled and answered. "Yes ,Simone?"

"And how are you?"

"I'm OK. I thought I was supposed to start working for you today."

"I know, and I'm sorry. I had to get some stuff organized, and I didn't have a chance to call you earlier on . . . sorry."

Antonio sighed.

"Um . . . . you OK?"

Again Antonio sighed, contemplating whether or not he should tell Simone about Greg. "I'm just tired."

"I see. Do you want come over to your place so I can stroke you down?"

Antonio laughed. "Again you quoting songs."

"Problem?"

"Did I say there was a problem?"

"But you are insinuating that there is a problem."

"The only thing that you are insinuating is me thinking there is problem when there isn't."

Simone giggled. "I love it when I get you worked up."

"Yes, I'm sure you do." Antonio felt his body tense up. Greg's disappearance bothered him.

"You know what Simone, there is a problem."

Simone paused. "What is it?"

Antonio let out a sigh and starting walking. "It's Greg. No one hasn't seen Greg in the last couple of days."

Simone cleared her throat. "So you are talking to him now?"

"Simone, things are just not adding up."

"What do you mean?"

"I mean everything. Larry goes missing, then he's dead. Greg is now missing. I am still getting harassing calls, and . . ."

"And *what*, Antonio?"

Antonio paused as he stood outside Greg's apartment. "This is just too much for me."

"Want me to come over to your place?"

Antonio smiled. "You know what, I am tempted to say yes, but it wouldn't do any good. I am not in the mood."

Simone hissed. "Don't be ridiculous. You know want it."

Antonio rubbed his head as he headed towards his car. "Honestly Simone, I think I should just be alone for a bit."

Simone didn't reply.

Antonio got into his car. "I'll talk to you later."

Simone paused. "OK, but if you need something, let me know."

"Thanks." Antonio hung up, started the car and drove off.

Simone stared at her phone and licked her lips. She rubbed the tip of her phone against her lips and purred. "Antonio, you don't know what I got in store for you."

Antonio's mind was in a daze. He couldn't think straight. Everything tossed and turned in his mind.

"This is fucking crazy bullshit," he said as he made sharp turn down Madison Avenue. Every time he thought of Larry and Greg he started to question himself about Simone. Was Simone being honest with him?

Antonio swung his car, making a left. Out of nowhere appeared a dazed figure walking towards his car. Antonio gasped and slammed on his brakes. The tires screeched as his car continued accelerating towards the figure. Within seconds Antonio heard the body slam against his car window and roll off to the side.

Antonio stopped and jumped out of the car.

"Oh my fuckin God!" Antonio shouted. He knelt down to the body. The person was covered in a black sheet from head to toe. Antonio thought odd about this but his quick apprehension and fear of him possibly killing someone erased that thought. His hands trembled as he slowly removed the cloth from the face. His face turned blue and his heart dropped. His hands shook violently as he stared into the dark, familiar eyes.

It was Greg.

"Jesus fucking Christ!" Antonio cried. He closed his eyes ,trembling.

A deep voice echoed. "Sir, tell me what is going on?"

Antonio opened his eyes and jumped up.

"Sir, I asked you what is going on?" the voice repeated. He turned towards the television set that was blaring an old Western. Antonio sat up from the couch and shook his head. His chest felt heavy and sweat dripped from his forehead. He wanted this insanity to be over.

CHAPTER THIRTY-THREE

Simone lay sprawled on her back with the tip of her cell phone pressed up against her breast. She yearned for Antonio but was afraid that her emotions and would ruin her ultimate goal . . . to take control. To take control of what she believed men had abused for too long. What she deserved: power and respect. Simone's father had been the owner of three real estate companies alongside other small businesses. Her father was loud, arrogant, bossy, and abusive. He treated Simone's mother worse than shit. Simone hated that. The torment, agony and abuse ended when one day Simone came home from school to see her father dead in the living room. It was decided that he had died of a heart attack, but Simone knew it was likely caused by something else. Something she swore she would not bring up or discuss. Men liked Simone's domineering attitude and determination, while women were jealous and despised her. She'd never had any real female friends—she hated the competition. Early on, she'd decided to take control of her destiny, her life, and most importantly, her men. She treated men like hand rags and used one after another. She thrived on promiscuity and didn't care if she hurt their feelings. She'd been married four times and didn't care about any of the marriages. All that she was after was money and power. Then Antonio walked into her life. Antonio was going to be another pawn in her game, the helpless prey in the black widow web, but she felt weak by Antonio's charm, charisma, and strong sex appeal. She'd never felt so much sexual tension and passion with another man. Antonio made her feel sensations that she thought she knew how to control. She knew Antonio's lovemaking was a disease, but she didn't want the cure. Simone wondered if she was losing her touch, losing her battle, losing her finesse. She couldn't let that happen. After all, if she didn't look out for herself, no one else would.

Her phone rang. She answered. "Hello?"

"Hey, how are you?" Antonio said.

Simone bit her lip. "Wanting you."

"Good." Antonio said. "Because I need you too."

Simone felt aroused. "When can I come over?"

"Now."

"I'll be over for in fifteen minutes."

"See you."

Simone hung up the phone, closed her eyes, and smiled in relief.

Antonio sat up from his bed and stared out of his bedroom window. He took a deep breath.

Simone arrived five minutes early, but Antonio didn't mind. Simone grabbed Antonio's warm hand and led him upstairs to his bed. She dropped her purse on the floor and Simone savagely ripped open his shirt. Antonio dragged her closer and pressed his lips hard against hers. She panted while her hands reached for his belt. Within seconds they were on the bed feasting off of each other. Simone felt lost and delusional, and Antonio couldn't stop. Their naked bodies intertwined with each other. Simone's felt her nails claw into Antonio's back as he licked, sucked, and teased Simone's ample breasts. Simone felt her inner thighs dampen to the touch of Antonio's tongue. She felt possessed and pushed his head between her moist thighs. Antonio immediately ravished her with his tongue. His tongue sent electrical pulses through her while he devoured her. Simone felt her body tense as Antonio devoured her harder and faster. She bit her lip and yelled out. "Fuck . . . oh fuck!" Simone arched back and her legs quivered with his force. Simone couldn't hold on and let out a loud scream. She hyperventilated as Antonio moved his head slowly from her thighs and up to her chest. She grabbed onto Antonio's hips and thrust him against her.

She stared deep into his eyes. "I want it . . . I want it now."

Antonio stared coldly into her eyes—it almost frightened her. With one slow thrust Antonio entered her. Simone's eyes shut and he covered her mouth teasingly. Antonio was on a mission and Simone was not going to argue. Every thrust, every stroke, and every glide Antonio made, Simone responded with a loud moan. The energy inside of Antonio was unbearable as he thrust harder. Simone's chocolate legs draped over his shoulders. Simone never felt so much pleasure and she was hoping this was not a dream. Antonio thrust harder and deeper. He then slowed down and then thrust faster. Slower, then faster. Slower, then faster. Simone closed her eyes. A million thoughts ran through her head. Why is this happening to me? This is too intense. Am I really in love with this guy? Simone's thoughts were interrupted by Antonio's harder thrust. Simone felt an orgasm coming and cried out in pleasure. Antonio felt himself quiver, and with seconds felt his orgasm overpowering him. They both lay on the bed, sweaty, exhausted, and exhilarated.

Simone took a puff from her cigarette. "You know Antonio, I think you are too much for me."

Antonio smiled, staring up at the ceiling. "I'm sorry. I've been very stressed out."

"I love it when you are stressed out."

"Simone, everything lately has been fucked up."

Simone nodded. "This is the real world, honey."

"Simone I am serious. I mean, ever since I met you . . . I don't know. This is gonna sound weird, but all this shit has been happening."

"You mean the phone calls and stuff?"

Antonio nodded. "Simone, come on. You can't tell me that ain't fucked up. Weird phone messages, Larry dead, Greg missing."

"I know."

Antonio grabbed Simone's hand and placed it on his chest. "Simone, can you do me a favor?"

"What?"

"I need your help."

"With what?"

"With everything. I need help finding out who is calling me. I would like to find out why Larry was killed and why is Greg missing."

"Antonio, I would love to help you, but . . ." Simone's phone rang. "Fuck ,who is calling me now?"

Antonio released her hand. "Go answer."

"Antonio I don't . . ."

"Go answer it," Antonio beckoned.

Simone got up and wrapped a towel around her, grabbed her phone and headed downstairs. She glared at the phone as she picked. "What the hell is it, Ronnie?"

"Where the fuck are you?"

"I'm busy."

"Listen, we have business to deal with here, and you are too busy fucking that artist boy. What the fuck is wrong with you?"

Simone spoke under her breath. "Ronnie, shut the fuck up! What the hell do you want?"

"I want your ass over here soon. We need to settle this shit."

"It's gonna have to wait."

"Why?"

"Because I am busy."

Ronnie let out a groan. "You know for a woman who claims to be in charge, you sure are letting some guy rule you."

Simone detested the comment because she knew it was starting to be true. "Ronnie, I'll be over when I'm over. Bye." Simone hung up the phone and walked upstairs.

Antonio stood by the edge of the bed puzzled staring at her.

"You look a bit confused," Simone said.

The puzzled look on Antonio's face quickly turned into disgust. "Yeah, I am."

Simone approached him and grabbed his hand. "Why?"

Antonio shoved a card in her face. "You wanna tell me why your driver's license says your name is Dana Robinson and that you are fifty-eight years old?"

Simone dropped her phone.

CHAPTER THIRTY-FOUR

Lisa yawned on her sofa. The sympathy cards and messages she received from everybody at work were stifling the living daylights out of her. She gazed at her computer monitor thinking about Antonio. It was quite obvious to her and her mother that she had more than a crush on him.

Lisa jumped up when the phone rang. She looked at the number.

"Who is calling me from an unknown number?" Lisa muttered. She yawned. "Hello."

There was no response.

Lisa rolled her eyes. "Hello?"

A hoarse voice whispered on the phone. "Lisa, shhhhh, it's me Greg."

Lisa jumped from her sofa. "Greg, where the hell are you? Everyone has been freaking out—"

"Lisa, listen to me carefully. You need to tell Antonio to get away from Simone."

Lisa screwed up her face. "Simone, that rich lady? Why?"

"She's psychotic. She's fucking sick!"

"Why?"

"She was the one who got Larry killed."

Lisa eyes widened. "What?"

"Lisa, you gotta to listen to me. Simone is not who she says she is. She's crazy. She was married to Larry's brother, who died shortly after. When Larry realized who she was, she killed him. Now she's after Antonio and might kill him."

Lisa stood up, shaking her head. "What? Are you serious? This can't be real."

"Lisa, I'm not lying to you. I'm telling you the truth."

Lisa didn't know what to say.

"Lisa, you gotta listen to me, you need to tell Antonio that—"

There was a click.

"Hello?" Lisa said. "Hello? Greg? You there? Hello?"

No one replied.

Lisa stared at her phone. She was dumbfounded by what Greg had said. She didn't know where Greg was or why he was saying this.

"This is crazy," she said to herself.

Lisa took a deep breath and dialed Antonio's phone number.

Greg's body shook as the 9mm pressed up against his forehead.

"Who the fuck were you calling?" Jazz said.

"Nobody really import—"

Jazz pressed the gun further into Greg's head. "Answer me, faggot, who the fuck where you talking to?"

Greg felt fear and anger mixed deep within.

"A friend."

"Who?'

Greg stuttered. "Someone you don't know."

"Listen to me, you piece of shit. I don't have time for this bullshit. You tell me who the fuck you were talking to."

"I told you. It was just a friend."

"It was Antonio, wasn't it?"

"No."

"Don't fucking lie to me, you piece of shit."

Greg felt his blood boil. "The only piece of shit in here is you."

Jazz laughed. "Oooh, now he has balls, guys."

The two bodyguards who stood at the corner of the room snickered.

Jazz glared at Greg. "I don't have time for this bullshit. I know you were informing on someone."

Greg spat in his face. He then spoke with an evil vengeance that took Jazz by surprise. "Fuck your mother."

Jazz's blood boiled. Within seconds the gun went off, its piercing sound echoing off the walls. Then there was silence.

CHAPTER THIRTY-FIVE

Simone stared at Antonio. "Antonio where did you find that?"

"I found it on the floor." Antonio said. His voice was emotionless. "So you want to explain this?"

Simone grabbed her driver's license from Antonio. "It's a long story."

"I've got all night." Antonio spat back.

Simone felt her chest tighten. "Antonio, you really don't want to hear about this now, do you?"

Antonio sat on the edge of the bed. "Gee, I don't know. I've been making love to a woman old enough to be my mother, and I've also found out that she's been using a fake name."

Simone glared at Antonio. "Excuse me? Your mother? How dare you say that."

Antonio got up. "Excuse me? Excuse you! Simone or Dana or whatever your name is, you've lied to me!!"

Simone grabbed her clothes. "You know what? I don't need to discuss this now."

Antonio grabbed her arm. "Well I do, so let's talk."

"Let me go of me!"

"Not until you tell me what the hell is going on?"

"Nothing is going on."

"Bullshit!"

"Antonio, you are acting crazy!"

"Crazy? I am crazy. I don't even know the woman standing in front of me right now. This mysterious life of yours is something I don't understand."

Antonio clutched her arm harder. "So explain to me why was Larry acting that way at the gala that night."

"I told you why!" Simone snapped. "We went out and he used to abuse me."

Antonio glared at Simone. "I don't believe you."

"What do you mean you don't believe me?"

"I don't believe you."

"Well then, that's not my problem. Now let go of me."

"No, I want the whole truth!"

"That is the truth Antonio!"

"No it's not! You are not who you claim to be, and I can't just take that. Who the fuck are you, Simone?"

Simone glared into Antonio's eyes. "Antonio, I am going to say this one more time. Take your hands off me. "

Antonio eyes pierced into Simone's. His grip loosened. Simone grabbed her arm and rubbed it. She quickly gathered her clothes.

"I am going to leave now, and we are going to discuss this another time."

Antonio didn't respond.

Simone quickly put on her clothes headed downstairs.

Antonio followed her.

"I can't believe this." Simone said. "An hour ago we were ripping into each other and now you just want to rip my head off."

Antonio did not reply.

"What? Now you are not gonna talk to me?"

Antonio headed towards the door and opened it. "Here, you forgot this."

Simone stopped at the door. "What?"

Antonio handed her the card. "Your driver's license, Mrs. Dana Robinson."

Simone grabbed it and stormed off.

Antonio's phone rang. Closing the door behind him, he marched over to answer it. "What is it?"

"Oh, Antonio, is that you?" Lisa said.

"Oh, Lisa, hi. I'm sorry. I thought you were somebody else."

"Antonio, you need to listen to me and listen carefully."

"What?"

"You are in danger."

Antonio snarled. "Yeah, from having a normal life."

"No I am serious. You are in danger. Greg just phoned me."

"Greg? Where the hell is he?"

"I don't know, but Antonio listen to me. He told me that woman you've been seeing is not who she said she is."

Antonio clenched his teeth. "Simone, yeah I know. Don't even go there."

"Did you know that she was the one who killed Larry's brother?"

Antonio froze. "What?"

"Apparently she killed Larry's brother, and she might be the one responsible for Larry's death."

Antonio felt nauseated. "Hold on, hold on . . . what are you telling me, Lisa?"

"Simone is responsible for both of those deaths. I know this sounds crazy. I don't know what to make of it either. Greg was gonna tell me more, but the phone got disconnected."

"Where did he call from?"

"I don't know—the number was unknown. And he was whispering as if, like, he didn't want anyone to hear what he was saying."

Antonio shook his head.

"Tony, listen. This girl sounds psycho. Stay away from her. Call the police."

Antonio shook his head. "Lisa, I don't think the police can handle this one."

Another call buzzed on the next line. "Lisa, can you hold on? I got someone on the next line."

Antonio switched over. "Hello?"

No one replied.

"Hello?"

"No one answered.

"Listen, Simone, leave me alone. I have nothing to—"

"Mmmmm . . . sexy . . . so sexy . . ." purred the voice.

Antonio shouted. "Who the fuck is this?"

The voice continued: "I'm watching your every move, I know where you are and where you live."

Antonio felt his blood boil. "Simone, I know it's you, so you can stop with this psycho shit. It's insane!"

The caller hung up.

Antonio switched over to the next line. "Lisa, you there?"

"Yes." Lisa said.

"I think I have a psychopath on my hands."

* * *

Simone got out of her car and slammed the door.

Ronnie stood watching. "I guess I pissed you off, huh?"

"I am not in the mood right now, Ronnie. Let's just get this done and over with."

Ronnie smirked. "What's wrong with you?"

Simone stopped abruptly and turned to Ronnie. "He found out my real name."

"Who?"

"Who do you think, idiot?"

Ronnie lowered his eyes. "How?"

Simone sighed and rolled her eyes. "My driver's license fell out of my purse."

Ronnie shook his head and laughed. "Wait a minute. You never changed your name on your driver's license?"

"Ronnie, how can I? I still have ties with everything else, and changing my name would take forever."

"So you were just gonna play along with this game, knowing fully well that one day artist boy would find out what who you really are?"

Simone ignored his question. "Fuck, this is ruining everything. This was not supposed to happen."

"It wasn't." Ronnie interjected. "But you got your fuckin emotions involved with this. You knew what the plan was. You know what the purpose of this was and yet you decide to have an affair with this guy thinking that you would trap him into buying off this gallery that he's worked to build up. It wasn't supposed to go this far, Dana, was it? At this point in the game you already needed to have him killed."

Simone jolted at the thought.

Ronnie shrugged his shoulders. "Well?"

"Ronnie, please. I know what I'm doing."

"No you don't. If you did, you would—"

Simone quickly turned around, pointing her 9mm gun at Ronnie. "Ronnie, don't fuck with me."

Ronnie stood back and didn't reply.

Simone still pointed the gun. "Ronnie, now listen to me. I know what the hell I am doing and everything is still going according to plan. Soon I will take over the possession of that company, and Antonio will be non-existent, just like everyone else who tries to cross my path. Do I make myself clear?"

Ronnie rolled his eyes.

Simone clicked the gun, ready to fire. "I said do I make myself clear?"

Ronnie reluctantly nodded.

CHAPTER THIRTY-SIX

Antonio's mother answered the door. "Well, this is a surprise."

Antonio grinned. "I know, mom. Sorry for the unexpected arrival. Can I come in?"

Antonio's mother laughed. "Now what kind of question is that?" Antonio smiled and walked in.

His father emerged from the living room. "I thought I heard your voice."

"Hey dad," Antonio said.

Antonio's mom looked at her watch. "Son, shouldn't you be at work this morning? Is it your day off?"

Antonio didn't want to worry his parents about the details of his new job. "Took the day off. I needed to get away from the city."

"I am sure you did." Antonio's father said. "The city tires people out. We're glad it drives you out here once in a while."

Antonio laughed. "Dad, you make it seem like you and mom live like three hours away from the city. You're only twenty minutes away."

"Twenty minutes is far enough!" Antonio's mother laughed.

Antonio lay on his bed in his old bedroom. Everything was still the same. The Knicks poster of Patrick Ewing plastering the backside of the door was faded and curling at the edges. A couple of trophies and awards decorated the light-blue walls. A computer graphic artwork of a car hung over his bed. His old stereo system sat underneath the TV, blanketed with dust. Antonio took a deep breath and closed his eyes. His mind was in turmoil. Everything that he'd doubted seemed to be making sense. Larry's outburst at the gala kept replaying in his mind:

"You bitch. You fuckin' lying bitch."

"Tony. Listen, as a co-worker and a friend, let me just tell you this. Stay away from her, OK? Just stay away from her. She's sick . . . she's bad news."

Antonio's mind then switched to the fight he and Greg had:

"You think you got a real lady, huh? You honestly you think you do? Well get this. If she is such a real lady, I dare to check her driver's license."

"Bullshit? You think that is bullshit? Well try this on for size, Tony. Larry's brother who died, remember that? Did Larry tell you that his brother was married to Simone?"

"Fuckin' lies, Tony? Fuckin' lies? Tony, Larry told me that his brother married Simone after they got involved in a little business deal, similar to the one she has with you. Things didn't go right, and weeks after, he died in a car accident."

"Car accident?"

"Yes, Tony, a car accident. Larry's brother Shane died in a car accident. Apparently the brakes failed or some shit like that, and his car ended up hitting a tree."

Shane? That is the Shane she was referring to?

Antonio felt nauseous. He did not know what to believe or think anymore. He wanted everything to end but he knew he was far from that.

There was a knock on the door.

"Come in." Antonio groaned.

His father opened the door. "Everything OK?"

Antonio nodded.

"You sure?"

"Yeah dad, I am. Just needed to get away and clear my mind."

"Anything worth talking about?"

Antonio grunted at the thought. Telling his father that he was having a romantic affair with a woman old enough to be his mother and finding that she was a potential psycho killer was the last thing he wanted to share. "Nah, I am OK, just tired."

"Alright, well if you need anything let us know."

"Thanks dad."

Antonio's father closed the door. Antonio lay on the bed staring at the ceiling. He wanted to confront Simone, but a part of him rejected the idea.

His cell phone rang.

Antonio did not bothering looking at and answered it. "Hello."

"Hi."

Antonio reddened. "Oh . . . it's you."

"Antonio, we need to talk." Simone said.

"What? Is there more stuff about you that I need to be aware of?"

"Antonio, please . . . there is a lot going in my life that's difficult to explain."

"Simone please just leave me alone. The last thing I need from you is an apology. Just do me a favor and leave me alone."

"Antonio, would you stop being a prick and just listen to me for a moment?"

"Prick? How am I a prick? I don't even know who you are! I don't know even know what name I should call you. Simone, Dana. Fuck.. for all I know, you're a fucking transsexual . . . vampire!"

"Fine, you don't want to talk about this. Just fine," Simone said.

Antonio shook his head. "I can't believe this. You are giving me attitude because you lied about yourself to me."

"Antonio if you would just——"

"You know what? Forget it. Just forget it!" Antonio hung up.

Antonio's mother walked into the room. "Honey, is everything OK?"

Antonio got up from the bed. "Mom, I am fine. Just having a little discussion."

Antonio's mother nodded. "Very well." Antonio's mother left, closing the door behind her.

Antonio rubbed his hands over his face. "Why did I get myself into this shit? I can't get myself a girl, and the girl I finally get turns out to be this old psycho grandma." Antonio grabbed his jacket and stormed out of the house.

"Off so soon?" Antonio's mother yelled from the kitchen.

"I am going for a drive, mom. I'll be back," Antonio said, slamming the door behind him.

Simone stared at her cell phone and then at the 9mm gun on the passenger seat. She shook her head glaring out in the distance before she started her car and drove off.

The crimson sun tinted the clear evening sky. The warm breeze refreshed Antonio's mind as he drove down the freeway. He had driven for most of the day, stopping at different parks and just relaxing. He sat in his parked Nissan in an empty shopping mall and stared at his cell phone. He still didn't understand what was going on, and although he was afraid to, he knew he had no choice. Antonio took a deep breath and dialed the number.

A voice answered. "Metro police department. How can I direct your call?"

Antonio paused and took a deep breath. "Can I have officer Stevens?"

The line immediately transferred and a husky voice answered. "Officer Stevens."

Antonio cleared his throat. "Officer Stevens, hi, this is Antonio Madison. We were talking a couple of weeks ago regarding Larry's death."

Officer Steven's voice perked up. "Oh yes, yes. We are still on working on that case, Mr. Madison."

Antonio adjusted his collar. "That is what I want to talk to you about."

"What do you want to know?"

"Officer, how difficult is it to find out information about someone?"

The officer paused. "Depends. Why?"

"Will you do it if I were to tell you that I think I might know who's responsible for Larry's death?"

There was a pause on the phone.

Officer Stevens sighed. "Mr. Madison, when can you come to the station to discuss this?"

"Right now. I can be there in twenty minutes," Antonio said.

"Good. I will expect you here then." Officer Stevens said.

Antonio let out a deep breath. "Thank you."

The Mustang sat at the other end of the parking lot with its lights out. When Antonio drove off to the police station, the Mustang followed.

Officer Stevens closed the file folder. "Excellent, Mr. Madison. This should be enough for us to start doing some work."

Antonio leaned in. "So what do you make of the whole thing?"

The officer scratched his head. "Well, this is an interesting case, but there are a lot of loopholes that we need to look at. I've most certainly heard of Simone Jackson, but this new information is quite interesting."

"Do you think she had anything to do with the murders?"

"Mr. Madison, I don't know yet, and I can't answer that question. Like I said, there are a number of factors that we need to research here."

Antonio sunk into his seat. "Yeah, I understand."

The officer straightened his back. "Now what I am quite interested are these calls that you keep getting. You say you changed your phone number yet are still getting these calls?"

Antonio nodded.

"So other than Simone and Greg, who else has your new number?"

"Other than my colleagues at work, no one."

"And you don't suspect that anyone at work would do this?"

Antonio screwed up his face. "I can't see anybody doing that."

"Well, that is what you thought of Simone Jackson, right?"

Antonio didn't reply.

"Very well, Mr. Madison, I believe we have enough information to do some investigating. I can't make any promises if this will result in any new leads, but we will keep you informed."

Antonio asked, "And what happens if someone else dies in the meantime?"

The officer cleared his throat. "Then I guess we'll have a more serious issue to deal with, Mr. Madison."

* * *

The red Mustang sat at the corner of the police station. The black glove reached for the phoned and dialed a number.

"Yes?" The voice answered.

"I followed him. He's at the police station."

"What the hell is he doing there?"

"Who knows, but it doesn't look good."

"Keep on him."

"Shall I continue with plan as follows?"

There was brief pause. "Yes."

* * *

Antonio got into his car and drove down 12th Avenue. He felt that he'd made some progress but not enough to spark anything.

He shook his head. "How the hell did I get myself involved in this shit?"

Antonio turned on his car stereo. Maxwell's "Ascension (Don't Ever Wonder)" blared from the stereo. With the windows down and his moon roof open, Antonio allowed the cool evening breeze to rejuvenate his mind. His cell phone rang, but Maxwell's voice drowned it.

A pair of bright headlights appeared in his rearview mirror.

Antonio squinted and adjusted the mirror. "Geesh. Turn off your brights, buddy." Antonio switched lanes. The bright lights followed.

Antonio stared attentively at the rearview mirror. He quickly changed lanes again.

The lights behind him did the same.

"What the hell is this idiot doing?" Antonio said. He eased off the accelerator, slowing to twenty below the speed the limit. The car behind him slowed down as well.

Antonio pulled over to an empty parking spot along 12th Avenue. The car pulled up right behind him.

Antonio felt uneasy. Within seconds he took off again, speeding down 12th avenue. The red car followed closely behind him.

Antonio slammed on the clutch and moved it into fifth gear, taking a huge lead; however, the red car did the same and was now right on his bumper.

"OK, you know what? This is fucking enough." Antonio said.

He quickly turned off on a side road and pulled off to the side. The red car drove right up behind him.

Antonio got out of his car marched over the driver's side. "Buddy, what the fuck is your problem?" The windows were tinted black and Antonio could not see inside.

"Fucker, answer me!" Antonio screamed. The red mustang car just stood there idling, not moving. Antonio flipped him a finger and headed towards the car. "Whatever, you fuckin' idiot!"

Antonio reached for the car handle when he felt a gloved hand covering his mouth. Antonio yelled and kicked, but a sharp pain jabbing into his neck paralyzed his senses.

Then everything faded to black.

CHAPTER THIRTY-SEVEN

William Huntingwood ruffled through some papers nesting on his desk. The last couple of weeks at Mahogany had been quite odd, to say the least. Lisa's accident, Larry's death, Antonio's departure, and Greg's disappearance were too much to handle.

"Where is that goddamn file?" William Huntingwood cursed.

Monica appeared at the door. "Mr. Huntingwood, sorry to bother you. I just wanted to remind you about the meeting this afternoon."

William Huntingwood sighed heavily. "Can we not move it to tomorrow?"

Monica shook her head. "Mr. Huntingwood, these are the clients from Germany who came to see some of the art work."

William Huntingwood cursed under his breath. "Fine, I'll be there. What time is it now?"

Monica looked at her watch. "11:45am."

"I need a vacation!"

"You and me both."

William Huntingwood gazed at Monica. He adjusted his collar. "Yeah, I would like that."

Monica rolled her eyes. Monica knew that despite being married, William Huntingwood had a thing for her, and the thought always disgusted her. William Huntingwood was repulsive to Monica. His thin strands of hair and shiny bald head made her cringe. His beer belly looked like it would burst through his button-down shirt. His rosy red cheeks made him look like Santa's long-lost brother. William Huntingwood carried that "yeah I got a beer belly and I'm fat, but I can still get the ladies attitude" which Monica found funny, but pathetic and disgusting. Monica responded, "Yeah anyhow . . . the meeting's at 1pm, OK?"

William Huntingwood nodded. "Yeah sure."

Monica walked off. William Huntingwood stared at his opened door.

The phone rang. He answered it. "Yes, Monica?"

"I've got someone on the line for you."

"Tell them I am busy."

"Mr. Huntingwood, this person said this is an urgent call."

"Fine, send them through."

Monica transferred the call.

William Huntingwood cleared his voice. "William Huntingwood, how may I help you."

"William Huntingwood," the voice chirped. "How are you?"

"I am really busy right now. May I ask what the purpose of this call is?"

"I will like to set up a meeting with you."

"For what?"

"I'd rather not discuss this over the phone, Mr. Huntingwood."

"Then you are wasting your time. I really have to—"

"Have you ever considered extending your partnership with the gala?"

"Gala?"

"Your Art Gallery Business Mr. Huntingwood."

"I have many partnerships I don't need anymore thank you. Now if you excuse me I —"

"Mr. Huntingwood, I am going to make this simple. I am interested in your gala, and the type of business I run would benefit from your gala."

William Huntingwood rolled his eyes. "Look, I don't do business deals over the phone. Furthermore we are not a gala, we are a successful business art gallery company. If you are interested in meeting, fine, but I really don't have the time right now to—"

"How does a million-dollar offer sound?"

William Huntingwood laughed. "I beg your pardon?"

"You heard me."

"Yes, I heard you, but what kind of out-of-the-blue offer is that?"

"You're obviously not interested."

"You obviously don't know how to do business and did not do your research about Mahogany. We are one of the successful art gallery businesses internationally and we're ranked in Forbes Magazine as one of the top of successful businesses. Do you know how much profit we make annually? 100 times your pitiful offer!"

"Mr. Huntingwood, listen to me. I am interested in your company. All I ask is that we set up a time and date together to talk."

"I don't understand why you couldn't leave this information with my secretary."

"I don't deal with secretaries; I only deal with the main source."

William Huntingwood snorted at the comment.

"Are you interested in meeting or not?"

"OK, first of all, you call here unwilling to disclose your identity to the secretary, and now you're trying to strike up some deal with me to partner with my gala for a pathetic amount? Again, I am not interested."

"I guess you're right. Maybe I'm wasting your time. I mean after all, who would want to have a business relationship with a business that was responsible for the murder of one of its employees?"

William Huntingwood sat up in his seat. "I beg your pardon?"

"Must I constantly repeat myself?"

"Where did you get that information that our company was responsible for an employee's death?"

"Obviously *you don't know* about business, Mr. Huntingwood."

Sweat beaded on the man's forehead. "Well I'll ask again. Where did you hear that we were responsible for an employee death?"

The voice chuckled. "It is not where I heard it from. It's how it will affect your reputation."

William Huntingwood leaned in further. "Are you trying to bribe me?"

The voice did not reply.

"Listen, I don't have time for this bullshit. Who are you? And why are you harassing me?"

"I am an interested client. I would like to form a partnership with your company."

"Well all you're doing right now is annoying me."

"Fine. I'm sure that the news media will have a frenzy hearing about how you were responsible for your employee's death."

William Huntingwood spoke louder. "You don't scare me."

"But your clientele will be scared of you."

William Huntingwood sighed. His reputation was something that he cared for deeply, and the idea of having Larry's death ruin his career and the company horrified him. At the time of Larry's death, William Huntingwood had instructed everyone to keep everything confidential and not to tell anyone. Did someone disobey him? William Huntingwood did not want to think about the outcomes of a situation like this.

He shook his head. "Fine, fine. To make you happy, we'll set up this meeting. What is your name?"

The caller didn't reply.

"Hello? Are you there?"

The caller coughed. "Sorry, yes."

"Your name please?"

The caller paused for a moment and took a deep breath.

Ronnie sat in his blue van at the corner of Broadway and 8th waiting for Simone's phone call. He sang along to Billy Joel's "Uptown Girl", which was blasting from his car stereo. His silver aviator sunglasses rested on his sweaty nose as he checked himself in the rearview mirror. He ran his fingers through his hair and smiled. Ronnie hated waiting for Simone, but that was part of his job description whether he liked it or not. Every time he thought about Simone and this plot they had together, he shook his head in disgust. Things were not going according to plan and it annoyed Ronnie. Simone's love affair with Antonio was getting in the way and delaying their deadline—a deadline that was supposed to be very prosperous for Ronnie.

There was a tap on the driver's side window.

Ronnie looked over to see someone wearing a black trench coat and a black baseball hat. His face was scruffy and dark.

Ronnie rolled down the window. "What can I do for you?"

"You are in my parking spot," the man growled.

Ronnie took of his sunglasses. "I beg your pardon?"

"You heard me. You are in my parking spot."

Ronnie leaned out his window. "Buddy, I am parked on the fuckin' street. Is your name on here?"

The man did not reply.

Ronnie shook his head and began winding up the window.

The man leaned towards Ronnie's face. "I said to move out of my fuckin' space, asshole."

Ronnie snarled at him. "Fuck off, faggot."

"You are gonna regret saying that," the man warned.

Ronnie laughed. "Listen you little fuck head, I don't know who you are, but my van is staying right fucking here, and you can't do shit about it."

The man didn't reply.

"What the fuck are you staring at, faggot? Ronnie said. "Get outta here or else the only thing hard up your ass that you are gonna feel is a bullet."

The man smiled, shook his head, and stood back.

Ronnie leaned back in his car and rolled up the window. "Fuckin' idiot."

A loud pierce deafening sharp bang shattered the driver's side window. Car alarms from nearby cars blared in unison as people stood around wondering what had just occured. Blood splattered all over the windshield. A young lady quickly ran to her car that was parked in front Ronnie's blue van and noticed that Ronnie's van windshield was shattered. Apprehensive, the young lady looked inside. She held her hand to her mouth and screamed loudly causing everyone to gather around her. As a pool of blood formed underneath Ronnie's driver seat. Everything in the van was motionless.

Billy Joel kept on singing.

CHAPTER THIRTY-EIGHT

Simone sat on her deck sprawled out on a lawn chair. The warm sun baked her chocolate skin.

Simone's cell phone vibrated against the concrete floor.

She ignored it and sighed, allowing herself to relax.

Minutes later one of the twin towers, Juan, approached her.

"Mrs. Jackson, I've got Jazz on my cell."

Simone sat up and removed her Armani sunglasses. "Tell him that I am busy."

"He said that it would be wise if you took this call." Juan said.

Simone sighed. "Fine, send it. I'll take the call."

"Actually, Mrs. Jackson, he's here."

Simone furrowed her eyebrows. "Here? Then why would he call?"

Juan shrugged his shoulders.

"Send him here."

Juan nodded and marched off.

Simone quickly sprang up and grabbed her robe. She took out a cigarette from her breast pocket and lit it.

Jazz strolled into the patio deck with Juan following him.

He smiled. "Aren't we looking' sexy."

Simone sneered. "Jazz, you say that to everyone you meet."

Jazz approached her and gracefully grabbed her hand. "No, but Simone, you are something special." He kneeled down and kissed her hand.

Simone laughed. "Jazz, if you are looking to receive an Oscar for your performance, you are in the wrong business."

Jazz laughed. His spiked platinum hair and snake tattoo that ran up his pale, freckled neck made him look a punk rocker. "I have a weakness for chocolate. What can I say?"

Simone rolled her eyes. "OK, enough with this 'blacker the berry, the sweeter the juice' crap. What do you want?"

Jazz's smile flattened. "We need to talk."

"About?"

"About everything that has been happening."

"Ok, what do you need to know?"

"I think someone tipped us."

Simone leaned in. "Are you sure?"

"Yes."

"How do you know?"

"Because we saw them leave from the police station."

"And who is this?"

Jazz swallowed before he spoke. "It's your boy toy Antonio."

Simone rolled her eyes. "I am not worried about him."

"But I am." Jazz said. "He could screw things up."

Simone paused briefly, then sighed. "Did you do what I asked you to do?"

Jazz slowly nodded. "Lucky took care of that for you."

Simone smiled. "Good. Now I have one less problem to worry about."

Jazz scratched his head. "Simone, I still don't understand why you wanted to get rid of Ronnie."

Simone flicked her hair. "Because he was a glitch in my plan. He could easily go to the police and rat on me, and he had already threatened me once. I can't have that."

Jazz screwed up his face. "Simone I still don't get it."

Simone rolled her eyes. "Jazz, are you forgetting about Ronnie's history?"

Jazz shrugged his shoulders.

Simone shook her head. "Jazz, Ronnie used to be a cop, remember?"

Jazz nodded but was unsure of Simone's response. He smiled and grabbed her hand. "You know, Simone, I really think you should forget this business deal shit. You should join with me. You'll be even richer."

Simone pulled her hand away. "Jazz, your kind of money is illegal."

"So is yours."

"Yeah, but mine doesn't involve people being ruthlessly murdered."

"You still kill, Simone."

Simone paused. "Jazz I don't kill. I get revenge."

Jazz laughed. "Is that what you call it?"

Simone sat down on the lawn chair. "Are you done interrogating me?"

Jazz knelt down beside Simone and caressed her shoulder. "You know, you are wasting your time with that Antonio fuckhead. You need a real man who can make you scream."

Simone glared at Jazz. "Antonio does that for me already."

Jazz whispered in her ear. "You know, there is a reason women call me Anaconda."

Simone rolled her eyes. "The same reason why the guys in the jail called you that?"

Jazz wasn't amused but laughed anyway. "See, that is why I like you. I like your style and finesse and energy."

"Jazz, listen. As much as your coming on to me is intriguing, I don't mix business with pleasure. And besides, I am too old for you."

"Too old? Simone you're only forty-two years old. That's not old at all. Fuck it, I'm thirty-five. Besides, I heard older women are freaky in bed."

Simone bit her lip. "Don't let the numbers fool you."

Jazz smiled.

Simone didn't.

* * *

The sounds of gunshots made Antonio's eyes blink. He tried to move his arms, but they felt heavy and numb. Antonio slowly rolled over and the bright lights stung him. His body felt weak and his head was dizzy. Black masking tape covered his mouth, making breathing difficult. Antonio could not make out where he was except that he was in a foul-smelling room. The pungent smell made him nauseous but too weak to vomit. Everything around him seemed like an illusion. He was unaware of where he was or why he was there.

The door of the room flung wide open. The bright light from the entrance way made Antonio squint as a large figure appeared in the door. He marched over to Antonio.

The large man leaned over and smiled. "I see our guest is awake."

Antonio stared blankly.

He dragged Antonio to his feet and pulled him forward. "Come along with me."

Antonio remained silent and allowed his weak body to be dragged along by the fat man.

The room was then empty.

* * *

Jazz stood at the front door entrance. "OK, so everything is set. Are you sure you want to continue with this?"

Simone glared at Jazz. "When a woman says yes, she means yes."

Jazz shook his head and leaned in. "You sure you don't want some cream in your coffee?"

Simone gently pressed her index finger on Jazz's lips and whispered seductively, "Fuck off, Jazz."

Jazz stood back and smiled. "You say that now, but . . . ."

"Jazz, leave," Simone said, opening the door.

Jazz nodded. "Fine. Don't say I didn't' try."

"I'd sure won't," Simone said.

Jazz nodded. "I guess I'll see you later."

Simone nodded and closed the door. She glanced at her watch and quickly darted upstairs into her bedroom to change. So many exciting thoughts were running through her head. Things were finally going as planned, and she would be safe soon. She felt her self-doubt melting away.

There was a knock on the door. "Mrs. Jackson?" George's voice questioned.

"What is it? Simone yelled from behind the door.

"You have another guest."

"Tell them I'll be there in a moment."

"Very well," George said. Simone quickly changed into her business suit jacket and skirt and made sure her briefcase was with her. As she approached the stairs, she adjusted her tight-fitting skirt and walked down the stairs.

Simone beamed. "Oh, well, what a surprise. So glad you could make it."

William Huntingwood stood at the door and adjusted his tie. "Let's make this fast and worth my time because I don't tolerate bullshit."

* * *

"I told you I didn't say anything." Antonio groaned.

Antonio sat strapped in a chair in a dimly lit room. Beside him towered two large men in black suits with their arms folded. They both had jet-black hair tied in long, greasy ponytails. One of them had a mole on his forehead.

"You're fucking lying!" said the guy with the mole.

"I don't understand why you have me here and why this is all happening!" Antonio said.

Both men laughed.

Antonio got nervous.

The guy without the mole leaned in close. "The boss told us to bring you here."

"Which boss?"

"Oh, you know who it is."

Antonio shook his head nervously. "No I don't. I don't know what you're talking about."

The guy with the mole laughed.

Antonio's voice croaked. "What's so funny?"

"You don't know what is in store for you, do you?"

Antonio shrugged his shoulders. "Listen, guys, I don't know want you're talking about. Honestly."

A cell phone rang.

The guy with mole answered. "Yeah? . . . OK, for how long? Alright." He hung up and turned towards Antonio.

"The big boss is gonna be here in an hour."

Antonio shook his head. "Who is this big boss?"

The guy with mole smiled. "You'll see."

* * *

Officer Stevens yawned. "I am not getting anywhere with this case."

A younger blond freckled officer sat across from the table and handed him a report. "Did you take a look a this?"

Officer Stevens grabbed the file. "What is this?"

"Some information on that Simone Jackson woman."

"Who?"

"Check it out."

Officer Stevens read through the file. His mouth gaped open. "Well I'll be damned."

"Interesting, don't you think?"

"She sounds like a handful."

The blond officer nodded.

Officer Stevens sprung up from his chair. "Shawn, I want you to do a thorough check on Simone Jackson. I want everything—details, financial statements, relationships, business partnerships, the whole works."

Officer Shawn nodded. "Yes sir."

Officer Shawn grabbed a couple of files and darted out the room. Officer Stevens sat at the table with an incandescent light illuminating his bald, graying head. He grabbed the telephone and started dialing, leaving a message when no one picked up:

"Antonio Madison, this is Officer Stevens calling if you can please contact me immediately at the police station. I have some very interesting news to tell you about the information that you gave me. Thank you."

Officer Steven hung up and stared at the stacks of information that lay in front of him. He was baffled by the information he read. Two different names seemed to be referring to the same person: Simone Jackson and Dana Robinson. Quickly Officer Stevens logged into his computer and started searching his database for Dana Robinson. As he continued going through his hits, he discovered something that made him sit back in his chair in disbelief. His eyes widened.

"Holy smokes," Officer Steven said. "I can't believe this!!"

A tall figure stood over the Antonio's answer machine. He yanked the plug out of the socket and threw it across the room. He continued his way through Antonio's apartment.

* * *

A cell phone rang.

Antonio watched as the big guy without the mole answered.

Antonio scanned his body movements. The man quickly nodded and hung up.

He glared at Antonio. "The boss is here."

Antonio stomach turned.

Soon there was a knock on the door. The man with the mole jolted quickly to the door to answer it. His massive size towered the figure that was in front of him.

"Boss, how great to see you."

The boss did not reply.

The man moved out away and Antonio's eyes widened. He felt his head pound and his blood boil.

The voice replied. "Hello, Mr. Antonio Madison."

Antonio glared at the figure standing in front of him. "Simone."

CHAPTER THIRTY-NINE

Simone walked slowly to Antonio and stood in front of him. "How are you doing?"

Antonio glared at Simone. "What is this? A sick joke?"

Simone paused. She undid one button from her blouse and knelt down towards Antonio. "I've come to collect what is rightfully mine."

Antonio lowered his brow. "Um, what?"

Simone laughed. "Antonio, you foolish boy. Like I've said to you a number of times, never underestimate a woman's work. "

"OK, really and truly, I don't understand what this is all about. Is this supposed to be some way of getting back at me? Because if it is, and if you want me to apologize, then I will. But this is completely crazy."

Simone stepped back. "You think I've taken it too far? How so, Antonio?"

Antonio lost his temper. "Fuck this bullshit. Simone, what the hell is going on? Why are you doing this? You fucking kidnapped and drugged me!"

Simone laughed. "Antonio, you were the missing link in my plan."

"What plan?"

"The plan to take over . . . everything, basically. I met up with your boss today."

Antonio paused. "William Huntingwood?"

Simone nodded.

"And?"

"I've signed a partner deal with him."

"William Huntingwood? You signed a deal with him? That must have been difficult."

Simone turned back towards Antonio. "Actually, it was quite easy."

"How?"

Simone paused and then laughed. "Well I mentioned to William Huntingwood that it would be quite a shame if his company were to be involved in a certain scandal."

Antonio tried to adjust himself in his chair. "What scandal?"

"Larry's death."

Antonio's eyes widened. "You bribed him?"

Simone smiled.

"So where do I come into this?"

Again Simone laughed. "Well, you were my catalyst, and I thank you for that."

"So basically, you used me."

"You can say it that way. Yes, I guess I did."

Antonio clenched his teeth and blurted out the first thing that was on his mind. "You are a fucked bitch, you know that?"

Everyone in the room fell silent. Simone giggled.

"Oh Antonio, you see that is where you are totally wrong." She grabbed her silver 9mm, approached Antonio, and held it against his head. "See? I am not just a fucking bitch. I am a bitch with a gun. A conniving, business-minded fucking bitch."

Antonio could not believe what was happening. "You killed Larry, didn't you?"

Simone didn't reply.

"And Larry's brother, and your first husband. You killed them too, didn't you?

Again Simone didn't reply.

Antonio shook his head in disgust. "I can't believe this. Larry and Greg were right." Antonio straightened his back. "Greg. Where is Greg? You did something to him, didn't you? You killed him!"

Simone rolled her eyes. "Don't exaggerate."

"Simone don't fuck with me right—"

Simone pressed the gun harder against his temple. "Don't make me have to pull this trigger so soon."

Antonio felt himself shake.

"Did you go to the police station?"

Antonio didn't reply.

Simone pushed the barrel harder against Antonio's temple. "Answer me, goddamn it! I asked you if you went to the goddamn police."

One of the bodyguards interjected. "Mrs. Jackson, Jazz is here."

Simone smiled. "Good."

Antonio screwed his face? "Who?"

"A special guest."

Within seconds, Jazz walked into the room. He stopped in front of Antonio and then turned to Simone. "Yeah, that's him."

Antonio was confused. "What the hell is going on here?"

Simone grabbed Antonio by the face. "Antonio, my friend Jazz said that he saw you go to the police station."

"Yeah, because of those crank calls I was getting."

Simone shook her head. "You're lying."

Antonio wanted to scream, but he knew nothing would come of it. Standing in front of him was the same woman he'd held down screaming as she reached orgasm. Now she was pushing a 9mm gun against his temple.

Antonio closed his eyes tight. "Simone, why are you doing this?"

Simone sighed and then took a deep breath. "Because I love you."

"Because you love me?"

Simone nodded and began laughing hysterically. "Oh my dear Antonio, the things you do to me, and the things you say."

Sweat beaded down Antonio's forehead. "Simone, think about what you are doing."

"Oh I have." Simone hissed.

* * *

Lisa startled at the sound of her phone ringing. She threw her book on the sofa and walked across the room to answer it.

"Hello?"

There was no reply.

Lisa made a face. "Hello?"

A raspy voice whispered. "5676 O'Connor Drive."

"I beg your pardon?"

"5676 O'Connor Drive. Antonio is there in trouble. Call the police."

Lisa's hands shook. "What?"

"Call the police."

"Who is this, and what's going?"

"Call the fucking police!"

Lisa felt a chill up her spine. "Greg, is that you?"

The person hung up.

Lisa felt her legs wobble. She quickly dialed Antonio's number. There was no response. Who the hell was this? Was this a joke? Lisa quickly hit redial but noticed the number was marked private. She dialed Greg's cell. It went straight to his voicemail. That wasn't a voice of someone playing a joke. She quickly wrote down the address she'd heard, grabbed her jacket, and dashed out the door. Lisa didn't question her compulsion to go to Antonio's house. She just followed her gut instinct. Her mother always told her to follow her gut instincts . . . she shook her head as she scurried out of her apartment building. "Antonio is in danger," she frantically repeated to herself. "Antonio is in danger!"

CHAPTER FORTY

Lisa sped down Broadway to Antonio's loft in her red Ford Focus. She wanted to assure herself that he was at his place. She knew she was in no condition to drive, but her concern for Antonio outweighed everything. She'd only officially been to his place twice, but she'd occasionally driven past it—something she'd been ashamed about, but hell, it was sure coming in handy now. She always fantasized about just showing up to his apartment one evening. She didn't want to come off as some obsessed, crazed girl, but there was something about Antonio that made Lisa feel kind of crazy. And she felt crazier that he didn't even seem to notice her. She wanted Antonio to pay attention to her like he paid attention to Simone. She wanted to be that date that Antonio brought out at galas and to dinner. She wanted to hold Antonio's hand. She wanted to be like the two lovers in his paintings. She wanted to be on his mind like he was on Simone's. She wanted him. She wanted Antonio.

She arrived at his place and buzzed up.

No answer.

She buzzed again.

No answer.

Lisa squinted through the glass door in front of her. Her eye caught a piece of metal that was jammed on the side of the door. She looked around before attempting to open the door.

The door opened freely.

Lisa quickly headed towards his apartment.

* * *

Antonio eyes twitched as the gun pressed harder into his temple.

Simone laughed. "You know Antonio, I love to see a man squirm and sweat under my control."

Antonio squirmed more in his chair.

Simone slowly and seductively walked towards Antonio. "Do you like what you see?"

Antonio raised his brow. "What?"

"You heard me. Tell me, do you like what you see?"

Antonio shook his head, confused.

Simone approached Antonio and straddled his lap. She grabbed his face and brought it close to hers. "Seeing you like this just turns me right on."

"Simone, seriously, stop . . ."

Simone pressed her lips against Antonio's. Her strength overcame Antonio and Antonio felt himself give in. Simone gyrated her hips as her tongue explored Antonio's mouth.

Jazz stood by the corner clenching his fists.

Antonio stopped abruptly. He gazed at her. "You're completely crazy."

Simone laughed hysterically.

"Simone, please tell me what you're doing is some sick joke."

Everyone in the room laughed, including Simone. Jazz approached Antonio, pushed Simone aside, grabbed his jaw and glared at him. "You are in so much fucking trouble."

Simone pushed Jazz out of the way. "Jazz, relax." Again she straddled Antonio's lap and glared into his eyes. She looked sinister, hysterical, and hungry.

She spoke softly and deeply. "Fuck me."

Antonio's eye twitched. He cleared his throat. "I beg your pardon?"

Simone grabbed Antonio's face. "I said fuck me."

Antonio's red tired eyes pierced into Simone's hazel eyes. He shook his head. "You want me to fuck you in front of these guys?"

Simone laughed hysterically. "You think they'll mind? They may even join in on the action."

The thought made Antonio nauseous. "You are not the same woman I thought you were."

Simone got up abruptly. "Antonio, I've always been the same woman. The problem is that you never bothered to explore the real me."

"Simone, 'the real you' is psychotic," he said, trying to free himself.

"I am a woman, Antonio. You don't get that. And you can keep wiggling all you want," Simone said as she lifted the gun towards his forehead.

"Simone, please. You are acting crazy."

Simone smiled.

"Simone please, stop this."

Simone's finger was on the trigger.

"Simone!"

Simone arms were straight like an arrow aiming at her prey.

"Simone! . . . Si—"

Antonio's plea was shorten by the loud thunderous gunshot.

The room fell silent.

* * *

Lisa got to Antonio's loft and noticed the door was cracked open.

Her heart stopped. She closed her eyes and with a little courage pushed the door open.

Lisa scanned Antonio's apartment. A half glass of orange juice sat on the kitchen counter. A pillow from the couch lay peacefully on the ground. Lisa slowly crept into the living room. An eerie feeling shot through her body as her footsteps echoed throughout the empty apartment.

"Hello? Antonio, are you here?" Lisa said. Her voice echoed off the walls.

There was no response.

Lisa cautiously and slowly walked through the apartment. Antonio's artwork hung proudly on his walls. His huge collection of CDs and DVDs were stacked neatly on shelves. Lisa saw a light piercing from the washroom and heard the buzzing of the ceiling fan. She slowly approached it and peeked in.

No one was there.

She turned around and decided to walk back to the main living room. She looked up the staircase.

"Antonio? Are you up there?"

The serenity in the apartment made Lisa apprehensive. Her heart raced. She grabbed on the railing and walked upstairs. At the top of the stairs was Antonio's bedroom.

Her jaw dropped.

Her eyes gazed in fear at the smeared red writing across Antonio's bed:

~~DANA~~ SIMONE AND ANTONIO FOREVER!

Lisa shook her head. "What the hell?"

She edge closer to the bed scrutinizing the message.

"Why is 'Dana' scratched out?" she asked herself.

There was a thud from below.

Lisa jumped.

"Police!" shouted a voice. "Is anyone in here?"

Lisa ran downstairs towards the officer.

"Ma'am, is this your place?"

Lisa cleared her throat. "Officer, this is my friend's place, but something is wrong."

The officer adjusted his hat. "And you are?"

"Lisa."

"And you're friends with the occupant who lives here?"

"Yes, but I think my friend is in trouble."

"We just got a call that there was a break and enter."

Lisa froze. "Break and enter?"

"Yes, ma'am," the officer said, taking off his hat. "Someone called and reported a robbery here."

"Well I came here to see him, and the door was cracked open."

"It was cracked open?"

"Yes, when I arrived the door was open."

The officer grabbed his pad and pen and started scribbling.

Lisa scratched her head. "Break and enter?"

The officer ignored her statement. "How long were you here, madam?"

"Ten minutes."

"Any signs of distress in here?"

"No, but officer you need to look at this," Lisa said, beckoning the officer to follow her upstairs.

Lisa showed the officer the bed. He placed a curled index finger on his lips and nodded slowly.

"And you saw this when came up here?"

"Yes."

The officer examined the sheets. His nose twitched.

Lisa watched.

"Still smells like perfume. Smells like someone was just in this bed."

"What do you think they were doing?"

"Can't be sure, but your friend may have a real wacko lover."

Lisa pursed her lips. She took out a piece of paper and handed it to the officer.

"What is this?" the officer said.

"Officer I received a call from some unidentified number, and they gave me this address. They said my friend Antonio who lives here is in trouble."

The officer took the paper and read it. "When did they call you?"

"Before I arrived."

"Male or female voice?"

"I don't know. It was like they were whispering."

The officer wrote down the address and continued searching around. He then stopped and paused. His eyes widened. "Ma'am, did you see this?"

"See what?" Lisa said.

"That," the officer said, pointing on the opposite side of the bed.

Lisa walked over and froze.

"OH MY GOD!" she screamed.

Lying on the floor beside the bed was a black revolver and a lifeless body. It was Greg.

CHAPTER FORTY-ONE

Everyone in the room stood back with guns drawn aiming at the door.

"What the fuck was that?" Jazz yelled.

A muffled voice echoed from the stairs below. "Police! Put your fucking weapons down!"

"Shit, the cops!" one of the bodyguards cursed.

"The cops? Who the fuck tipped them off? How the fuck did they know we were here?" one of the men in the room said.

"Go, go, go!" Jazz ordered as the men raced out through a back door. The men shoved each other out of the room as the heavy footsteps of the officers grew louder.

"Police—open up!" shouted one of the officers behind the door.

No one replied within in the room.

Without hesitation the officers burst into the room and prepared to shoot. The room was empty.

"There's no one here!" exclaimed one officer.

From an open window, they could hear the loud rumble of engines.

One of the officers approached the window and pointed. "Fuck, they're getting away!"

Another officer ran to the window and stopped. He turned to his men. "Follow them!"

Antonio sat in the passenger seat while Simone veered down Columbia Avenue with her gun pointed at Antonio's head.

"Simone, why the fuck are you doing this?"

Simone didn't reply.

"Do you realize what you're doing?"

Again Simone did not reply.

"Simone, why do you want to kill me?"

No reply.

"Simone, please talk to me—this is too fucking crazy. You can't just kidnap and drug someone and take them as hostage and . . ."

Simone turned to Antonio. "Antonio. Listen to me. I am doing this for the both of us."

Antonio leaned back. "The both of us? You are doing this for the both of us? Explain to me how the fuck do you plan to this for the both of us when an hour ago you were ready to blow my brains out?"

Simone grimaced. She spoke with a lifeless voice. "I like to create shock value."

"And killing Larry and your previous husbands was shock value too."

Simone grew angrier. "Antonio, I told you what happened."

"Simone, you tell me a lot of things that, quite frankly, I don't know if I should believe," he said sarcastically.

"Antonio, don't get me cross."

Antonio felt a fuse blow inside of him. Anger and exasperation overwhelmed him, and he lost control. He quickly grabbed the gun from Simone's hand and flung it in the backseat. Simone swerved the car, trying to control Antonio, but Antonio clenched on to her wrists. The Mercedes Benz swerved back and forth between lanes causing cars to honk and slam on their brakes.

"Antonio, let go!"

"No!"

Simone dug her nails into Antonio's fists, but he wouldn't relent. Antonio quickly grabbed the steering wheel and veered to the left, narrowly avoiding a dump truck.

"Antonio, let go of the steering wheel!"

Antonio's blood boiled hotter, and he smacked Simone across her face. Simone slammed on the brakes, causing the wheels to screech and the car to jolt to a stop.

She slowly turned to Antonio and glared at him. "You fucking slapped me!"

Antonio returned the glared back at her. "You fucking tried to kill me!"

Police sirens echoed behind them, and car horns blared furiously.

Simone gazed deeply into Antonio's blood-boiling eyes.

She pulled him towards her. "Kiss me."

Antonio pushed her away. The cars continued their furious noise.

She grabbed him again. "Antonio, kiss me, just one more time."

Again Antonio pushed her away and tried to open the passenger door.

The sirens grew louder. Instantly Simone pressed on the gas pedal and veered down the street, causing Antonio to slam back in his seat. The sirens and flashing lights were now chasing her. Simone eyes remained fixed on the streets—diving in between cars, going through intersections, and nearly missing other cars and pedestrians. Antonio held on to his seat, dumbfounded. Cars honked and screeched. A police cruiser raced up on the driver's side and tried to block her, but Simone went faster. Lights, buildings, signs all whizzed by like strobe lights. Simone quickly veered her car to the left into a narrow alleyway. The cruisers followed behind, blaring their sirens. Her eyes were fixed on their destination: to get out, take control, and be on top. Adrenaline rushed through her veins, and she loved every minute of it. Antonio sat in the passenger seat, holding on to dear life. His mind flashed back to the meeting at the art gallery, the dinners, and the passionate sex. Now he was being held hostage in Simone's car, nearly being killed so she could go seek a dream he couldn't understand.

"Simone, look out!" Antonio yelled.

Simone quickly veered her car to the right, avoiding a large rusty pipe that was sticking out from a dilapidated building.

Simone glanced at Antonio.

Antonio slowly turned to Simone.

"I've always wanted to do this," Simone said.

"Simone, for fuck's sake, *listen* to me! You can't do this! What you are doing is crazy! Can you please . . ."

Antonio didn't have time to finish his sentence. Everything happened so fast. The screech of the brakes echoed throughout the dilapidated alleyway as the car headed straight into truck that was backing up. Broken glass and pieces of metal flew everywhere, followed by a thunderous crash. Silence pervaded the dead, lifeless air.

And then everything faded to white.

CHAPTER FORTY-TWO

William Huntingwood sat at home at his desk, staring at the agreement. He wondered if he was making the right decision. It seemed odd that someone would take such a huge interest in this gallery. He also couldn't decide why they would try to blackmail him into signing into this agreement on accusations that he knew were totally false. How on earth had he got himself involved in this mess? The more he thought about it, the more it irritated him.

"Honey, dinner will be ready soon," shouted a voice down the hallway.

"Thanks, dear," William Huntingwood shouted back. He took another deep sigh before he left his desk and strolled down to the kitchen.

His wife sat at one end of the dinner table. Her short, dark hair nuzzled behind her pale ears. Two empty chairs sat across from each other between Mrs. Huntingwood and where William Huntingwood was going to sit.

William Huntingwood plopped on the chair. "Where are the kids?"

"Billy has soccer practice and Katie is at her friend Joanne's place."

William Huntingwood grinned. "So I guess it's just the two of us, huh?"

Mrs. Huntingwood immediately started to apportion the meal. "So, how was work today?"

William Huntingwood grunted. "Fine."

"Is that right?"

"Yep?"

"Anything new?"

William Huntingwood paused while serving his food. "Wow, that's a first."

"I beg your pardon?"

"You hardly ever ask me about my day at work."

"Well, today I am asking."

"Yeah, but why?"

"Bill, stop being an idiot."

William Huntingwood took a sip of his drink. "Oh, so now I am idiot for asking why you're interested?"

"Actually, I find it quite insulting."

"Well, I don't think you're making any sense. How 'bout that, Joan?"

"You know, I was trying to be nice to you, Bill. You could at least show me some consideration."

"I just find your curiosity quite odd, that's all."

Mrs. Huntingwood dropped her fork to answer the phone that rang. "Just forget it, OK?"

William Huntingwood shook his head and started eating again. "Alright, whatever you say."

Mrs. Huntingwood approached him with the phone. "It's for you."

"Who is it?"

"Work."

William Huntingwood grabbed the phone and answered. "Hello?"

"Mr. Huntingwood it's Monica."

He smiled. "Hello Monica. How are you? Why are you . . . ?"

"Mr. Huntingwood, I think you should go to the hospital."

"The hospital? For what?"

Monica paused before she started sobbing hysterically.

* * *

Lisa sat on her chair in the hallway of the hospital looking pale, drained, and dazed. She slowly massaged her right temple, attempting one more time to understand what had occurred. She sighed, shook her head, and sobbed.

Her cell phone rang and she picked it up. "Hello?"

"Is this Lisa?"

"Yes, who's this?"

"This is officer Brian from Mr. Madison's apartment. I am afraid I have some horrible news."

Lisa slowly stood up from her chair. "Horrible news? About what?"

Officer Brian paused before he spoke deeply and slowly. "Your friend Antonio was just involved in a pretty bad car accident downtown."

Lisa paralyzed. "What? Car accident? What car accident?"

He and another occupant had an accident with a . . . . truck."

Lisa starting walking slowly. "But he's OK . . . he's OK, right officer? Antonio is OK, right?"

The officer paused.

Lisa felt a weight press on her. "Officer, please . . . tell me! Is he OK?"

The officer sighed. "Things don't look good right now."

Lisa dropped her phone and collapsed.

* * *

The dark room and the hissing of the oxygen machines made the ICU feel like a death chamber. There were two chairs in each room. All but one bed was empty. IV tubes, wires, and oxygen tubes all plugged into the wall onto the bed. Antonio laid captive, lifeless, and weak. With black bruises spotting his body, Antonio looked like a corpse laid out for display in a gallery. The visitor froze in shock and astonishment and wiped away a tear. Slowly she approached Antonio's bed and gazed at him.

"This wasn't supposed to happen," the person whispered. More tears starting flowing. "Oh, Antonio, this wasn't supposed to happen!"

CHAPTER FORTY-THREE

Both Antonio's mother and father came rushing into the emergency room.

"Where is he?" Antonio's mother yelled. "Where's my baby?"

A red-haired nurse approach them. "Madam, please calm down, who are you looking for?"

"My baby!" Antonio's mother sobbed. "My baby! He's hurt."

The nurse turned to Antonio's father. "Who are you both looking for, sir?"

Antonio's father spoke softly. "Our son. His name is Antonio Madison."

The nurse was familiar with the name. "He's in the ICU. Please follow me."

The nurse took them to the ICU unit where Lisa, Monica, and William Huntingwood all stood by Antonio's bed.

Antonio's mother cried. "Oh my God, Antonio! Baby!" She ran to the bed.

Lisa and Monica saw her reaction and stood back respectfully.

Antonio's mother turned to the nurse. "Nurse, please tell me he is going to be OK. Please, please tell me."

"Mrs. Madison, we are not too sure as yet. He has suffered a lot of damage, and right now we have him under observation."

Mr. Madison walked over to Lisa, Monica, and William Huntingwood and nodded.

"Nice to meet you too," Lisa said softly. "We all worked for him."

Mr. Madison raised his eyebrow. "Where's Greg?"

Lisa closed her eyes, bit her lip, and took a deep breath. "Mr. Madison," her voice shook. "Greg was found unconscious at Antonio's apartment."

Mrs. Madison looked over. "What?"

Lisa slowly approached Mrs. Madison. "I got a strange call from someone telling me that Antonio was in some kind of danger. When I went to his place, I found the door open. Apparently, somcone had called the police, reporting a break and enter. When the cop arrived, he apparently found Greg's body in Antonio's bedroom."

Mrs. Madison closed her eyes and shook his head. "I don't believe it."

"I know, Mrs. Madison, nothing adds up. We don't know what is going on. Everything has been crazy the last couple of months. "

"Maybe I can explain," a voice echoed from behind a curtain.

Everyone startled.

"Who's there?" William Huntingwood asked.

The figure walked out of from behind the counter.

William Huntingwood's face darkened. "What are *you* doing here?"

The person nodded. "Yes, William, it's me."

"What's wrong, do you know her?" Lisa asked him.

William Huntingwood nodded. "Yes, she is Simone Jackson."

Simone nodded.

"But I heard that you and Antonio were both in that car . . . and . . ."

"I know what you heard."

Lisa stood back. "Wait, aren't you Antonio's friend?"

Simone did not reply.

"OK I am confused here. What is going on?" Mr. Madison said.

William Huntingwood shook his head in fear. "This can't be. You were in that car with Antonio, according to the police. How can you be standing here in front of us?"

Simone paused. Tears welled up in her eyes, and she lifted her head before everyone. "It wasn't me in that car."

Everyone looked at each other puzzled.

"What do you mean, it wasn't you?" Lisa said. "Two bodies were identified in that crash. Antonio's and yours. If it wasn't your body, whose was it?"

Simone trembled as the tears flooded. "Antonio and Dana were in that crash. Dana Robinson. My twin sister."

The room fell silent.

CHAPTER FORTY-FOUR

Antonio's parents stood vigilant by Antonio's bed. William Huntingwood and Monica remained outside in the hallway.

Simone sat on a chair in the waiting room with a hand on her jaw, staring down at the floor.

Lisa brought her a glass of water.

"Thanks," Simone replied.

Lisa cleared her throat. "So let me get this straight. Your have a twin sister Dana who's been pretending to be you?"

Simone sighed. "Dana is . . . she was a very jealous, deceitful person."

Lisa leaned forward in her seat. "Was? You make it sound like she's dead. You know she's in another hospital being treated at . . ."

Simone raised her hand. "To me, she's dead."

Lisa shook her head. "I don't get it. Why would she do all of this?"

Simone took a deep breath. "Dana and I grew up with an overbearing father and a weak mother. He abused her. Dana and I grew up despising men because of what he did to her. And then when he died, Dana confessed to me that she was the one who killed him. She was always the black sheep, too. Growing up, everyone in school liked me but detested her. Her hatred for men shaped all of her relationships. She used men for whatever she could, and a lot of them abused her right back. She ended up getting herself in trouble and mixing up with the wrong crowd, dating drug dealers and doing a lot of bad, stupid stuff. Through all this, though, she still dreamed . . ."

"Exactly what was her dream?" Lisa said.

"Her dream was to be rich and powerful, even—or *especially*—if it involved hurting and harming others. She pretended to be me because she knew that I would not get into any trouble."

"What exactly did she do?"

Monica rushed in and interrupted Lisa and Simone. "Lisa! Lisa! The doctor just said that Greg is awake!"

Lisa and Monica huddled over Greg's bed as Greg groaned in pain.

"Where am I?" he moaned.

"In the hospital, Greg." Monica said, "But don't speak so much. You are still weak."

Greg moaned. "How long have I been here for?"

Lisa smiled. "A good while."

"Why am I here?"

Lisa glanced at Monica, then back at Greg. "Greg, you were found unconscious in Antonio's apartment."

Greg screwed up his face. "Huh?"

Lisa nodded. "You were found at Tony's place unconscious."

Greg slowly shook his head wincing at the pain. "Why was I there?"

"We don't know." Lisa said.

Greg moaned. "Someone must have saved me."

Lisa and Monica raised their eyebrows. "Saved you?"

"Yeah. I was held hostage in some run-down place. These four guys kept harassing me about Antonio."

Lisa felt uneasy. "What guys, Greg?"

"There were a bunch of them. Four, like I said. One guy had bleached hair. He kept asking me these questions about Antonio and I think Simone."

Lisa gasped.

Greg lowered his eyebrow. "What's wrong?"

Lisa cleared her throat. "Greg how much do you know about Simone?"

Greg tensed. "Enough—I know that she's a psycho bitch who killed Larry and is going to kill Tony." Greg then paused. "Tony. Where is he? Does he know that—?"

Monica leaned in. "Greg, Antonio was involved in a serious car accident with Simone. He was admitted here and he is in the ICU. Things don't look so great."

Greg paused. "What? Car accident? How did that happen?"

"We don't know as yet, but we found someone who can give us some answers," Lisa said, opening the curtains. Simone slowly walked out of the from the corner.

Greg started squirming and appeared extremely agitated. "Her! That's her. She's . . . hold on. You were in the car accident with Tony? How are you standing here right now?"

Simone took a deep breath. "Greg that was my twin sister in the car."

Greg face went pale.

Monica spun around with her finger on lips. "So let me get this straight. Dana, your twin sister has been using your ID so she can basically rob and murder?"

Her head down, Simone nodded.

"And she is responsible for the death of Larry, his brother, and her first husband?" Greg interjected.

Again Simone nodded.

William Huntingwood shook his head. "So that explains why she wrote her first initial on the agreement and then wrote your name."

Again Simone nodded.

"Simone," Greg said. "In all due fairness, aren't you partly to blame? I mean, you were helping her, weren't you?"

"Not really," Simone said. "She would ask me if she could borrow stuff, but I didn't realize it had gone this far. When I heard she went to the art gallery and was involved with Antonio, I had to stop it."

"So wait," Lisa said. "How did you know about Antonio in the first place?"

Simone bit her lip before speaking. "I was actually the one that Antonio met that day."

The room fell silent.

Simone played with her hands. "See, I met Antonio and was so strongly attracted to him. My sister found about him and wanted him for herself."

Lisa shook her head in disgust. "And you let her?"

"She threatened to kill me . . . I just did not know what else to say."

"What a psycho." Monica said.

Greg raised his hand weakly. "Hold on a second. I have a question. Antonio was getting these weird messages on his phone . . ."

Simone lowered her head. "That was me."

Greg shook his head. "You did that? Why?"

Simone reddened and a tear rolled down her cheek. "Because I wanted to fuck up things between Dana and Antonio and make him leave her. I was finally becoming attracted to someone that I found interesting, smart, and . . . well, perfect. There was such passion between us. But Dana made it difficult and often would make plans with him more than I could see him so Antonio often was with Dana more than me. I only ever saw him twice. The first time was when I saw him at the gallery and the second time was for a lunch date. Everything after that was Dana."

Again Greg held his hand up. "Hold on, so he was intimate with Dana and not you?"

Simone closed her eyes and nodded in shame.

Everyone in the room made small movements indicating their discomfort.

Greg shook his head. "OK, so how did I end up in Antonio's apartment?"

"Yes," Lisa interjected. "How did Greg end up there?" Lisa stopped. "Wait! You were the person who phoned me with the address, weren't you?"

Simone sighed and nodded.

Monica and Greg shrugged their shoulders.

Simone let out a deep breath. "Yes, I was the one who phoned you."

"How did you get my number? And how did you know where he was?"

Simone brushed a strand a hair from her face. "Antonio was kept in a place that I know all too well. It's an old dilapidated building where Dana's drug dealers and hustlers hang out. She never keeps them around the estate. Greg, when I heard that she had kidnapped both you and Antonio, I knew right where they'd be."

Lisa narrowed her eyes at Simone. " Why did you allow your sister to do this? Why did you allow her to ruin your life like this? This makes no sense. Why did you allow this to happen?"

"Because my sister threatened my life if I did not co-operate with her. Looking back, I realize that I was still being a coward. I should have done something sooner . . . somehow."

"So what made you change?" Greg said adjusting himself in the bed.

Simone took another deep breath. "After hearing what she really planned to do to Antonio, I knew I had to act. I couldn't have her mess up something good for me, so I decided to screw over her plans." Simone swallowed and turned to Greg. "Greg, I found out where you were being kept and managed to get some guys who can never tell the difference between Dana and I to secretly move you into Antonio's place and lay you besides Antonio's bed. I painted those words 'Simone and Antonio forever' so the police would think Dana did it."

Lisa felt a chill go up her spine.

Simone sat down and turned to William Huntingwood. "I also overheard Dana talking about killing you."

William Huntingwood froze. "What?"

Simone nodded

"Wait, so how did you have access to all of this information?" Greg asked.

Simone half smiled. "When you are surrounded constantly by Dana's people, you tend to befriend a number of them."

"So Dana's entourage doesn't know she has a twin? And what about Larry? Did he know this too? What about his brother and the other previous husbands? No one at all did not know this?"

"Some do, some don't. It's stupid, I know. Listen, I am really sorry for everything, but this was not supposed to happen. It was supposed to be—"

Antonio's father burst into the room. "Guys, come with me quickly!"

"What's wrong?" Lisa said.

Antonio's father trembled. "It's Antonio. Something is wrong. I don't know, All these doctors and nurses are working over him. The machines are beeping. Something is wrong!"

Nurses and doctors surrounded Antonio. Machines and lights were beeping and blinking excessively.

"His blood pressure is dropping!" shouted one nurse.

Everyone gathered outside the room, watching in horror.

"Give him 3ccs of heparin now!" shouted one physician.

Simone stood at the end of the hallway in horror of what was happening. She felt helpless and weak. Everything around Antonio seemed to be happening in slow motion. The shouts, the screams, the hands gesturing, the noises, the stress were all surreal. Within seconds, everything had slowed down. The nurses and doctors all simultaneously stared at the monitor with dejected, melancholy looks on their faces. One of the doctors went over to everyone gathered outside. A couple of them already knew and started weeping. The cries seemed to fade away in oblivion as everything around Antonio dissolved into a white wave.

Then his eyes opened.

CHAPTER FORTY-FIVE

Antonio's eyes fluttered against the bright lights in the room.

His mother approached the other side of the bed. "Hi honey, are you OK?"

Antonio felt weak. "Where am I?"

"You are in the hospital. You just came back from surgery," his mother said.

"Surgery?" Antonio mouthed.

"Yes honey, surgery. You were involved in a serious car accident and they had to perform emergency surgery on you."

Antonio still had a hard time processing what was being told to him. "Surgery? This is gonna sound weird but I remember faintly hearing doctors and nurses shouting and panicking over me as if I were dying."

A tear emerged from Antonio's mother. "Yes dear you were in the intensive care you unit and you nearly died on us. They had to perform an emergency surgery on you."

"You mean I'm not dead? I feel dead," Antonio said.

Antonio's mother smirked. "No honey, you ain't dead yet."

Antonio moaned in pain. "But I heard everyone around me—nurses, doctors . . . everybody."

"Honey, you must have been hallucinating or dreaming or something." Antonio's mother said.

Lisa appeared at the door and cleared her throat. "Hi, Antonio."

Antonio smiled. "Lisa, what are you doing here?"

"Um, it's a long story—a complicated, long story. But I don't think you want to hear it from me."

Antonio looked confused. "Huh?"

Lisa stepped back. "I think someone here needs to explain a lot of things to you."

Simone walked in the door, and Antonio was immediately agitated.

"Why the hell are you here?" Antonio gasped, trying to fight off his pain. "You're psycho! Get away from me."

"Antonio, please, you have to listen to me."

"Why the hell did you guys bring her here? She nearly had me——" Antonio stopped. "Wait a minute, you were in the car with me too. How was I the only one hurt?" Antonio winced from his pain.

Simone bit her lip and tried to fight a tear from her eye. "Antonio, that wasn't me in that car with you."

Antonio was even more confused. "Huh?"

"That was my twin sister, Dana."

The words shot through Antonio like a 9mm bullet.

* * *

Antonio shook his head. They were alone now, and Antonio wondered why his family had left him with her. "This has be to some crazy joke, right?"

Simone stared off through the window.

Antonio closed his eyes and slowly shook his head. "I can't believe this. I can't believe I got involved with you. I'd have been better off dead," Antonio snorted.

Simone snapped her head towards him. "Don't you ever say that!"

Antonio chuckled. "Why not?"

"Antonio, stop it! You think this was easy on me? Having my own sister threatening to kill me?"

"So what are you saying Simone? If this accident had never happened, you would have killed your own sister?"

Simone hesitated.

"You know what?" Antonio said. "I don't want any part of this. Get out!!"

Simone grabbed Antonio's hand. "Antonio, please. Don't leave me. I need you."

Antonio shoved Simone's hands away. "Simone, I can't be with you! I don't even know who I was intimate with! Get out!"

Simone walked towards the door. "I guess this is it, then?"

Antonio ignored her.

Simone reached behind and closed the door. "Antonio, I do want to ask you a favor."

Antonio straightened his back. "Yeah."

Simone slowly walked over to Antonio. "Can I get a from kiss you? Just one more time?"

Antonio's stomach knotted. He was all too familiar with this.

Antonio shook his head. "Simone, Get out!!"

Simone closed her eyes and walked away. "I understand. Can I visit you tomorrow?"

Antonio did not reply.

Simone smiled. "I will visit you tomorrow regardless."

"Whatever."

Simone sighed. "Anyhow I have some family matters that I have to take care of and settle."

"What do you mean?"

Simone opened her eyes and gazed at Antonio with such intensity it almost frightened him. "I need to make sure that my sister is really dead."

* * *

Simone sat in her blue Lexus listening to the hum of the engine as she drove. Her thoughts were confused, but she felt electrified that Antonio was still alive. She had a knot in her stomach and knew she needed to put an end to this crazy episode in her life. She swung a left on Thornton Avenue and headed east across town on the expressway. With the windows down, moon roof open, and warm breeze cleansing her soul and mind, Simone let out a deep sigh before she took the exit towards Lexington

General Hospital. As she parked her car, she opened her purse and stared down at her revolver.

Tears trickled down her face despite her efforts to remain calm. "Why, Dana? Why are you doing this to me?" She quickly wiped her tears before closing her purse and exiting the car. She calmly walked towards the main entrance of the hospital towards the information desk. An elderly man with white hair and liver spots on his face looked up at her.

"May I help you?" he asked.

"Yes, I am looking for my sister Dana Robinson. She was admitted here."

The elderly man slowly clicked on the keyboard and studied the monochromatic screen. His eyes lit up. "Yes Dana Robinson, she is in Emerg . . . no wait she is in ICU. ICU is just down the hallway."

Simone smiled. "Thank you."

The old man nodded.

Simone took a deep breath before heading to face her sister.

CHAPTER FORTY-SIX

Dana's lifeless body lay on the bed among a web of wires and tubes. Her heavy bandaged face was unrecognizable, and the beeps of the machine around her were the only signs indicating that she was alive.

Simone stood at the doorway with tears stinging her eyes. She hated her sister for everything that she'd done: for ruining her life, for ruining her relationships, and for killing those she'd loved. Now she would get the revenge that she deserved. Simone clutched her purse to her chest as she quietly walked in and closed the door behind her. She approached Dana and stared at her.

"Hi Dana, it's Simone."

Dana did not respond.

"Dana, I can't help but wonder how you got yourself into this mess."

Again Dana did not reply.

"All I want to say to you, Dana, is fuck you! Fuck you for ruining my life. Fuck you for taking what was mine and making it yours because you were a jealous bitch. A hateful, jealous bitch."

Dana's lifeless body provided no reaction.

"You have made my life a living hell! I lost everyone I loved. My husbands, brother, Larry, and now I almost lost Antonio . . . because of you! Why did you do this to me? I was always so good to you! And what do I get in return? Being used and abused for no reason whatsoever."

Dana's lifeless body continued to lie there.

Simone's eyes filled with tears. "This was because of mom and dad, right? I know dad was a bastard, but that doesn't mean you have to hate all men, especially men that I like, Dana! Dana, I have been nothing but good to you, and all you did was destroy it. You even almost destroyed Antonio. A man that I actually was . . . was falling in love with."

Dana's eyes flickered open.

Simone stood back.

Dana' s eyes continued to flicker until she opened her mouth. With a faint voice, she replied. "Antonio thinks you're a fucking psycho." Dana continued. "Simone you are nothing. I am everything."

"I'm alive standing here, aren't I? I'm *normal*. You, Dana, are not normal. You are sick! You are a jealous, conniving, psycho, sick bitch and you always wanted what was mine."

Dana laughed faintly. "Get over yourself, Simone. You're fucking schizophrenic. That's why you had to be locked away."

"Yeah, so you could pretend you were me and run the estate!! You jealous bitch!"

"Jealous? Me? Jealous over a psychotic, schizophrenic, suicidal bitch like yourself?"

Simone eyes continued to flow with tears. "It is true! I got everything—I always got the good grades and the good guys. I got everything that you hated because you hated dad."

"He was a fucking bastard," Dana said, raising her voice.

"I know he was a bastard, but you can't kill him again and again with every new man!"

"I wish I could kill him again, that motherfucking bastard. Remember the stuff he did to mom? Pushing her down the stairs? Slapping her so much she would black out? How could you not forget that Simone? You think that any person deserves that?"

"And you think that all men are like that, Dana?"

"All men are the same. You know that. They use women, and I use them back."

Simone shook her head. "Dana, for fuck's sake, this is not some fucking film noir . . ."

"I don't care how it sounds! He deserved to die. I should have pushed him down the stairs like he did to our mother. That would have been a painful more death. Or better, just shot him. That would have been more sweet than just giving him cyanide."

"Dana stop it! Stop it right now."

"What? Am I making you uncomfortable? See, your problem, sis, is that you are such a weakling. You let men control and abuse you. No wonder you ended up in the mental ward. I never let any man do that to me. If they want what's between my legs, they need to pay for it."

"So in other words, you're calling yourself a whore?" Simone said, folding her arms.

"A smart whore who knows how to trick men into doing what she wants them to do."

"Including men that don't belong to you, Dana?"

Dana felt a sharp pain shoot up her leg but fought it off as she reached for the bed rail to raise her head. "Simone, Antonio did not belong you."

Simone shook her head. "I met him first." She felt herself falling into Dana's trap.

Again Dana laughed. "You silly child. Simone, you are forgetting some important information here. How did you find out about Antonio Madison?"

Simone shifted her eyes. "That is none of your business."

"Answer me, Simone. How did you find out about Antonio?"

Simone remained silent.

"You see, you can't even answer that question, can you!"

Simone's makeup was running down her face with her hot tears. "You conniving bitch," she spat. "You conniving bitch."

"I'm a conniving bitch? Why am I conniving bitch when I was the one who told you about Antonio in the first place?"

"Drop it, Dana."

"No, I won't drop it, Simone! When you were interested in Larry, did Larry not mention that he worked for an art gallery?"

Simone didn't reply.

"And Simone, didn't Larry mention that he had an artist friend named Antonio who made great paintings?"

Simone remained silent, clutching the bag to her chest.

"And, Dear Miss Simone, was it not yours truly who told you to tell Larry to contact Antonio? But you were too scared so I had to do the digging myself?"

"Fuck off!"

"Oh, knock it off, Simone. If it wasn't for me getting that number and information, you wouldn't have known about Antonio. Simone, I got all the information about him because you couldn't do it yourself. Fuck, you were even nervous that day to go see him. You brought Juan and Zeus to come with you, didn't you? And furthermore you did not even tell Larry what your real name was. In fact, you were too chickenshit that you did not even go out with him. You always cancelled out on him so he never saw what you looked like."

"So what? I never wanted to be this demanding monster like you.."

"Well honey, Antonio likes it when I'm demanding."

The words stabbed Simone like a venomous spear. "I hate you."

"Simone, it is a shame that Antonio wasn't with you in bed because honey, you would have love it."

"Stop it, you bitch!"

"And by the way, how the hell did you get out of the ward? You were not supposed to be out so soon. I thought they would have drugged your sorry ass enough that you wouldn't be able to escape."

"Shut up, Dana."

"Let me guess, you killed one of the nurses or workers? Wow, you are so smart and daring Simone. I am sure daddy would have been proud of you."

Simone's blood boiled. "Bitch!"

"Simone, Antonio's dick filled me up so right that I was having g spot orgasms. Would you imagine a woman of my age having G spot orgasms? Damn, I soaked those sheets!"

Simone's hands trembled.

"Too bad he wouldn't have had any fun with you. I'm sure you could have given good head, but face it, sis, when it comes to hot sex, I would make all the guys come back for more. How do you think you were so popular in school?"

Simone's eyes widened in disgust. "What?"

Dana let out another weak laugh. "Oh come on, sis, like you didn't know I was sleeping with your boyfriends? Wow, you are dumber than I thought."

Simone couldn't believe what she was hearing.

Dana giggled. "Simone, honey, all the guys thought you were the hottest girl in bed—too bad they didn't know it was me. I mean, face it. I'm better."

Simone convulsed. "I hate you! I fucking hate you!"

"Tell them all about it at the mental institute, Simone!"

Simone shook her head. "If my conscious didn't bother me so much, I would kill you right now."

"Why don't you? What do you have to lose? If I die, you will have nothing in the estate."

"What are you talking about?"

Again Dana giggled. "Simone, my dear, naive sister, you have nothing. Everything on that estate has been transferred to me. While you were running around lusting after Antonio and these other fools, I had all the documents signed over in my name."

Simone was confused. "Bullshit. How could they have done that?"

"Simone they had to. Don't you think I know by now how to fuck over a couple of dumb husbands? They were idiots who couldn't protect their assets, so I took them."

"I can't believe I am hearing this. You are now telling me this on your fucking deathbed!" Simone yelled.

Dana chuckled. "Deathbed? Oh Simone, this is not my deathbed. This is my revival bed. Even if you were to kill me right now, you would be left with nothing. No estate, no money, no earnings, no inheritance, and of course no man. "

"I love Antonio and you know it!"

"Like Antonio is gonna go after you after all this bullshit. Please, you are tainted, and your mind is all fucked up. He'd never want you."

"I'm not the psycho one, Dana, you are!"

"Is that why I still have the upper hand in this and you don't? I suggest you go dry your eyes and pull yourself together. Antonio doesn't want you. He doesn't like you. I tainted him and you will never have him back."

A cold wave of emotion drowned Simone's thinking and rational thoughts. Quickly she grabbed her revolver from her purse and aimed it at Dana.

Dana smiled. "Oh, I see. Here's the part where you act brave and shoot me."

Simone's hand trembled. "I will shoot you!"

"Please, you are just as the weak sister—" Dana's sentence was cut off by a loud deafening bang. Blood spattered all over the wall as Dana's lifeless body slumped back in her bed. Loud beeping noises from the machines that were connected to Dana echoed profusely as Simone quickly shoved her gun back in her bag and ran out of the room. As she ran down the hallway she could hear nurses and staff running into Dana's room, following by an ear-piercing scream from one of the nurses.

Simone quickly darted out an emergency exit and hurried towards her car. She jumped in and drove off.

CHAPTER FORTY-SEVEN

Antonio winced in pain as he reached over for the glass of water on the tray.

Lisa quickly grabbed it for him.

Antonio smiled. "Thanks."

Lisa smiled back. "No problem."

Antonio took a sip. "Lisa, listen I really appreciate your staying here and visiting me so much."

Lisa beamed. "No worries."

"But Lisa, I feel terrible. I didn't come to see you once when you were injured."

"Antonio don't worry about it. It's OK."

"No it's not. I feel like shit."

"Antonio, I was hit by car. You were involved in near fatal car accident. There is a huge difference."

"It does not make a difference Lisa. It really doesn't. Principle is principle. I should have visited you but I was too busy involved with . . ." Antonio couldn't find the strength or courage to say Simone's name.

Lisa touched Antonio's arm. "Antonio, I know. Don't worry. I understand. Believe me."

Antonio smiled weakly. "Thank you."

There was a knock on the door.

"Come in!" Antonio shouted.

A big beefy male nurse came in. "Antonio, what's up buddy? I've got to give you your injection again."

Antonio sighed. "Oh good Lord, here we go again."

Lisa smirked. "It has to be done."

As Antonio eased up for the nurse to give him his injection, he tapped Lisa. "Lisa, how is Greg?"

"Greg is doing OK, but he still has a lot of healing to do."

Antonio winced as the nurse injected him. "I feel so horrible. I nearly had him killed. And for what? Over a woman."

The male nurse smirked. "Women can do a lot, my friend."

Antonio eased back when the nurse was finished. "Buddy, you do not want to know what this woman did."

"What did she do?" the male nurse asked as he took off his gloves and threw away the syringe in the disposal container.

"Let's just say that my friend and I nearly got killed because of her."

The male nurse's eyes widened as he scratched goatee. "Woah. No comment."

Antonio nodded. "Yes, no comment indeed."

* * *

Simone sat at the desk in her office digging through her files and signed agreements. One by one, she looked at each agreement. They were all signed by "D. Robinson." Simone felt totally overwhelmed. She picked up a briefcase that had a combo on it. She carefully entered the combo, and the suitcase unlocked. The documents of the will and estate lay peacefully in the centre of the suitcase. Carefully, she picked them up one by one and read each signature. Each time she read the signature she felt a stab of deceit penetrate her heart. "D. Robinson" was scrawled across the bottom of every page. Simone felt hysterical.

"That fucking bitch!" Simone cried hysterically. "That fucking bitch!"

Frantically, Simone tore through all the other documents in the office. She ripped through the drawers and opened sealed envelopes, all bearing the same scrawling signature.

Simone let out a pained scream that echoed through the room and upstairs. She continued screaming her lungs out. "I fucking hate her! Why? Why!!"

George rushed into the room. "Madam, is everything OK?"

Simone sobbed on the floor. "George, go away."

"But madam, I rushed because . . ."

"Go away!" Simone ordered.

George shrugged his shoulders and left the room.

Simone continued sobbing, wondering how and why this was meant to be. She instantly thought of Antonio and the pain and sorrow that Dana had put him through. She needed to make peace with him. She needed to let him know what had occurred so she could be with peace with herself. Quickly, she grabbed her purse and bolted out the door.

As she was driving down her street, she noticed two police cruisers driving in the distance towards the mansion. She immediately figured that they were either coming to question her about Dana's death or to let her know about the fatal incident. Simone couldn't help but smile as she veered down the street towards the expressway.

* * *

Lisa laughed. "Antonio, I don't think that would make any sense."

Antonio shook his head. "Lisa I am cursed. That is the end of the story."

There was faint knock on the door.

"Come in!" Antonio shouted.

Simone quietly walked into the room.

Antonio felt a wave anxiety roll through his body. Lisa sensed it too.

Simone spoke softy. "Hi, Antonio."

Antonio nodded.

Simone turned to Lisa. "Lisa, can I speak with Antonio in private."

Lisa gave an Antonio look. Antonio looked at Simone. "Um, yeah sure."

Lisa cleared her throat. "I'll be in the waiting room if you need me."

Antonio smiled slightly as Lisa walked out the door. Simone closed the door behind her before turning around and sighing heavily.

"What's up?" Antonio said.

"Antonio, I want to be clear with you about everything," Simone said as a tear trailed down her face.

"Simone I really don't have the energy for this."

"Dana is dead."

Antonio jolted in his bed. "Oh, I'm sorry to hear that."

"I'm not."

Antonio sensed her coldness. "I guess not if she pretended she was you."

"Antonio, my sister is more than what you thought she was, and I never told you everything about us."

"Simone, I told you. I really do not want to get into this. I think it is best that . . ."

"I killed her, Antonio."

Antonio's eyes widened and he winced in pain. He stuttered. "What did you just say?"

CHAPTER FORTY-EIGHT

Simone wiped the tears from her eyes. "I was locked up for no reason! Do you know what that's like? I was placed in that mental ward because of her, not me!"

Antonio remained frozen, afraid to say or do anything.

Simone sniffled. "Antonio, all I wanted was to be normal, but she robbed that from me. She hated all men and was jealous of me. And now I am left with no estate, no home . . . nothing. All because of that psycho bitch. She killed my husbands, she killed Larry, she killed my father, and now she tried to kill you."

Antonio's dry throat ached for water. He finally spoke with a hoarse voice. "Simone, I don't know what to say."

"Say that you will forgive me."

"Forgive you? Apparently you didn't do anything. It was your sister."

"But if wasn't for me buying those paintings, then none of this would have happened!"

Antonio shook his head. "Simone, that's not true. You didn't know that your sister was going to do this to you. You didn't, and quite frankly, blaming yourself is not going to solve anything. Just face the facts."

Simone shook her head. "I can't! I just can't!"

"Simone, what is in the past can't be changed. You have to move on forward."

"But I have nothing right now."

"Simone, I am sure that, legally, you can get those documents reversed."

"After killing Dana? I seriously doubt it."

"Simone, I am sure you're going to get through this."

"I can't do this alone."

"Why can't you?"

"I can't make it on my own, I need your help."

Antonio raised his eyebrow. "I beg your pardon?"

"I need your help."

"Help? How am I gonna help you?"

"I need you to be my friend."

Antonio was uncomfortable. He didn't want to have anything to do with Simone. He shook his head. "Simone, I need time to think about this."

"To be my friend? You need time to think about that?"

"Simone, I was in a relationship with your sister, not you."

The words jolted Simone, and Antonio sensed it.

Antonio lowered his voice. "I'm sorry, Simone."

Simone stood back. "No, I guess you're right."

"Simone, I really can't be your friend right now. I still have a lot to settle in my head. I was nearly killed."

"Don't remind me."

"Well, unfortunately, looking at you reminds me of Dana. I'm sorry Simone, but mentally and emotionally I cannot do this."

"Then can I ask for one more favor?"

"What?"

"Please kiss me, Antonio. Please just one kiss."

Antonio hesitated. "Simone, no."

"Please? I feel like if you kiss me it will complete everything."

Antonio's stomach knotted. "Everything?"

"Yes, everything."

"I'm sorry. I don't follow."

"There is nothing to follow, Just kiss me one more time."

Antonio's stomach knotted more. He slowly slid his hand underneath the sheet and grasped the call bell button.

Simone approached his face. "I need you to complete me, Antonio."

"And if I don't?"

"Then we will both regret it."

Antonio's premonition grew stronger. His index finger was right over the button. "How?"

Simone got up from the bed and turned to the door, ensuring it was closed. She drew her gun from her pocket and aimed it straight at Antonio.

Antonio's heart sank. *Push the button,* Antonio thought to himself. *Push it now.*

Simone's hands trembled as she pointed the gun at Antonio. Tears gushed from her eyes. "Please, Antonio, don't let me do this."

Antonio finger felt heavy. Quietly and calmly he pushed the button. "Simone, you are not going to do anything."

"Why do I always end up losing?" Simone sobbed.

Antonio shook his head. "Simone, you are not a loser."

"Yes I am!" She wailed. "All I wanted was to be happy."

Antonio watched as Simone broke down sobbing uncontrollably. An eerie sensation crept up Antonio's spine. He wondered if the abuse Simone had talked about only happened to her mother, or if she had also been involved.

The door flung open. Simone jumped nervously and fired. A young Asian nurse fell to the ground as blood poured from her chest.

Antonio gasped. "Simone!"

Simone stood in horror watching the unconscious nurse splayed on the floor in a pool of blood. "Oh my God," she repeated. "Oh my God! Oh my God!!"

A slew of people rushed into the room. Simone panicked.

"Get away from me!" she shouted, waiving her gun. "Get away from me or else I'll shoot!"

Lisa heard the commotion from down the hallway. She turned to Monica who had just arrived to visit Antonio. "What the hell is going on?"

Monica got up from her seat. "I don't know, but it looks like it's coming from Antonio's room."

Lisa sprang up from her seat and followed Monica to the commotion.

"Ma'am, put down the gun!" shouted a security guard who was already in the room.

"Leave me alone or else I'll shoot again!" Simone screamed hysterically.

Antonio tried to calm her down. "Simone, Simone listen to me! You need to put down the gun. You've hurt one person already."

The security guard spoke into his transceiver. "We have a nurse who has been shot in room 508."

"Everyone stay away from me!" Simone shouted, waving the gun. The gun went off again, shattering a light fixture. More people rushed into the room, and a couple people started screaming. Three officers moved in. "Police! Drop your gun now!"

Simone did not budge. Her voice took on a heavy, unnatural tone. "Drop yours."

"Drop it now or we'll shoot."

"No!" Antonio said. "Don't shoot her! Please don't!"

Lisa and Monica pushed their way into the room. Lisa's mouth dropped open. "Oh my God!"

"Leave me alone!" Simone screamed, waving her gun. "I will shoot the next motherfucker who tries to bother me!!"

"Simone!" Antonio screamed. "Listen to me! You are hurting yourself! Your sister is already gone now, and you're gonna do this to yourself?"

Simone sobbed. "All I wanted was to be happy! She hurt me and took everything away from me!"

Antonio lowered his voice. "Simone, you will be happy soon."

"But I want to be happy with you." Simone said.

Antonio shook his head. "You can't be happy with me when you are waving a gun like this."

"Drop the gun now!" shouted one officer.

Antonio gazed at Simone. "Simone, listen to me. You like my paintings, right?"

Simone nodded slowly.

"Well you can enjoy my paintings some more, but you have to put the gun down first."

Simone cried. "Your paintings are so beautiful! So beautiful! I remember the first painting that I bought from you—the naked lovers. It reminded me so much of me and you!"

Antonio let loose a smile. "Yes, I am sure it does."

Simone sniffled. "I think about that painting everyday. Until my fucking sister stole it from me!"

"Simone, calm down. I want you to take it easy. You can't do anything until you put the gun down."

Simone eyes filled with tears. "Why is this happening to me? Dear God, why is this happening to me?"

"Put the gun down now!" shouted one of the officers.

Simone quickly waved her gun at the officers.

Antonio shouted. "Simone, stop it! Please!"

Simone slowly gazed back at Antonio.

Antonio slowly nodded his head.

Simone weakly nodded hers.

Antonio smiled weakly.

Simone closed her eyes and smiled.

It all happened too fast. Within an instant, Simone had pointed the gun at herself. A loud bang ricocheted through the room followed by the crimson blood that sprayed everywhere. Screams deafened Antonio's ears as the police and security rushed over to Simone's swaying body. Antonio screamed in horror. Lisa stood frozen. Simone's body collapsed onto the bloody floor as the police tried to revive her.

"WE NEED A DOCTOR IN HERE NOW!" yelled a staff member.

Antonio froze, unable to move, speak, or breathe. He felt like he had witnessed his own death. The doctors rushed in before he could fully believe what had happened.

Lisa squeezed through the crowd to Antonio and hugged him.

"Are you OK?" Lisa said.

Antonio slowly shook his head. He felt like a lifeless body. He gazed at Simone's body laying in a pool of blood. He squeezed his eyes shut trying to erase the image from his head. A tear trickled down his face. "No. No, I am not OK."

CHAPTER FORTY-NINE

Greg leaned back in his chair, sipping on a beer. "Tony, any words from those clients?"

Antonio stared at his cell phone and shook his head. The bright sun shone into the bar they both were sitting at during the busy lunch hour. U2's "With or Without You" blared throughout the bar with Bono's voice wailing, "And you give yourself away . . ."

Antonio gazed up into the blue sky through the window next to him.

Greg sighed. "Tony, I know I am gonna sound like an insensitive bastard, but you really need to put the past behind you. It's been six months. It's unhealthy to think about it."

Antonio chuckled and turned to Greg. "Greg, how can I not? Larry's dead, you and I nearly got killed by some psychotic women. I've had very interesting year so far, Greg."

Greg patted Antonio on the shoulder. "Hey, well at least you have me."

Antonio laughed. "Yeah, I guess."

Greg rolled his eyes. "Gee, thanks for the comfort." Greg took another sip from his beer. "I'm serious, man. That was a true test of friendships here."

Antonio pondered the idea. "Yeah, as scary and stupid as that sounds, I know."

"At least now you know that when your friends tell you something that is not right, you should listen to them."

Antonio half-smiled. "I wish Larry was still with us, man. He didn't deserve this. Greg, if it wasn't for me, he wouldn't have . . ."

"Antonio, stop it right there. You are doing this again to yourself. You are blaming yourself for something you had no control over. You did not know that woman, whoever she was, knew Larry. And furthermore, you just thought of her as a simple client."

"But I fell for their trap Greg, I fell in love with Dana."

"No you fell in love with Simone."

Antonio cringed. "Can we change the subject now?"

Greg nodded. "Fine, let's talk about something else. You know Lisa finds you attractive, right?"

Antonio smirked. "Yeah right."

"Tony, I am serious. She has a serious crush on you. Are you forgetting all that time she spent with you in the hospital?"

"Yeah, and I still feel bad that I didn't do the same for her when she was in the hospital."

"Tony, we didn't know she was in the hospital until days later. Stop beating yourself up."

"Lisa is not interested in me."

"How do you know?"

"Because I know."

"Bullshit! Have you asked her? Have you shown any interest in her?"

Antonio didn't reply.

Greg smiled. "I rest my case."

Antonio leaned back in his chair and shook his head. "If I didn't meet up with Simone, I probably would have been . . ."

"Less rich and successful?" Greg interjected.

Antonio screwed up his face. "Man, what are you talking about?"

"Tony, remember how much money she bought your paintings for? And look at Mahagony now. The demand for your work is crazy high because of all this nonsense."

Antonio nodded. "True, but then why do I still feel like shit?"

"Because you witnessed stuff that you weren't ready to see." Greg said.

Antonio took a deep breath and let it out slowly. "Again, we find ourselves talking about this. Let's change the subject."

Greg looked at his watch. "We'd better head back before Huntingwood starts getting upset."

"I don't think Huntingwood will give us a hard time."

Greg laughed as he threw a twenty dollar bill on the bar counter.

"I'll meet you outside," Antonio said.

Greg nodded, grabbed his coat, and headed outside.

Antonio sat at the bar. He slowly dug into his pocket and stared at the ring that Dana had given him. It sparkled and glistened from the bar lights above Antonio's head. He held it up and stared at it, reflecting on all that had occurred. The dinners, the walks, the passionate nights, the first purchase of his paintings, the auctioning, the deceits, the lies, the torture, the deaths, and the realization. He then closed his eyes and clenched the ring tight into his hands. He let out a sigh, got up, and grabbed his jacket. On his way out, he passed by a garbage can. He paused, took out the ring, and dumped into the garbage.

His cellphone rang. He answered. "Hello?"

There was no response.

Antonio cleared his throat. "Hello?"

Again, no response.

He zipped up his coat. "OK I don't have time for this, who the fuck is this?"

Again there was no response.

Antonio hung up the phone, paused, shook his head, and headed outside where Greg waited for him.

Lisa sat staring at the receiver. A tear trickled down her cheek.

Bono kept on singing.